*The Renaissance Stage*

*Books of the Theatre Series*

***Number 1*** ***December 1958***

A Rare Books of the Theatre project of the American Educational Theatre Association

# THE RENAISSANCE STAGE

## Documents of Serlio, Sabbattini and Furttenbach

Translated by

*Allardyce Nicoll,*
*John H. McDowell,*
*George R. Kernodle*

Edited by *Barnard Hewitt*

UNIVERSITY OF MIAMI PRESS
Coral Gables, Florida
1958

Library of Congress Card Catalog Number: 58-14141

*Printed in the United States of America*
*McGregor and Werner, Inc., Washington, D. C.*

# *Preface*

This book presents in English the three major sources of information about stage scenery and scenic practice in the Italian Renaissance theatre. It serves well to introduce the American Educational Theatre-University of Miami Press Series of Theatre Books, which aims to make available to students and lovers of theatre important works which have not been readily accessible.

The Series exemplifies the work of the American Educational Theatre Association at its best: it is the realization of an idea conceived by one member, developed and implemented by a Work Project, and brought to fruition by the efforts of members and officers of the Association. Walther R. Volbach had the idea that the Association should sponsor the publication of significant writings about the theatre which have been either out of print, unavailable in English, or extant only in manuscript. He presented this idea to our Advisory Council and was appointed chairman of the Rare Books Project charged with developing it. He enlisted the aid of other members of the Association; librarians and theatre authorities suggested titles and submitted manuscripts; translations which had long awaited publication were discovered.

While the Project sought publishable works, Professor Volbach, Kenneth L. Graham, Executive-Secretary-Treasurer of the Association, and Delmar E. Solem, its Administrative Vice-President, conducted a vigorous search for publishers, which culminated in the decision of the Executive Board to authorize a contract with the University of Miami Press by which one book will be published each year.

His idea thus realized and his purpose promised fulfillment, Professor Volbach, under the pressure of increased academic duties, turned over the chairmanship of the Project to Barnard Hewitt, who has become Editor-in-Chief of the Series.

By the fortunate circumstance that this project, begun

and developed in previous administrations, has come to public attention this year, the President of the Association in 1958 is privileged to pay tribute to those who preceded him in the office. The Rare Books Project was organized in 1956 when Frank Whiting was President, and it was energetically fostered by Jack Morrison, President in 1957. He is privileged also to express the Association's gratitude to all who worked to produce this book and to those who are preparing future volumes for the Series.

The Rare Books Project of the American Educational Theatre Association consists of Barnard Hewitt, chairman, H. Darkes Albright, Helen Krich Chinoy, Wallace Dace, George Freedley, Mary Grahn, Russell B. Graves, Mary Virginia Heinlein, Orville K. Larson, John H. McDowell, Constance Ruys, Nurredin Sevin, Walther R. Volbach, and George E. Wellwarth.

EDWARD C. COLE, *President*
AMERICAN EDUCATIONAL THEATRE ASSOCIATION

# *Foreword*

That English-speaking students have paid so little attention to the origins of the modern theatre or to continental stage practice contemporary with the Elizabethan theatre is due in part to the fact that, although the Italian Renaissance theatre was well documented, the important treatises of the time have not been easily available.

The three treatises included in this volume are the most important. Serlio's short treatise of 1545 is the first published account of the modern theatre. Sabbattini's of 1637 and 1638 is the fullest description of Renaissance practice before the developments that characterized the Baroque theatre. The several passages from Furttenbach, written between 1627 and 1663, supplement the Italian accounts in important ways and show how Italian practice was established in northern countries.

The present translations grew out of Allardyce Nicoll's seminars in theatre history at Yale in the years 1934–1936. Professor Nicoll had sketched out a translation of Serlio and started one of Sabbattini. John McDowell took charge of the Sabbattini and George Kernodle of the Furttenbach translations. Many points of interpretation were discussed and investigated in the seminars. On difficulties in the Italian text Sarita Hopkins, James F. Mormile, Lawrence Carra, Salvatore Castiglione, and the late Professor Angelo Lipari were consulted; and for the German, George Nordmeyer and Visiting Professor Max Forster. Later the translations received a thorough check by that very able theatre scholar, the late Dr. Franz Rapp. In the case of Furttenbach, his help was indispensable. Furttenbach wrote in a very prolix and repetitive German. The English text is often much shorter than the German, but it is hoped that no essential information is omitted.

# *Contents*

# GENERAL INTRODUCTION

## *The Renaissance Stage*

The Renaissance theatre was created as a part of the ornamentation and display of the princely courts of Italy. A performance on a platform stage with perspective scenery was rarely a separate integral function. It was usually only one of the festivities for the celebration of an important event. The birth, betrothal, marriage, or accession of a prince called for days of lavish display and entertainment. The visit of a prince with his court party required the services of the best poets, musicians, costumers, and architects to celebrate the occasion and properly honor the visitors.

The indoor functions especially, such as balls, banquets, and foot tourneys, required new paintings and hangings on the walls, elaborate pavilions for the royal party, ingenious little scenes built in three dimensions on stands or in niches along the walls, and chariots and pageant platforms for presenting the performers in the midst of the guests. The perspective stage really grew up as one of the temporary side ornamentations built in the palace for such festive occasions.

The court theatre developed as its most characteristic form a type of short musical spectacle or *intermezzo* intended to be combined with other forms of entertainment. In Italy the *intermezzi*[1] were performed between the acts of plays, at court balls, and with tournaments, both foot and horse. In France and England the combination with the masked ball of the court party

1. The nature of the *intermezzi* is discussed by Allardyce Nicoll in *The Stuart Masques and the Renaissance Stage* (London and New York, 1938), pp. 60 ff.

received especially elaborate development in the *Ballet de Cour* and the *Masque*.

As spectacle was the primary purpose, the stage developed many elaborate scenic effects: painted settings that would change in the twinkling of an eye; brilliant, glittering lighting; devils, gourd vines, and mountains that came up through trap doors; marvelous, highly colored clouds that descended or moved across the stage; rising pink dawns; and waves, ships, whales, and monsters, or thrones, or moving processions at the inner stage. The theatre belonged to the architect. The poet, the musician, the actor was merely an assistant in the presentation of the spectacle.

Our modern theatre originated in the perspective theatre of Italy. The auditorium, the stage setting, the proscenium, the curtain, the musicians' pit — the whole tradition took form between 1500 and 1650 and has undergone only a gradual evolution since. The treatises of Serlio, Sabbattini and Furttenbach show the experimentation in the formative years.

## AUDITORIUM

The form of the auditorium of the Italian court and academic theatres was primarily a result of the adaptation of the Roman *cavea*, as studied in extant ruins and as described by Vitruvius, for temporary wooden construction in the great halls and courtyards of the Renaissance palace. Rising tiers of seats were built around a semicircle, and a small space was left between the structure of the seats and that of the stage.

For the best acoustics, Vitruvius prescribed a colonnade back of the seats to raise the structure of the auditorium to the height of the proscenium. The colonnade in the Renaissance palace was one of the ancestors of the balcony. When the *cavea*, originally an outdoor form complete as a structural unit, was put indoors in the rectangular hall, it was not integrated with the structure of the hall, but remained merely an independent system of seats. Between it and the walls were corner spaces, and sometimes there was a back space. Although Serlio does not show a colonnade, he does make use of the space above and behind the tiers of seats as a kind of balcony for extra seats. Later developments expanded the balcony function. The Teatro Olimpico at Vicenza and the Teatro all' Antico at Sabbioneta were both very close to the Vitruvian form, with a single colonnade behind narrow curving tiers.[1]

Serlio and Sabbattini both deal with the early form, a simple row of tiers around a semicircle. Here, as in the case of the flat wings, Sabbattini ignores the new development of the balconies, which had appeared well before this time and which were to dominate the later theatre.

The Royal Seat was the central feature of the auditorium. It was the characteristic form distinguishing the auditorium of the Renaissance court from the Roman, from that of the academies, and from the professional theatres that appealed to the general public. Both the unique importance of the duke or prince in the court and the mathematical basis of the perspective design made his seat the center around which both the audience and the stage performance were planned. As the forced perspective scenery was designed to be seen from a single point opposite to and near the level of the vanishing point, the Royal Seat was opposite the center of the stage, on a raised platform, either in the orchestra or cut into the Vitruvian tiers of seats. There behind a balustrade and framed by columns, canopies, and heraldic devices, sat the family and the most important guests of the prince.

The proper seating of the other guests according to rank was only less important than the seating of the prince. A performance was a major social event. The ushers or marshals of the field were careful to seat the ladies in the most important places, according to beauty and age. To facilitate this, Sabbattini suggested that the ushers be acquainted with the members of the audience.

The importance of the ladies in the whole spectacle is shown in the description of the performance of *L'Ermiona* in Padua in 1637. Five balconies, one above the other, were built around an open field for the performance of alternating tourneys on the field and short operas on the stage. Before the first opera began a little social spectacle was enacted on the field.

"Along the ground of the theatre were set up two banks on which were arrayed eighty Padovan ladies of surpassing beauty

1. Any complete story of the origin of that balcony must consider late medieval and sixteenth century forms that were not influenced by the ancients: the tribunes and seats for the mystery plays, tournaments, civic gatherings, courtly balls and banquets, as well as the inn-yards. Cf. Thornton Shirley Graves, *The Court and the London Theatres* (Chicago, 1913), pp. 43 ff.

and majestic manners, who, because of the excellency of their noble bearing and the luxury of their adornments, seemed to be worthy of being invited to the wedding of a goddess. To the onlookers their eyes seemed more luminous than stars when they began a stately dance to the music of violins and viols. When this was over and they had returned to their seats, the banks where they sat moved up by means of hidden wheels to a position facing the scene. Then various concerts of musical instruments made the auditorium resound. The most noble senses were so enraptured with the beautiful sight and the sound of harmony that the spectators could believe they had ascended to the skies. Then while the spectators were overwhelmed by the many delights, the music changed and the action on the stage began".[1]

## PROSCENIUM

A picture stage has to have a frame, but the proscenium frame was not always in one single piece.[2] A frame for painting is very old, though many medieval mosaics and wall frescoes kept the frieze form of art, where there is no formal frame but only architectural elements to separate one scene from the next. With the full development of perspective in the fifteenth century the concept of the single framed picture as a complete unit prevailed. That concept assumed a picture plane through which the entire perspective space was viewed, and usually assumed a frame. But when the three-dimensional perspective stage appeared at the beginning of the sixteenth century, the problem of space and a formal frame was a little more complicated. Many small theatres of the fourteenth and fifteenth centuries had had frames, and those theatres brought down two traditions of their own. One was that the acting area included space in front of the frame, and the other was the related tradition that the proscenium itself was a scenic emblem. Many medieval mansions had arches that permitted an inner room or inner stage to show. But the actors also used the platform in front of the mansion, and often the mansion itself was a particular building, not a formal frame. In the well known puppet stage illustrated in the mid-fourteenth century manuscript of the *Romance of Alexander*, the proscenium arch is a castle, with two towers spanned by an arc.

1. Pio Enea Obizzi, *L'Ermiona* (Padua, 1638), pp. 8 f.
2. Cf. George R. Kernodle, *From Art to Theatre* (Chicago, 1944), chaps. I and VII.

Since the whole stage was a temporary construction set up in a ballroom, the proscenium was often treated as a setting in itself. When part of the space of the floor extended forward beyond the first side wings, there were several places where a framing element might be placed. Serlio shows a parapet at the front of the stage painted with stonework as though a part of the structure of the street. His first houses, well back of the front edge of the stage, serve to define the sides of the picture — themselves part of the picture. Though he does not show it, he assumes a masking valance above with lights for the sky. Then in his ground plan and in the design for the Comic Scene he shows a flat forestage that is not considered part of the scenic picture. Hence his first houses serve to define the picture plane, and to frame the picture in from the sides. Sabbattini discusses the difficulty of changing a setting framed by side houses, themselves part of the setting, and prefers the full formal proscenium. Such formal frames for the whole scene were certainly used for some perspective scenes early in the sixteenth century. Sheldon Cheney, who advanced the theory that the Teatro Olimpico was the origin of the proscenium frame, himself published an engraving of a complete frame that can be dated 1560,[1] twenty years before the Olimpico was begun.

Yet along with the complete frame persisted the separate parts. In the accounts of English masques we read of the separate "pilasters" and "pillars" at the sides and an "arch" at the top. Only gradually did the idea of a unified frame, the "ornament" or "frontispiece," prevail. Even when permanent theatres were built in the seventeenth century, some relics of the partial proscenium persisted in the forestage, the parapet in front of the orchestra pit, the unchanging scenic *tormentor* or *return*, and the valance above.

Most Renaissance court spectacles called for dancers to come down by steps from the stage to the floor of the ballroom. From Furttenbach's account, however, we learn that when no real steps were needed, they were sometimes conventionally painted on the parapet. Hence the presence of steps in any design does not necessarily indicate that part of the performance took place on the floor of the hall.

---

1. Sheldon Cheney, *The Theatre*, p. 261.

## THE CURTAIN

In order that the scene might have the fullest effect, it was covered by a curtain until time for the play to begin. Furttenbach tells how sounds and music increased to a loud climax of drums and trumpets, and how the curtain then suddenly dropped to disclose the scene. This main purpose — to keep the perspective scene hidden until it should be revealed to the impatient audience — is clearly stated in the account of the *Ballet des Effets de la Nature* given in Paris in 1632: "Considering that those things which take one by surprise always have the most powerful appeal to the senses, it is advised to cover the front of the stage in such a fashion that neither from the amphitheatre nor even from the galleries can anyone see the scene before the ballet begins. For this there should be a great cloth hung in front extending from the ceiling to the floor. It will keep the audience in an impatient desire to see what it is hiding. When the moment comes to let it down, it will disappear in a trice, and discover the scene."[1]

When the Teatro Olimpico was opened with a very elaborate production of *Oedipus* in 1585, a curtain covered the entire stage until the play began. Then, "The hour of lowering the curtain having arrived, first there was a very sweet odor of perfumes, to indicate that in the city of Thebes which was represented odors were dispersed, according to ancient history, to soften the disfavor of the gods. Then the trumpets and drums were played, and small fireworks were set off as well as four large pieces. Then in a twinkle of an eye the taut curtain fell before the stage. Here it would be very difficult to express in words, or even to imagine, the great joy and the immeasurable pleasure which came upon the spectators at the sight."[2]

Both for this effect of disclosing the scene to the waiting audience and as a beautiful cloth, the curtain was an important part of the spectacle. Several handsome examples are described in the accounts of early sixteenth century court performances, as especially the curtain Raphael painted for the performance of *I Suppositi* before the Pope in 1518, with a figure of "Father

---

1. Paul Lacroix, *Recueil de Ballets et Mascarades de Cour* (Geneva, 1868), IV, 194. Cf. Richard Southern, *Changeable Scenery* (London, 1951), pp. 20–21.

2. The letter was first published in *Raccolta Milanese* in 1756–57 and again in *Due Lettre descrittive l'uno dell ingresso . . . l'altro della recita nel teatro Olimpico dell Edippo di Sofocle nel MDXXXV* (Padova, 1830). Cf. A. M. Nagler, *Sources of Theatrical History* (New York, 1952), p. 85.

Mariano with a crowd of devils gamboling about him."[1] Furttenbach gives designs of four stage curtains for one production, to be let down one at a time for different parts of the play. He suggests that the painted cloths would be useful at other occasions besides the play. A similar use of several successive curtains appears in the production of the *Ballet d'Alcine* in Paris in 1610.[2]

The medieval stage used a cloth over the opening of a mansion, or over the entire mansion, but apparently never over the entire stage.[3] The medieval use of a small hanging over an alcove or opening continued in the practice of the London and Parisian public theatres to the middle of the seventeenth century.[4]

The curtain that covered the whole scene appeared almost as soon as the earliest productions of secular drama in the Renaissance courts. Curtains were drawn for small plays on classical themes on two occasions at the court of the Duke of Burgundy — at the banquet at Lille in 1453 and at the Duke's marriage to Margaret of York at Bruges in 1468.[5] In the *tableaux vivants* of the fifteenth and sixteenth centuries, the different stations of the medieval stage were separated and were conceived of as unit scenes. Those of Brussels in 1496 used curtains over complete little scenes.[6]

The Roman *Siparium* was mentioned by Donatus, whose treatise was printed in many Renaissance editions of Terence. Hence many people who were concerned with the production of plays knew of classical authority for the curtain. Like the Roman *Siparium*, the curtain of the early Renaissance fell, usually into a pit, to disclose the scene.

The curtain must have been frequently used with the perspective scenes in Italy in the early sixteenth century. Yet Serlio

---

1. Lily Bess Campbell, *Scenes and Machines on the English Stage During the Renaissance* (Cambridge, 1923), pp. 52 ff., and W. J. Lawrence, "The Story of a Peculiar Stage Curtain" in *The Elizabethan Playhouse and Other Studies* (First Series, Stratford, 1912), pp. 114 ff.

2. Henri Prunières, *Le Ballet de Cour en France avant Benserade et Lully* (Paris, 1914), p. 148.

3. Cohen suggests that a curtain may have covered the entire stage for the Mystère of Saint Louis. S. Wilma Holsboer, *L'Histoire de la Mise en Scène dans le théâtre français de 1600 à 1657* (Paris, 1933), p. 139.

4. Chambers, *Elizabethan Stage*, I, 155 ff. H. C. Lancaster, *History of French Dramatic Literature in the Seventeenth Century* (Baltimore and Paris, 1929), I, ii, 715–717.

5. Kernodle, *From Art to Theatre*, pp. 199 f.

6. Max Hermann, *Forschungen zur deutschen Theatergeschichte des Mittelalters und der Renaissance* (Berlin, 1914), pp. 373 ff.

does not mention one. It is possible that he intended one to be used with his scenes and merely failed to mention it in this brief account, which he admitted was far from complete. In his use of the phrase "the unveiling to our view of a stage setting," he seems conscious of the contemporary use of the curtain. None of the other writers on perspective who devote a few pages to the stage in the sixteenth and early seventeenth centuries mentions a proscenium or a curtain. They seem to be concerned only with the organization of the scene by the laws of perspective and with the relation of the scene to the different seats in the auditorium.

The use of the curtain over the entire scene is to be found in court performances in many parts of Europe wherever there was a single unified scene on a platform, even if there were other parts of the setting dispersed about the hall. At a disguising at Greenwich in 1527, a setting was revealed "by lettyng doune of a courtaine."[1] In the *Ballet de la Royne* performed in Paris in 1581, the settings were dispersed around the hall, but the central structure was opened by a curtain. As soon as the practice began of uniting the décor on a perspective stage at one end of the hall, one or more curtains were used to reveal the scene suddenly to the audience. Falling curtains were used at the productions of the *Ballet d'Alcine* in 1610, the *Delivrance de Renaud* in 1617, and the *Ballet de Madame* in 1619.[2] Since the proscenium was usually considered part of the scene, the main curtain often covered it as well as the perspective setting.[3] Then there might be another curtain inside the frame.

Rising curtains (as well as doors on hinges) were used to disclose the interior of the scenic castles built for the *tableaux vivants* to welcome Charles V in Bruges in 1515; but they seem scarcely to have been used for the indoor court productions until well into the seventeenth century. Sabbattini discusses both types of curtains and describes a large cylinder above the stage to raise the curtain quickly. The accounts of the earlier English masques describe the falling of the curtain, but accounts of those of the 1630's indicate the rising type.[4] Furttenbach, even late in his life, makes no mention of the rising curtain.

---

1. Chambers, *Elizabethan Stage*, I, 155.
2. Prunières, *Le Ballet de Cour*, p. 156.
3. Nicoll, *Stuart Masques*, pp. 42 f.
4. Lawrence, *Elizabethan Playhouse* (First Series), pp. 114 ff. and Nicoll, *Stuart Masques*, pp. 39 ff.

Once removed, the curtain was not used to hide the changing of scenes. The accounts of Sabbattini and Furttenbach, and the descriptions of many productions, show the great ingenuity exercised in making quick changes. The object was to create a great effect of wonder in the audience that the scenes could be transformed so suddenly before their very eyes — or while they were momentarily distracted. The scenes were carefully planned so that during the change no part of the backstage space would be exposed. Either the *periaktoi* turned quickly or one wing was slid directly over another. Even if the operation took several seconds, there would be no such disillusioning exposure and derangement as would be seen in a modern theatre. Scenic changes, except for rare elaborate effects, regularly took place in sight of the audience throughout the seventeenth century.[1]

## PERSPECTIVE

Perspective was the fundamental principle of the Renaissance court stage. To show a large street or square with many houses, churches, roofs, and arches, all designed to appear exactly as they would seem to a person at a single point, was the joy of the architect and the audience. For the first time since the classic theatre a large stage was designed to represent a single unified place. For the first time in the European theatre the scene was designed to create a complete illusion — a purpose which the theatre has held ever since.

The principle of perspective dominated Italian painting from the fourteenth and fifteenth centuries, but it was not applied to the stage until the beginning of the sixteenth century.[2] In both painting and the theatre it gradually transformed space from a wide shallow area very near the plane of the picture to a deep space leading to seemingly unlimited depth. The relationships between buildings or other objects represented were changed from a horizontal axis parallel to the picture plane to an axis going into the depth perpendicular to the picture plane. In both painting and the theatre the change was gradual. In painting great depth was not achieved until the end of the fifteenth century, and in the theatre a century later.

---

1. Cf. Richard Southern, *Changeable Scenery*, pp. 17–24.
2. Cf. the close relationships in forms and principles between Renaissance scenery and the traditions of painting studied in Kernodle, *From Art to Theatre.*

The "house" at the side, the main unit of structure of the perspective scene, began the system of "wings," the characteristic feature of the theatre from the early sixteenth century almost until our day.

In the texts of Serlio, Sabbattini, and Furttenbach we see the different experiments in the development and use of the two earlier types of Renaissance wings — first the angle wing and then the *periaktoi*. The third type, the flat wing, which in the seventeenth century displaced both the earlier kinds, had been used in unimportant positions long before it became the standard type.

The angle wing, built with a front face and a side (perspective) face, appeared in the structure of the late medieval stage when a house at the end of the platform required only two faces. The illustrations of many of the academic Latin plays and of some of the early *commedia dell' arte* scenes[1] indicate one two-faced house at each side of the stage. The perspective scene merely doubled and multiplied that side house into a row of reduplicating houses one behind the other — just as fifteenth century painters had already doubled and repeated the side house for great depth in painting.

The principle of the angle wing was the reproduction on the stage in three dimensions of the visible parts of an actual house, reduced only as much as was necessary by the conventions of perspective design. It was most effective when built solid with three-dimensional cornices and ornaments in a theatre such as Serlio's and the Teatro Olimpico, where the scene was not expected to be changed. But Sabbattini gives methods of changing a light form of the angle wing.

For swift changes of scene the triangular wing or *periaktoi* that turned on a pivot was developed.[2] This was the only form of the wing that had classical precedent. Vitruvius mentions it as having tragic, comic, and satyric scenes painted on the sides, but he is not very clear about its use. Palladio showed one at each of the main openings of the *frons scenae* in Barbaro's edition of Vitruvius.

---

1. Cf. the early prints and drawings with *commedia dell' arte* figures in a perspective scene, and the attempt to represent "houses" on the back cloth of mountebank stages. John H. McDowell, "Some Pictorial Aspects of Early Mountebank Stages," *PMLA*, LXI (March, 1946), 84–96.

2. Cf. A. M. Nagler, "The Furttenbach Theatre in Ulm," *Theatre Annual*, XI (1953), 49–54.

Furttenbach's method of using a pair of *periaktoi*, each with two long sides, placed to come together to form a corner like a corner of the angle wing, would be much the most effective. It was the only method he considered. But many variations on the device were tried before it gave way to the flat wing. Besides his equilateral three-sided prisms, Sabbattini mentioned a quadrangular form as being in such common use that a description of the process seemed unnecessary. Five-sided *periaktoi* had been tried in Nantes, France, in 1586.[1] Dubreuil recommended the use both of four-sided *periaktoi* and of two-sided.[2] These two-sided *periaktoi* with pivots in the center seem to have been used at the sides of the stage at a performance of *Candy Restored* in a private house in England.[3]

It was the flat wing that survived the Renaissance. Scenes made up entirely of flat wings appear in drawings of Aleotti very early in the seventeenth century.[4] Of course one or two flat wings at the back of the stage had been used by Serlio and others on the principle that objects at a distance lose their thickness, and the wings on the inner stage were flat. But the type did not become established for the whole stage until well into the seventeenth century. Inigo Jones changed from angle wings to flat wings between 1635 and 1640.[5] The fact that Sabbattini, writing about 1637, does not mention them shows that he was completely out of touch with contemporary Italian practice.

The *periaktoi* disappeared from the theatre, to reappear only in a few isolated revivals. The angle wing persisted in provincial theatres and in occasional scenes for many years. It left one important vestige in the tormentor and return[6] that preserve to the present a front face attached to a side face.

The triumph of the flat wing marked the triumph of the stage painter over the stage architect, for it presented in two-dimensional painting what the architect had built in three dimensions. The persistence of the flat wing in the theatre since the Renaissance shows the continued dominance of the painter up

---

1. Holsboer, *L'Histoire de la Mise en Scène*, p. 137.
2. Jean Dubreuil, *La Perspective Pratique* (Paris, 1642–49), Traité IV.
3. Nicoll, *Stuart Masques*, pp. 63, 151, 152, 154.
4. Franz Rapp, "Ein Theater-Bauplan des Giovanni Battista Aleotti," *Schriften der Gesellschaft für Theatergeschichte*, XLI (1930), 79–125.
5. L. B. Campbell, *Scenes and Machines*, pp. 178 f. and 188 f.
6. The word "return" was used by draftsmen for any face of an object that vanished into the depth of the picture.

to the recent appearance of designers who again deal with three-dimensional space.[1]

## INNER STAGE

The alcove or inner stage is a curious form of the Renaissance theatre. The wall at the back of the main scene was made so that it could be removed — usually as shutters that slid to the sides — to show a smaller inner scene. Sometimes that little scene was just an extension of the main one. Sometimes it was the inside of the building or inclosed area shown on the shutters. On some occasions the scene "discovered" in this way presented a place far away from that of the main stage. Occasionally on the continent, as on the Elizabethan stage, when the inner stage was established as an interior scene, the characters could walk out onto the main stage, which was normally an exterior, and still be considered as part of the interior scene. Indeed there are many points of similarity between the structure and conventions of the inner stage in the Italian tradition and the inner stages of the English and Spanish theatres.

The Renaissance inner stage derived directly from the medieval houses. Interiors were traditionally shown by opening a small house, often at the back of the main playing area. Side houses that opened to show interior scenes came down into the seventeenth century in France. But the Italian perspective tradition, except for a few open shops in side houses, for the most part placed the interiors in the inner stage behind the back shutters.

The explanation of the similarity among theatres of several countries, as well as of many of the conventions of the inner stage, may lie in a study of the conventions of medieval and early Renaissance painting. There interiors were shown as small inclosed scenes opening onto an exterior scene. There also small distant scenes were shown through one or more arches at the back of the main scene.[2]

The early sixteenth century perspective stage was probably too shallow to permit extensive use of an inner stage. Serlio

---

1. Kernodle, "Farewell to Scene Architecture," *Quarterly Journal of Speech,* XXV (December, 1939), 649–57.
2. Kernodle, *From Art to Theatre,* pp. 190 f.

does not include it as a structural part of the whole stage; but he uses the concept on a small scale when he plans a procession of small cut-out figures to be shown behind some upstage arch.

By the end of the sixteenth century the inner stage was a well established feature of the theatre. The Teatro Olimpico had small inner stages with permanent scenes behind each of the five openings of the formal façade. The Teatro Farnese provided for the inner stage a section of the building almost as large as that for the main stage. The different methods of opening the back shutters are discussed by Sabbattini in Chapters 13, 14, 15, and 16 of Book II. The small inner scenes on the ground plans of Inigo Jones show several small wings and another set of shutters. Ingegneri recommended discovering the Ghost in a small inner stage by means of a cloth soaked in aqua vitae that would burn away when ignited.

Furttenbach gives us our most important information about the inner stage. He calls it the rear pit, from its most frequent use as a place for the sea-machines, the boat- and fish-machines, and processions, which would either operate on the lower floor or require that the stage floor be removed for operators to work from beneath. He indicates that on occasion the principle could be extended, and a second inner stage behind the first be shown.

Furttenbach shows us that the inner stage was the chief means of presenting an interior. He speaks of it as an inside room. His description of a "tapestried room" suggests interesting comparisons with the curtains hung for the inner stage in England and in Spain.

The loose floor of the inner stage that permitted the sea to be shown at the back accounts for the many scenes in Baroque spectacles showing a row of wings — buildings, trees, rocks, or even ships — leading back to the open sea at the rear.

The inner stage lasted well into the eighteenth century both in England and on the continent; but after the Bibienas began setting large back drops at a diagonal, it became less important.

## MACHINES

Machines and effects played a very important part in the spectacle of the Renaissance theatre. Like the sudden disclosure of the scene by the removal of the curtain, and the quick change of scene, they contributed to the "wonder" and "surprise" considered so important for the audience. Stage tricks were a new toy of the court, and the novelty and wonder lasted for centuries.

The most spectacular were the cloud machines. Already popular in religious plays and at banquets and indoor tourneys, these devices became one of the chief ornaments of the perspective scene. Between the sections of the heavens were lowered white, pink, or purplish clouds varying from a few feet in diameter to a size large enough to cover the whole stage. Sometimes a simple cloud was lowered or drawn over a section of the heavens as an ornament or to indicate a change of weather. Often the cloud machine bore a person, and sometimes whole celestial choirs and orchestras were let in to make music from the heavens.[1] Sabbattini was much interested in clouds that would change size and shape, move across the stage, or separate into several parts as they descended and unite as they rose. Drawings in the Archivio di Stato and in the Biblioteca Palatina at Parma show machines designed to present a large number of singers seated on separate clouds. By means of pulleys and levers, the formation of the clouds would change to new patterns, to the delight of the audience.

Besides the regular cloud machines, the *glory*, a special machine for bringing down heavenly beings or for disclosing a figure in a nimbus, also was inherited from the religious plays and from the church itself. In the church it consisted of a series of frames diminishing by perspective, with hidden lights, to frame a cross or figure. Both Furttenbach and Sabbattini describe *glories* with cloud frames, to be let down from the heavens.

The cloud machine probably figured in nearly every production of *intermezzi* or musical spectacles of the princely courts. Both the mythological and the Biblical themes that were the main interest of the producers gave frequent opportunity for the arrival of heavenly figures or groups of celestial musicians. While the bare perspective stage practically lost the vertical extension of acting area that towers, houses, and upper stages gave to the

1. Even in the Restoration theatres of England, where effects were not nearly so elaborate as in Italy, spectacular cloud machines were usual. Cf. the glorious temple that descended to earth bearing spirits of the happy and suddenly disappeared in Otway's *Alcibiades* in Dorset Gardens, 1675. Lawrence, *Elizabethan Playhouse* (Second Series, Stratford, 1913), pp. 167 f.

medieval and Elizabethan theatres, yet that vertical extension was regained in the more spectacular form of the cloud machines. Here, as well as in the case of the scenery, the Baroque stage substituted a changeable, moving, illusionistic cloud for a static, architectural heavens.

The amount of attention given in these treatises and in the printed souvenir *descrizioni* to sea machines, trap doors, rising suns, processions, flowing rivers and fountains, smoke and flames from heaven and hell, wind, thunder, and rain, as well as to the many lighting effects, shows again that the Renaissance theatre was a theatre of spectacle and its dominating force the architect-designer. The play, the dancing, and the music were merely adjuncts to the spectacle.

## LIGHTING

The primary purpose of the Renaissance spectacle was to add brilliance and sparkle to a festive occasion. Since the performance on the floor of the hall of dances, combats, and tourneys was often as important as anything on the stage, the auditorium required brilliant lighting both for the performance and for the well-dressed audience. The theatre architect took over the three types of lighting already used in the great halls of palaces: chandeliers from the ceiling, brackets on the wall, and stands on the floor. Candles were most frequent at first, but torches and oil lamps were also used. Sabbattini goes into detail about methods of lighting and caring for the lamps.

As the performance came to be concentrated more and more behind the proscenium, there was less necessity for brilliant light in the auditorium. The audience would expect some light throughout the performance, for not until recent years would there be the means or the convention for the audience to see a performance from a dark auditorium. Often, however, in these texts, as in the *Dialogues* of Leone di Somi,[1] we see a growing desire to leave the auditorium dark and to concentrate the lighting on the stage.

In stage lighting the early idea was brightness, sparkle,

1. These *Dialogues*, probably written between 1556 and 1566, will be found translated into English in Allardyce Nicoll, *The Development of the Theatre* (New York, 1937 and 1947), Appendix B.

and wonder. Serlio tells us of shimmering suns, moons, and stars, of highly colored windows and lunettes, of many small, variously shaped openings in the scenery through which colored lights shone and sparkled like jewels, of bottles that acted both as lenses and as color mediums. His designs show flames at the top of buildings, which Leone di Somi tells us established the bright mood for a comedy and also for the beginning of a tragedy.[1]

For his scene and actors Serlio used the standard hanging chandeliers. Besides these he seems to indicate that candles were placed on the stage at the front in the position of footlights. Later workers show less interest in these highly colored lunettes and sparkling lights and more interest in producing a full warm glow on the setting by means of hidden lamps. All possible positions were utilized to secure that illumination which would make the time "seem like full day." At the front came the "footlights," placed at the center of the pit when the musicians occupied a position behind the scenes. Even when the musicians were placed in the pit, it seems that often as many lamps as possible were concentrated at each end immediately behind the parapet. Sometimes a low board at the front edge of the stage concealed a row of lamps. The back of the proscenium, both at the sides and the top, was hung with many lamps. Rows of lamps were put between the curved sections of the heavens. The back pit, or pits, allowed light from above and below to flood the back shutters and any special effect at the inner stage. Lights were put at the back of each wing to light the wing behind, sometimes fastened to the wings, sometimes set on poles let through the stage floor to the floor of the hall to keep the lamps from shaking with the dancing.

Beyond this even glow, the architect was concerned, as we see in these treatises and in the *Dialogues* of Leone di Somi, with the more "modern" problems of controlling the intensity of the light (for mood and dramatic effect) and the direction of the light (to give plastic relief to the setting). Sabbattini planned more lighting from one side than from the other so that the shadows would give plastic relief.

For this control, and for the many special effects such as the *glory*, sunrise, and hell, specialized lighting instruments were needed. We find Furttenbach experimenting with lamps, with

---

1. Cf. Kernodle, "The Magic of Light," *Theatre Arts*, XXVI (November, 1942), 717–22.

mixtures of oils for fuel, and with reflectors, in an effort to devise the most effective instrument for each position on the stage. As modest and old-fashioned as some of his scenic effects were, yet in lighting Furttenbach showed the germs of creative thinking that has borne full fruit only in the recent theatre of spotlights, projectors, and dimmers.

## SEBASTIANO SERLIO, 1475–1554

# *Introduction*

Sebastiano Serlio was the first important writer on architecture to combine a knowledge of Vitruvian and Renaissance architectural principles with a detailed study and measurement of the remains of ancient architecture. The several books of his work on architecture show the characteristic Renaissance antiquarianism which served as a basis and stimulant for creative activity. His presentation of both theatrical and architectural ideas indicates a close knowledge of Vitruvius and of ancient example, interpreted for contemporary practice.

Serlio[1] was born in Bologna the sixth of September, 1475, the son of a mediocre painter of ornaments. After working as a painter in Bologna and Pesaro, Serlio went to Rome and worked for several years with the younger but more famous Baldassare Peruzzi. Here he acquired his interest in studying the monuments of antiquity. Later at Venice he won favor as an architect and painter, and it must have been at this time that he built the wooden theatre at Vicenza to which he refers as "the largest of our times." After another sojourn at Rome, where Peruzzi was building the Palazzo Massimo on the site of the old theatre of Marcellus, he again settled down in Venice and began the publication of his *Architettura* in 1537 with Book IV, the *Regole Generali di Architettura.* It was dedicated to Ercole II, Duke of Ferrara, and bore a letter of commendation by Pietro Aretino.

The book was an immediate success. New Italian editions were called for in 1539, 1540, and 1544, and it was translated

1. This sketch is based on Leon Charvet's *Sebastian Serlio* (Lyons, 1869), and on the accounts of writers of the Renaissance gathered by G. K. Loukomski in *I Maestri dell' Architettura Classica da Vitruvio allo Scamozzi* (Milan, 1933).

into German in 1542. Serlio sent a copy to Francis I, King of France, and received a gift of 300 *écus d'or*.

Here in Venice, in 1540, he published Volume III, the *Libro Terzo*, perhaps the most characteristic book of his entire work. It contained the first important descriptions and drawings of the remains of monuments of classic architecture to be published. Peruzzi had been the guiding spirit in the detailed study of the remains of antiquity, and he had left his drawings to Serlio. Vasari and Cellini would give most of the credit for the book to Peruzzi, but more recent writers defend Serlio's part in the study and his good faith in completing the work of his companion. As Vitruvius, whose work had become the Bible of the architects, did not discuss the principles of all the types of ancient architecture, this study became an important supplement to the classic work. Indeed the whole *Architettura*, including the short section on stage scenery, was conceived as a commentary and enlargement on Vitruvius.

Serlio was next engaged to come to Paris. Francis I, a political ally of the Venetians, was very much interested in Italian art and architecture and had already brought many Italian artisans, including Benvenuto Cellini, to work on the palace at the Louvre and the new palace of Fontainebleau. Serlio was engaged for 400 livres a year, and set to work at Fontainebleau. He seems to have been well liked for a while, as he is mentioned by a co-worker as "le bon veillard," and is spoken of in an expense account as "notre cher & bien aimé Bastionnet Serlio." He was associated with the famous French architect Philibert de l'Orme, and stayed in the establishment of the Cardinal of Ferrara, who was also the patron of Cellini. The busy but disordered life of the many workers at this lavish court is vividly described in the autobiography of Cellini.

Here in Paris in 1545, Jean Martin brought out Book I and Book II of the *Architettura*, the treatises on Geometry and Perspective, in a single volume with continuous pagination. It is printed in both Italian and French, the French translation following each paragraph or small section of the Italian. In the dedication to the later Book V, Serlio states that the books on Geometry and Perspective were written in the solitude of Fontainebleau while the King was at war.

Serlio spent his last years in less favor. When Francis I died in 1547, and the staff was reorganized, Serlio lost his position. Starting toward Italy he stopped at Lyons, sick and at the end of his resources. For several years he engaged in minor building projects in the Midi and helped plan the rebuilding of the Lyons Loge au Change. Here in 1551 was brought out his Book VII, the *Extraordinario Libro* of the *Architettura*. Here also he designed the Arcs de Triomphe for the entrance of Cardinal de Touron, the Archbishop of Lyons, in 1552. Again the Renaissance architect was providing spectacles for official celebrations.

Back in Fontainebleau for the last few years, he probably died toward the end of 1554, and his widow is mentioned in Fontainebleau records for several years.

The book on Perspective, which contains our text on the theatre, was of tremendous influence. It proved so important that new editions and translations were soon called for. There is one Venice edition dated 1551; and another, undated, which possibly, though not probably, antedated the Paris 1545 edition, is found bound with the other books of the *Architettura* printed in 1551. At Antwerp a French edition appeared in 1549 and a Dutch in 1553. Within seventy-five years, besides many Italian editions, it had appeared in French, Dutch, Latin, German, Spanish, and English.

The English edition, rendered from the Dutch, was published for Robert Peake in 1611, taking rank as the first extensive treatise on architecture in English. Indeed this version of Book II was for fifty years the only account of perspective in English, and for two hundred years it and a few other translated continental works provided the only extensive accounts in English of stage practice. The 1611 translation, unfortunately, was inaccurate and often obscure — a fact apparently recognized by contemporaries. At any rate, Joseph Moxon, writing the next considerable treatise on perspective, complains strongly that one or both of the Serlian translators knew little of the subject. He wrote in 1670: ". . . as yet nothing of this nature had been published in English except Sebastian Serlio, who though he were a man of skill and fame, yet his book being originally written in Italian was first translated into Dutch and afterwards from Dutch into English; one of which translators (if not both) doubtless understood the language better than the Art; for therein (as the generallity of Ingenuous Artists do with me confess) the Words are translated, but not the science."[1]

1. Joseph Moxon, *Practical Perspective* (London, 1670), "To the Reader."

As a special problem in perspective, the theatre is given incidental treatment in a brief section at the end of the Book II. The subject is included because it was one of the many duties of the court architect to provide stages, auditoriums, and scenes for the entertainments of the prince. Although Serlio speaks with great enthusiasm about his experience in building scenes, he brings the book to a close with a much shorter account than he had intended. The section shows every evidence of hasty writing. He repeatedly says that there is more he could tell. In a notice to the reader at the end of the volume, he complains that lack of time forced him to "give such a sudden end to this book of perspective." "So many things come to my mind," he adds, "that I could have made a much larger book." Hence the absence of anything from Serlio's account can not be taken as evidence of its non-existence at the time. Even the designs are suggestive and not complete.

Brief though it is, as the first published account of modern theatrical practice it exercised great influence on later stage activities. The plates, the first regularly published scene designs, were copied and repeated in many books on architecture which touched on the stage. In 1547, two years after they first appeared, Jean Martin, who made the French translation of Serlio's text, used them in his edition of Vitruvius. In 1552, they appeared in the second edition of the Vitruvius of Philander, a pupil of Serlio. Barbaro used them in 1568 for his treatise on scenery in his *Prospettiva*, which was also based closely on Vitruvius. Although many designers varied from the strict interpretation of the three types of scenes, yet the influence of Serlio's interpretation of the Vitruvian Tragic, Comic, and Satyric types may be seen not only in Italy but also in the sketches of Mahelot and of Inigo Jones.

## *From "The Second Book of Architecture" 1545*

In the following design I propose to deal with the construction of theatres and the making of scenery. My task is not an easy one, for it is hard to demonstrate how and where the vanishing point (the horizon) should be placed for a scene, since the rules are different from those which I have already stated. It seemed advisable first to present a cross section, but, since the ground plan and the cross section explain each other, the best plan is to study the ground plan first, with reference to the cross section for any details which are not clear. I shall begin with the forestage[1] C. This should be flat and raised to eye-level. From B to A the stage slopes up a ninth part of the length. The broader vertical line from A to M indicates the back wall of the

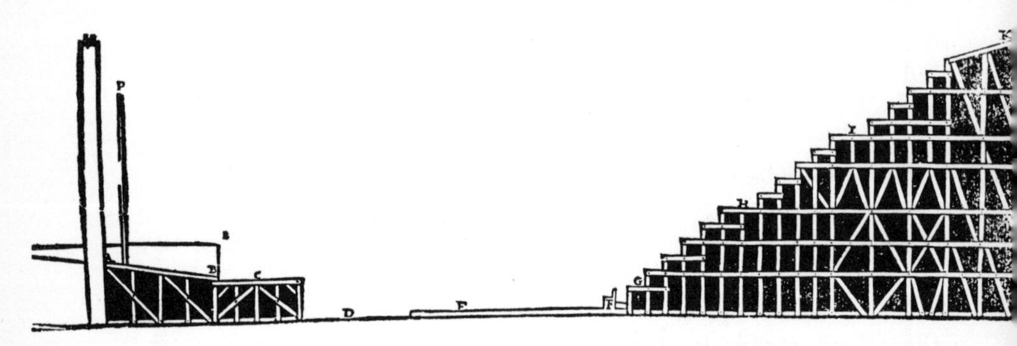

*Cross Section of a Theatre*

hall[2] in front of which the scene is to be made. The narrower vertical line at P indicates the back wall of the set.[3] O is the vanishing point. The point where a line drawn to O parallel to the floor of the hall cuts the wall P is the point of intersection. This point serves for the perspective of the back wall only. The line L to O is used for finding the points of intersection for all the front faces of the houses. The vanishing point for the perspective faces is at the point C. It will be understood, of course, that if the houses have two sides,[4] these two sides will have different vanishing points. So much for the scene itself.

The proscenium[5] is marked D. E is the orchestra,[6] raised one-half foot from the ground. F indicates the seats reserved for the nobility. The first tiers, which are marked G, are for the

1. English ed. 1611, "scaffold."

2. English ed. 1611, "hall or other place."

3. English ed. 1611 adds, "that a man may go between it and the other wall."

4. English ed. 1611 adds, "(as they must be built that men may see out of them on both sides)."

5. Italian 1545, "proscenio." In the edition of 1566 and in later editions, this is changed to "la piazza della scena." The same change is made in Book III in the plates showing Roman theatres. The English, 1611, has "post scene."

6. Italian 1545, "orchestra." In the edition of 1566, this is changed to "la piazza del teatro," and the same change is made in Book III.

most noble ladies; the ladies of lesser rank are placed higher up. The broader levels marked H and I are passageways between which are tiers reserved for the noblemen. Men of lesser rank

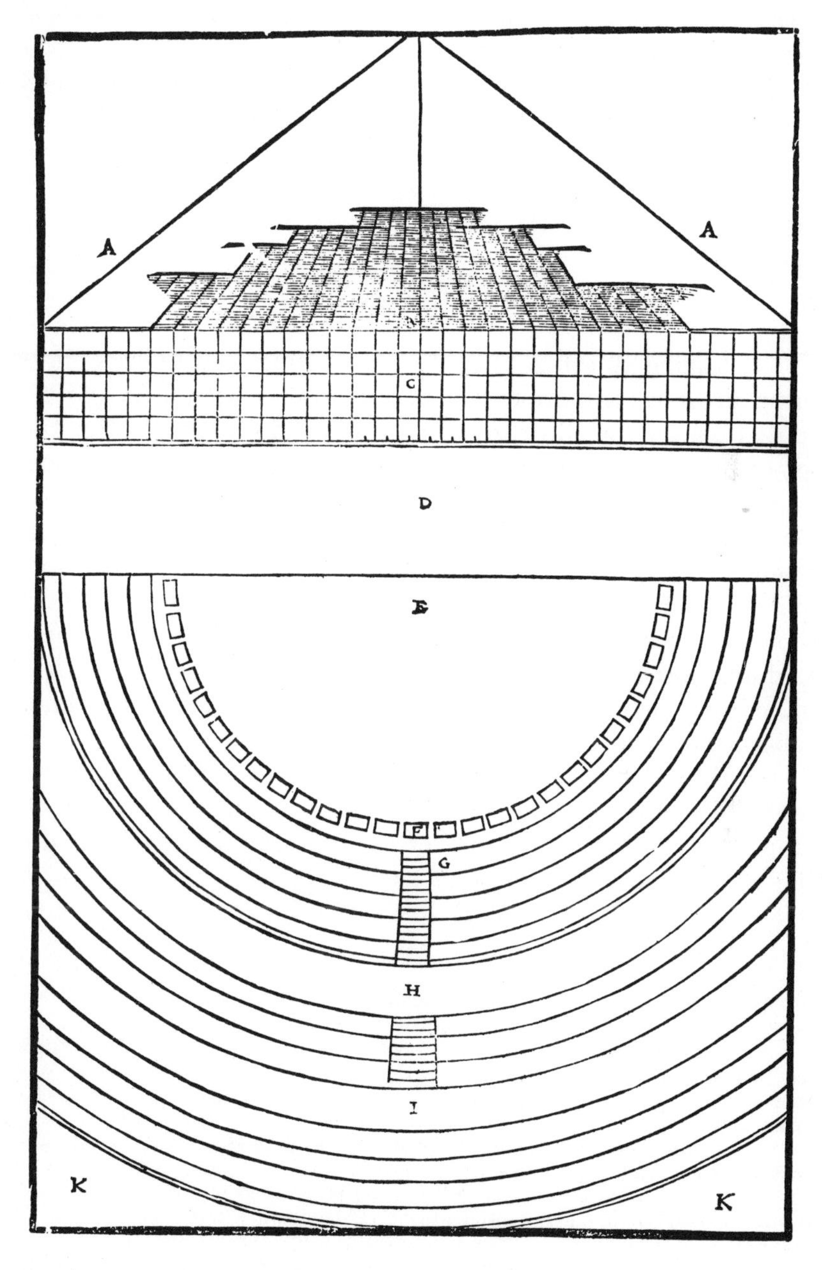


*Ground Plan of a Theatre*

will sit on the tiers above. The large space marked K is for the common people[1] and may vary in size according to the dimensions of the hall. The auditorium and stage that I built in Vicenza were planned approximately in the way I have described. Because the auditorium was set in a large courtyard I was able to make it eighty feet[2] long; but the stage space was more restricted because it was built against a loggia. The scaffolding and framework were constructed as described above, and since there was no supporting wall for the auditorium, I contrived to give it greater strength by reinforcing it with buttresses around the outside.

## THE STAGE

Among all things made by hand of man few in my opinion bring greater contentment to the eye and satisfaction to the spirit than the unveiling to our view of a stage setting. Here the art of perspective gives us in a little space a view of superb palaces, vast temples, and houses of all kinds, and, both near and far, spacious squares, surrounded by various ornate buildings. There are long vistas of avenues with intersecting streets, triumphal arches, soaring columns, pyramids, obelisques, and a thousand other marvels, all enriched by innumerable lights (large, medium, small, according to their position), at times so skillfully placed that they seem like so many sparkling jewels — diamonds, rubies, sapphires, emeralds, and other gems.

Here the horned and lucent moon rises slowly — so slowly that the spectators have not been aware of any movement. In other scenes the sun rises, moves on its course, and at the end of the play is made to set with such skill that many spectators remain lost in wonder.[3] With like skill gods are made to descend from the skies and planets to pass through the air. Then there

1. English ed. 1611, "common officers and other people."

2. English ed. 1611, "eight and twenty."

3. "That there was a definite relation between the idea of the 'artificial day' which was being advocated at this time as the manifestation of the unity of time and this sun rising at the beginning of the play and going down at its close 'most artificially' seems certain." (L. B. Campbell, *Scenes and Machines*, p. 41, note 4) A moving moon is called for in the production of *La Mélite*, 1630 (*Le Mémoire de Mahelot* (ed. Lancaster, Paris, 1920) p. 76 f.) Suns and moons were frequent in England. The inventories of the Admiral's Men in 1598 (*Henslowe Papers* 117) include "the clothe of the Sone and Moone" (Chambers, *Elizabethan Stage*, iii, 77, n.1) Part II of the *Contention*, scene V, 9, requires that "three sunnes appeare in the aire." *I Troublesome Reign*, Scene xiii, 131, states: "There the five Moones appeare" (Chambers, *Elizabethan Stage*,. iii, 76) For elaborate sun and moon effects after the

are presented diverse *intermezzi*, richly staged, in which performers appear dressed in various sorts of strange costumes both to execute morris dances[1] and play music. Sometimes one sees strange animal costumes worn by men and children who play, leap, and run, to the delighted wonder of the spectators. All these things are so satisfying to the eye and the spirit that nothing made by the art of man could seem more beautiful.

Since we are dealing with the art of perspective, I will proceed with the subject further. The general art of perspective we have hitherto considered was concerned with flat planes parallel to the front, while this second perspective method is concerned with plastic scenes in relief. Obviously the latter must follow different rules. First of all, it is usual to begin the platform at eye level; from front to back this is raised a ninth part; i.e., the depth is divided into nine parts and the stage raised at the back as much as one of these parts. The platform must be made very even and strong to accommodate the dancers.

This slope of the platform I have found from experience to be effective. For in Vicenza, the richest and proudest among cities of Italy, I built an auditorium and stage of wood, perhaps — nay, without doubt — the largest erected in our times, where for the marvellous *intermezzi* which were presented there, introducing chariots, elephants, and diverse morris dances, I built in front of the sloping stage a level floor, the depth of which was 12 feet and the width 60 feet. This I found to be both convenient and effective. As this front platform was level, the floor was marked out with perfect squares (not in perspective), but on the sloping platform the squares diminished as they approached the horizon.

There are some who have placed the vanishing point at the back wall of the scene, in which case it must be placed on the stage itself at the bottom of the wall. This produces a very bad effect, for the houses all seem to run into one. It is my practice to carry the vanishing point further back.[2] This I have found so very successful that I have always held to it and always advise it to others.

---

Restoration see Montague Summers, *Restoration Theatre*, p. 194 ff. Cf. the sun at the center of the glory described by Furttenbach in *Mannhaffter Kunstspiegel* (See below). Cf. Nicoll, *Stuart Masques*, p. 137.

1. Serlio, like some other Renaissance writers, uses morris dance as a general term for theatrical dancing.

2. English ed. 1611, "place the Horizon before the doore."

The scenes for plays are of three kinds — Comic, Tragic, and Satyric.[1] First I shall deal with the Comic. The houses for this scene should be those of private persons. These scenes generally are set up at one end of a hall with rooms behind to accommodate the actors. There one sets up the stage as I have demonstrated in the cross section and the plan.

The part C is the level platform with squares, let us say, of two feet. The sloping floor is marked B with similar squares that diminish in perspective starting from two feet. As I have said above, I do not purpose to place the vanishing point at the back of the scene, but to carry it back from there to a distance equal to the distance from the edge of the sloping platform to the back of the scene. Then all the lines are carried to this back vanishing point. The two lines of points mark the wall at the end of the hall.[2] The houses and other objects will show better in the foreshortening when all the squares approach the same vanishing point and diminish according to their distance. On the squares are erected the houses, both those with faces parallel to the stage front and those in perspective, as indicated by the heavy lines of the plan. Such houses I have always made of frames over which I have stretched cloth,[3] making the openings for doors on either face as occasion required. At times I have heightened the effectiveness of the scene by making some parts of wood, cut in relief, as I will explain in due time.[4] All the space between the setting and the wall, marked A, is the off-stage space for the performers. Care must be taken that the back of the set is at least two feet from the rear wall so that the performers may pass from one side of the stage to the other without being seen. A

---

1. Serlio takes his classification of scenes directly from Vitruvius. The same classification existed, of course, in Aristotle's *Poetics*, but Aristotle had emphasized the two types of Comedy and Tragedy. The Renaissance did not know a satyr drama like that of the Greeks, but the plays of the popular pastoral tradition had similar scenes of woodlands and meadows, and characters equally low in social rank. Serlio has in mind the classical concept of rude and free-spoken peasants. But the two concepts were soon confused; Leone di Somi speaks of satyr plays and eclogues in the same breath, as reflecting "that simplicity, purity and joy of the early ages." Serlio's design for satyr plays became a model for pastoral plays.

Later Italian designers and others such as Mahelot and Inigo Jones frequently used the three types of scenes Serlio gives, but many other types were added, and the neat distinction of the three according to social class and appropriate setting was broken down in actual practice.

2. In the elevation drawing the wall is represented by two solid lines.

3. English ed. 1611, "spars, or rafters or lathes, covered with linnin cloth."

4. English ed. 1611, "I have also made some things of halfe planks of wood which were great helpe to the Paynters to set out things at life."

point is established at L at the edge of the platform B of the same height as the vanishing point, and thence a horizontal line is drawn to the vanishing point. The point at which this line cuts the back wall of the set is the vanishing point for that wall. But this line will not serve as a guide in constructing any other part of the set, except that it is of use for determining the size of the objects depicted on faces parallel to the back wall. The first vanishing point, which is behind the wall of the hall, is to serve for all the perspective faces of the houses. Since in order to use this vanishing point in the making of actual measurements it would be necessary to break through this wall — a thing not possible — I have always made a small model of cardboard and wood, carefully executed to scale, from which I could easily and correctly execute each piece separately in the large. Although this procedure may seem difficult to some, nevertheless much time and care may profitably be devoted to the making of such models and in practice, so that by careful application of principles the method may be mastered.

Although halls (however large they may be) could not accommodate theatres such as the ancients had, nevertheless in order to follow the ancients as closely as possible, I have included in my plan such parts of the ancient theatre as a great hall might contain. Thus the part D corresponds to the *proscenio,* the circular part marked E corresponds to the *orchestra,* raised one step from the *proscenio.* Around it are the seats for the most noble persons at F. The first tiers, G, are for the most noble ladies. The parts H and F are a passageway. The other tiers are for the less noble men, with steps for easy access. The large spaces marked K are for the common people, and will be larger or smaller according to the size of the hall. The greater the hall, the more nearly will the theatre assume its perfect form.

This first scène, the Comic scene, has houses appropriate to private persons, as citizens, lawyers, merchants, parasites, and other similar persons. Above all, the scene should have its house of the procuress (*ruffiana*), its tavern, and its church. I have already shown how these houses are placed in position, and I now discuss the details of their construction. In a small print, of course, I can do no more than suggest some details certain to please, such as an open portico with arches in the modern style leading to another house. The balconies, called *pergoli* by some, by others *renghiere,* give an excellent effect on the perspective

*The Comic Scene*

faces, as do the cornices whose ends, cut on the inside, form projecting corners on the houses. For the same reason those houses which have projections are especially successful — such as the tavern of the moon in this design. Above all else one must select some smaller buildings to be placed in front, so that over their roofs the other buildings may be seen, such as you may see above the house of the procurer (marked by the sign of the hooks, commonly called *hami*). The superior height of the houses further back gives the appearance of grandeur, and better completes the scene in that part, which would not be the case if each house were lower than the one in front.

Although the detail is painted with shadows as from a single light at one side, nevertheless it is better to illuminate the scene from the middle because of the greater power of a light hanging at the center. Those roundels and squares that appear throughout the scene are all transparent artificial lights of various colors; the means for making these I will give at the end of this book. It will be well to put light behind the windows in the front faces, but an especially good effect will be secured by making these of glass or paper or painted cloth. If, however, I were to make all the suggestions I could concerning these things, I should be considered prolix. Therefore I will leave them to the imagination of those who are interested in such things.

The Tragic scene is for the representation of tragedies. In this setting the houses must be those of great persons, because amorous adventures, sudden accidents, and violent and cruel deaths such as we read of in ancient and modern tragedies alike have always taken place in the houses of lords, dukes, grand princes, and particularly kings. Therefore, as I have said, you must introduce here none but stately houses, such as those indicated in the following figure; you must note, however, that, because of the limitations of space, I have not been able to sketch those grand edifices of kings and lords that I could show in more ample space. The architect concerned with these things needs no more than a suggestion of the general method, which he may adapt according to the setting and subject called for. As I have said in the section on the comic scene, the builder must take care to arrange the parts of his setting in such a way as to give the best impression to the spectators, placing, for instance, a small building in front of a higher one.

I have made all my scenes on flat frames. Since these sometimes fail to appear convincing, it is necessary to avail oneself of wooden relief — as in the building on the left side of the stage, the pillars of which rest on a base with several steps. In this case the base must be made of low relief raised above the floor, and upon it are set two frames, one facing the audience, the other in perspective. They extend upwards only to the top of the parapet which runs above the first arches. Now because the second arches are set back so as to make room for this parapet, the two upper frames also must be set back so as to produce the effect desired. What I say of this building applies also to others which have certain parts set back — especially to the houses near the front of the stage. If the house is set very far to the back, however, one frame will be sufficient, so long as all its parts are skillfully designed and painted.

De M.Sebaſtian Serlio.

*The Tragic Scene*

Concerning artificial lights enough has already been said in the section on the comic scene.

All the superstructures on the roofs, such as chimneys, belfries, and the like, although they are not indicated on the illustration, are to be made of thin board and cut in profile and drawn and colored with skill. Similarly, statues supposed to be of marble or bronze will be made of thick cardboard or even thin wood, cut to size, and shadowed. They are to be so placed in the distance that the spectators cannot see them from the side.

Some artists are in the habit of painting supposedly liv-

*The Satyric Scene*

ing characters in these scenes — such as a woman on a balcony or in a doorway, even a few animals. I do not recommend this practice, however, because although the figures represent living creatures they show no movement. On the other hand, it is quite appropriate to represent some person who sleeps, or some dog or other animal that sleeps, because no movement is expected here. I can recommend painting on the back shutter statues or similar objects supposedly of marble or of other material, as well as scenes of history and legend. Concerning the representation of living things having motion I shall speak at the end of this book; there I will tell how this is to be accomplished.

The Satyric scene is used for Satyric plays, in which all those who live licentiously are reproved and even castigated. In ancient satyr plays lines were spoken which referred, almost without respect to persons, to certain men known in the community to lead evil and vicious lives. Such license, however, as one may readily comprehend, would be conceded only to people who could speak without respect for rank — namely, rustics. Hence Vitruvius in dealing with scenery recommends that these scenes be composed of trees, rocks, hills, mountains, herbs, flowers, and fountains, — together with some rustic huts, such as those in the illustration. And since in our times these performances are generally given in the winter when few trees and bushes have flowers and foliage, these will have to be made artificially of silk, and will receive more praise than the natural objects themselves. Just as in the comic and tragic scenes houses and other buildings are to be imitated by the art of painting, so in this too, imitation is to be made of trees and bushes with flowers.

The more costly these things are, the more they are worthy of praise, because in truth they then express the generosity of rich lords and their enmity to ugly stinginess. Some time ago my eyes beheld such scenes carried out by the architect Girolamo Genga at the instance of his lord, Francesco Maria, Duke of Urbino. In these I witnessed as much liberality in the prince as taste and skill in the architect. Such beauty was there in the setting as I have never seen in any other similar work. Oh immortal God! what wonder it was to see so many trees and fruits, so many herbs and diverse flowers, all made from the finest silk of the most beautiful colors, the cliffs and rocks covered with diverse sea shells, with snails and other animals, with coral branches of many colors, with sea crabs among the rocks, with so great diversity of beauteous things that to write about all of them would take too long. I will not speak of the costumes of satyrs, nymphs, and sirens or of the shapes of monsters and strange animals, skillfully constructed to be worn by men and children according to their size. The movements of the actors seemed to bring these animals to life, each according to its own nature. And if it were not that I should prove too prolix, I should tell of the superb costumes of some shepherds made of rich cloth of gold and silk, furred with the finest skins of wild animals. I could speak also of the costumes of some fishermen which were no less rich than the others, whose nets were of thread of fine gold and whose other tackle was all gilded. I could also describe some shepherdesses whose costumes put avarice to shame. But all these things I will leave to the taste and judgment of the architects, who will always be able to make things of this sort when they find similar patrons, generously willing to give them full license to carry out all they desire.

## OF THE ARTIFICIAL LIGHTS FOR THE SCENE

Above, in the sections on scenes, I promised to describe the means of producing artificial lights of various translucent colors. First I will speak of the color of sapphire blue, much the most beautiful color. Take a piece of sal ammoniac, and have at hand a barber's basin or another basin of brass in which has been put a small quantity of water. Then grind this piece of salt on the bottom and around the basin until it is all dissolved, constantly adding a little more water as you grind, and if you want a more intense color increase the amount of sal ammoniac. Having made then a basinful of this solution, strain it through felt into another vessel, and it will come out a most lovely blue. If you want it lighter you can add some water, thus from one solution getting many shades, lighter or darker as you wish. If from this same solution you should wish to get an emerald shade, add some saffron according as you shall desire it darker or lighter. I am not giving the proportions of these things; experience will teach you to make various shades strong or light or dark. If you want to get a ruby color and are in a place where you can get light and dark red wines, you will find that these will produce both harsh reds and soft reds. If you don't have wines, cut some virgin wax[1] in small pieces, put them in a cauldron of water with some rock alum, set it to boil, skim it, and pass through felt.

1. English ed. 1611, "brazill." French 1545, "coppeaux de bresil."

You can add pure water if you wish a lighter shade.[1] If you wish the color of a Balas ruby, a mixture of white and red wines will give it to you. White wines of lighter or deeper tone will give the color of chrysoprase or of topaz. Pure water filtered through felt makes the best counterfeit of diamond. For all these colors you must have containers (*bozze*) made of glass, of special shapes with flat and rounded side to hold the water. There is a special way of placing these containers for the translucent colors. At the back of the painted houses where the lamps are to go is fastened a thin board pierced to hold the lamps separate,[2] and below it is another board to hold the glass containers. Then each of those *bozze* is placed with the curved part to the opening and made fast lest it be shaken down by the dancing. Behind every one is placed a lamp that the lights may all be even. The sides of the *bozze* toward the lamps should be flat or convex the better to receive and send out the light. In the same manner such lamps are to be put in the openings on the perspective faces. When you need a specially strong light you put a torch behind a glass and behind the torch a barber's basin well burnished. This will reflect a splendor like the rays of the sun. If some of these openings are square or of an almond or other shape, put in them plates of glass of various colors with lights behind.[3] But none of these lights have anything to do with the illumination of the scene. For this a large number of candles are placed leaning at the front of the scene.[4] Also above the scene are hung

1. English ed. 1611, "and use it with water and vinegar."

2. Serlio must have in mind the usual type of stage lamp. A glass globe which contained the fuel had a stem one or two inches long or a tapering bottom. It could be set into a hole made in wood or into an iron ring fastened to the scene, as Furttenbach describes in *Mannhaffter Kunstpiegel*. Cf. Nicoll, *Stuart Masques*, p. 134.

3. Compare the colored lights in the production of the *Masque of Flowers*, England, 1614: ". . . beautiful with transparent lights of variable colours . . . In the two first quarters were transparent lights resembling carbuncles, saphires, and rubies. In every corner of each quarter were great pots of gilly-flowers, which shadowed certain lights placed behind them and made a resplendent and admirable lustre"; of Ben Jonson's *Masque of Queenes*, 1609: "The Freezes [The proscenium arch and the parapet] both below and above, were filled with severall-colored lights, like Emeralds, Rubies, Saphyres, Carbuncles, etc. the reflexe of which, with other lights placed in the concave, upon the Masquers habits, was full of glory"; and of Ben Jonson's *Masque of Beauty*, 1608: "Behind them in the centre of the throne was a translucent pillar, shining with several colored lights that reflected on their backs."

4. The phrase "pendente davanti alla Scena" is usually taken to mean "hanging in front of the scene." The use of "also above the scene" in the following sentence leads us to think that Serlio is speaking of some kind of footlight perhaps similar to the "leaning light" described by Furttenbach. If so this is an important early reference to footlights. The French version, 1545, reads: ". . . flambeaux

chandeliers,[1] and above these chandeliers a vase of water in which a floating piece of camphor burns will give a very beautiful light and odor. Whenever you wish to show something burning you soak it well in the strongest aqua vitae and set fire to it with a taper.

Although much more could be said concerning fires, I wish to leave that for the present. Now let us speak of some other things which bring great delight to the spectator. For these times when the actors are not on the scene, the architect will have ready some processions of small figures, of an appropriate size, cut of heavy cardboard and painted. These are fastened to a strip of wood and pulled across the scene at some arch in a swallow-tail runway. In the same way can be shown musicians playing instruments or singing, and some one behind the scene will supply the music softly. At other times a troop of people passing over, some on foot, some on horseback, with the muffled sound of voices and drums and trumpets, will greatly please the spectators.

To make a planet or other heavenly body pass through the air, it is painted well on cardboard and cut out. Then far back in the scene, at the last houses, a soft iron wire is stretched across the scene with small rings attached to the back of the cardboard figure, which may be drawn slowly across, by a dark thread. But all must be so far back that neither the thread nor the wire can be seen.

Thunder, lightning, and thunderbolts will be needed on occasion. Thunder is made by rolling a large stone ball on the floor above the hall used for the theatre. Lightning is made by some one in a high place behind the scenes holding a box of powdered resin.[2] The top of the box is full of holes and in the center is a lighted candle. When the box is raised, the powder is thrown out and set on fire by the candle. A thunderbolt is made by letting down a rocket[3] or ray ornamented with sparkling gold[4] on a wire stretched at the back of the scene. Before the thunder

---

allumez penduz devant son appareil, & d'avantage certaines torches mises dessus les eschauffaux, & dessus aucuns chandelliers accommodez ou il sera requis, se pourront mettre quelzques vaisseaux."

1. Chandeliers were used for a scene in 1496 in the Brussels *Tableaux Vivants* of St. Lucas painting the Madonna. (Hermann, *Forschungen zur deutschen Theatergeschichte*, p. 399).
2. English ed. 1611, "powder of vernis or sulphire."
3. English ed. 1611, "squib."
4. English ed. 1611, "pure gold or chining lattin which you will."

has stopped rumbling, the tail of the rocket is discharged, setting fire to the thunderbolt and producing an excellent effect.

But if I were to discuss all the things I know about stage settings, I would never be done; therefore I shall say no more.

# NICOLA SABBATTINI, 1574–1654

## *Introduction*

Nicola Sabbattini was a native Italian architect and engineer (*ingegnero*) and his book entitled *Pratica di Fabricar Scene e Machine ne' Teatri* (1638) is a standard work on stage practice in the late sixteenth- and early seventeenth-century Italian theatre. He was not an inventor of the devices which he describes, nor was he a theorist in stage perspective. The machines described in the *Pratica* were well-known and had long been used; in fact, some were already out-of-date. The *Pratica* is a manual or handbook of Italian stage practice in the form of directions to an architect whose assignment is to turn a hall of state into a theatre, with auditorium and stage, along with scenery, machines, lighting and other effects. The study takes the reader backstage and reveals the secrets of the elaborate effects required for shows at the Italian ducal courts.

Biographical details about Sabbattini are lacking in precision. Thieme-Becker[1] lists him as an architect and a constructor and painter of scenery, who was born at Pesaro about 1574 and who died there on December 12, 1654. As an architect he was in the service of Francesco Maria II della Rovere, Duke of Urbino. His architectural achievements in the year 1598 include a chapel in the Church of the Madonna ai Servi at Pesaro,[2] the "Appartamento di Madama" in the Ducal Palace at Pesaro, and the Palazina di S. Angelo at Vado. He was also concerned with harbor construction. On October 4, 1614 with the assistance of Barigiani, he completed the Canale della Foglia (Channel of the

---

1. Ulrich Thieme-Felix Becker, *Allgemeines Lexikon der bildenden Künstler* (Leipzig, 1935), xxix, 284.
2. (Guiliano Vanzolini), *Guida di Pesaro* (Pesaro, 1864), pp. 169–170.

Foglia).[1] From 1630, he constructed court buildings at Pesaro; the Chiesa del Suffragio, built in 1637, is attributed to him.[2]

Thieme-Becker also credits Sabbattini with an unpublished manuscript on architecture.[3] In the foreword to the 1638 edition of the *Pratica,* this work is hinted at:

> "who knows, whether the author, according to this Practice of the Theatre, is not preparing also to impart his experience in civil and military architecture."

With his title as architect to the duke, Sabbattini's position was necessarily one of respect, and there is indication that he had some influence on others of his profession.[4]

Although Sabbattini was familiar with, and may have been associated with, the erection of numerous theatres, definite evidence points to the Teatro del Sole at Pesaro in 1637 for the production of *L'Asmondo,*[5] a tragedy with *intermezzi.*

In the last chapter of the *Pratica,* Sabbattini mentions this production and states that "The machines described in both these books have been to a great extent used in the very noble spectacles which recently were presented in the Teatro del Sole at Pesaro." As theatre architects usually began with a bare hall and built the entire structure, it seems reasonable to suppose that Sabbattini was responsible for this edifice.

Further activities in the theatre are uncertain. Flemming suggests that Sabbattini may have been drawn to Modena by Lucrezia d'Este, widow of Francesco Maria II, and may have erected the Theatre there in 1638.[6] Records from Modena indi-

---

1. From the map of Pesaro this project seems to have been the widening and deepening of the channel of the Foglia river so that shipping vessels could come up the river into the town. In the *Guida* this project is referred to as "la grand opera" done without regard to expense by the Duke. *Guida,* p. 63.

2. *Guida,* p. 170.

3. *Trattato di Architettura civile e militare.* Biblioteca Oliveriana, Pesaro.

4. The *Guida* refers to several architects taught by Sabbattini: "Sabbattini . . . che ci allevo il Capitano Zanchi G. B. juniore, Almerico Remoli Almerci, il Colonnello Girolamo Arduini, il Capitano Paolo-Emilio Mainardi, tuttu valenti architetti . . ." p. 71.

5. *L'Asmondo* (Venice: Angelo Salvadori, 1633; 1634, 1636) by Giovanni Hondedei, Patrizia de Pesaro; cf. Francesco Salverio Quadrio, *Indice Universale delle Storia, e Ragione d' Ogni Poesia* (Milan, 1743), iv, 88–89; Carlo Salvioli, *Biographia Universale del Teatro Drammatico Italiano* (Venice, 1903), i, 398.

6. Willi Flemming, *Anleitung Dekorationen und Theatermaschinen Herzustellen* (Ravenna, 1639), published at Weimar, 1926, in the *Nachwort* (p. 286) indicates that the date was obtained from Louis Leclerq [Ludovic Celler], *Les*

cate, however, that the Teatro Ducale, built for Francesco I, was designed by Gaspare Vigarani (1586–1663), and was not built until 1654.[1]

Scant though the records of Sabbattini's activities are, he was unquestionably a man with competent theatrical experience.

The first book of his *Pratica* was printed by Flaminio Concordia at Pesaro in 1637 and was dedicated to Sabbattini's new patron, Hieronimo Grimaldi. With the death of Francesco Maria II in 1631, the dukedom reverted to the control of the church and was governed by papal legates, whose residence alternated between Pesaro and Urbino. Consequently, Sabbattini was required to find a new patron. He selected Grimaldi[2], an Italian prelate, who was Governor of Rome in 1628, then ambassador to France and Germany, and later was made a cardinal by Pope Urban VIII. The choice was evidently not a happy one, for when the complete edition of the *Pratica*, including the original first book and the new second book, came out the following year (1638), it was printed at Ravenna by other publishers (Pietro de'Paoli and Gio. Battista Giovannelli) and dedicated to still another patron, Honorato Visconti. A six-page ode by Anton Francesco Tempestini is offered in praise of the new sponsor. No explanation is apparent for this shift in patrons.

In the first book of the *Pratica*, Sabbattini deals with the general problems of theatre construction, audience arrangement, scene building, scene painting, and lighting. He gives particular attention to perspective and the immediate problems confronting the architect in building the stage with proper attention to the duke's seat. Sabbattini developed his theory of perspective from his fellow-countryman, Guido Ubaldus (1540–1601), whose

---

*décors, les costumes et la mise-en-scène au XVII^e siècle* (Paris, 1869): "La salle du théâtre de Modène, bâtie en 1638, pour le duc François I^er dans son palais, fut, nous croyons, la première qui fut construite sur un plan arrondi." p. 48.

1. Allessandro Gandini, *Cronistoria dei teatri di Modena* (Modena, 1873), pp. 15–16; Girolamo Tiraboschi, *Storia della Letteratura Italiana* (Florence, 1812), 535; V. Tardini, *I Teatri di Modena* (Modena, 1902), iii, 862.

2. No references, however, identify Grimaldi definitely with Pesaro or Urbino. He is found with variously spelled first names: Gerolamo, Geronimo, and Jerome; he was born at Gênes, 20 August, 1597, and died at Aix, 4 November, 1685. *Enciclopedia Italiana*, xvii, 970; Michaud, *Biographie Universelle*, xvii, 549; *La Grande Encyclopédie*, xix, 428; Géraud Lavergne, *Archives de la famille Grimaldi-Regusse* (Monaco, 1911), 30, 277; *Nouvelle Biographie Générale* (Paris, 1877), 21–22, 74–75.

work was published in Pesaro in 1600.[1] In the introduction to the 1638 edition of the *Pratica,* Sabbattini gratefully acknowledges his debt to Ubaldus:

> "He who intensely desires to see the best theory for such practise should turn to the Archimedes of Italy, and read the sixth book of the *Art of Perspective* by the noble Sig. Guido Baldo dei Marchesi del Monte, whose eager student the author had the honor to be."

Sabbattini, as a pupil of Ubaldus, presents a unique method of locating the duke's chair, the vanishing point, and the groundplan for scenery, wings and shutters. Specifications are precise for painting wings, with particular attention to the difficult task of painting doors, windows, and balconies on the converging perspective faces of angled wings. He gives attention also to the problem of representing shadows in order to give the proper appearance of depth to the scene. Provision of seats for the accommodation of the spectators comes within his duties as chief architect. He even prescribes rules for ushers. Specifications for opening the front curtain are definite and precise to achieve an effect of wonder and awe. Lighting considerations complete the first book. Auditorium lighting, with the hazards of dripping wax, occupies considerable space. Within the scene, Sabbattini is concerned with the location and dimming of lights.

In the second book, Sabbattini treats of the *intermezzi.* For these allegorical episodes, which were displayed between the acts of a regular five-act play, devices for moving scenery, set pieces and for spectacular effects were required.

For Serlio and the Renaissance critics, the place either remained unchanged, or a change of locale was not associated with a change of scenery. By the last quarter of the sixteenth century, however, the *intermezzi* had become firmly established as a vehicle for spectacular entertainment; and the stage architect had to devise methods for quick changes and diverting effects designed to arouse delight and wonder as to how they were accomplished.

Sabbattini presents several methods for changing two-

---

1. *Perspectivae libri sex* (Pesaro, 1600). Ubaldus is variously referred to as Ubaldo, Ubaldi, and Guidobaldo Dal Monte. The last spelling is given in *Nouvelle Biographie Générale* (1877), 21–22, 562.

sided Serlian wings, *periaktoi*,[1] and shutters. He does not refer to the flat wing set nor the method for mounting it.[2]

Sabbattini describes hell scenes with fire effects, transformations achieved by means of traps, methods of representing the sea, ships and their manipulation, cloud machines, and methods of simulating rain, rainbows, thunder, lightning, wind, sunsets and cloudbursts.

This translation of Sabbattini's treatise, entitled *Manual for Constructing Theatrical Scenes and Machines*, is the first complete text in English. Several sources draw upon selected references and/or passages from the *Pratica*. Allardyce Nicoll in *Stuart Masques and the Renaissance Stage* (New York, 1937) has reproduced a number of illustrations from the *Pratica* to demonstrate the operation of machines used by Inigo Jones at Whitehall. Lily Bess Campbell in *Scenes and Machines on the English Stage during the Renaissance* (Cambridge, 1923) refers briefly to the *Pratica* in dealing with English masques. A. M. Nagler in *Sources of Theatrical History* (New York, 1952) has included an English translation of eleven out of a total of ninety-eight chapters.

The whole of Sabbattini's text has been translated into German and into French. The German translation by Willi Flemming, *Anleitung Dekorationen und Theatermaschinen Herzustellen* (Weimar, 1926), is printed with the facsimile reproduction of Sabbattini's originally printed Italian text. The French translation, *Pratique pour fabriquer scènes et machines de théâtre* (Neuchatel, 1942), is by Maria and Renée Canavaggia with an introduction by Louis Jouvet. French translations of selected chapters appear in Wilma Holsboer, *L'Histoire de la Mise en Scène dans le Théâtre Français de 1600 à 1657* (Paris, 1933). An attractive facsimile Italian edition, published by Carlo Bestetti (Rome, [1955]), has a biographical section by Elena Povoledo, along with illustrations from Sabbattini's notebook.

Sabbattini's *Pratica* is important not because it introduced

---

1. The earliest reference to *periaktoi* is given by Giacomo Barozzi da Vignola in *La due regole della prospettiva pratica* (Rome, 1583), who mentions *periaktoi* in operation in Castro, Italy in June 1543. They were built by Aristotile da San Gallo (1481–1551). In Florence, *periaktoi* were employed by Georgio Vasari (1511–1574), in 1565, by Bernardo Buontalenti (1536–1608) in 1585 and in 1589, and by Guilio Parigi ( ? –1635) for early seventeenth-century spectacles.

2. Aleotti is generally credited with the creation of the flat wing set at Teatro degl'Intrepidi (Ferrara, 1606). Notebooks in Biblioteca del Commune, Ferrara. Most certainly, flat wings were employed by Aleotti at the Teatro Farnese at Parma in 1618.

innovations but because it describes in detail the practices of the Italian stage in the late sixteenth and early seventeenth centuries, practices which other architects borrowed and introduced throughout Europe, and for the most part did not bother to explain.

# BOOK ONE

# *Manual for Constructing Theatrical Scenes and Machines, 1638*

## 1. *General Remarks On Stage Arrangements*

First of all, when you are planning to give a performance, it is necessary to select as convenient and spacious a hall as possible; this must have behind, at the sides, above and under the backdrop and scenery, space sufficient both for the various machines employed to present heavenly, terrestial, marine, and infernal apparitions and for such distant prospects and perspective views as may be deemed necessary. Take note that one must secure not only length but adequate height and depth as well (provided, of course, that one may have what one wishes). This brief reference to these things is obligatory because we recognize that they are all necessary or at least exceedingly useful in the arousing of wonder among the spectators, in the gaining of praise and in the imitating, so far as possible, of the natural and the real. After having made careful selection of the place where the play and the *intermezzi* are to be presented, the architect must go in person to inspect the site, taking with him good master masons and bricklayers in whom he has confidence, and diligently examine again the capacity of this place. After this the masons will look at the beams, the vaults and the roofs to see if they are sound and able to bear the weight of the stage floor, the machines and the spectators, and especially must this be done when princes are expected in the company.

When he has received the reports of the workmen, the architect will give order (should there be anything requiring remedy) to put matters to right, always maintaining a watchful eye himself and often going personally to supervise the work. He will show confidence in all, give good words to all, yet put complete trust in none, for often is one cheated either by the malignity of enemies or the ignorance of the incompetent.

## 2. *The Site Of The Stage*

In building the stage you must watch not to take up too much or too little space, otherwise one of two inconveniences will result: (i) because of the limitation in space the scenery will not show sufficient perspective distance and consequently will not prove so pleasing to the eye, besides which the restrictions of space will at times create great confusion among the actors in the *intermezzi* and among those who work on or superintend the action and the machines; and (ii) because by too much space the number of spectators will be curtailed, which is bad.

Thus you must consider well and carefully, as said above, what show is to be given, under what circumstances, and consequently select a space sufficient for the stage and scenery.

## 3. *How The Stage Should Be Built*

When you have, according to the advice given above, settled the length of the stage at the front; i.e., the lowest part nearest the spectators, you must mark on the walls at both sides this first height, which should not be less than 4 feet. Thence, there must be a rake up to the rear of the stage of ½ an inch to a foot; this marks the height at the back. The rake is to be in this proportion only when the stage is used for dancing. If there is not to be dancing on it then the rise can be ⅔ of an inch for by this means the scenery will be displayed to better advantage.

This done, a cord should be drawn from the height at the front of the stage to the height at the back and in accordance with this line holes are made in the walls to serve for the beams supporting the first stage scaffolding. These holes should not be further distant from each other than 4 feet. The beams are then to be placed in position, large, good beams, a foot square, made stoutly fast and carefully secured with many strong props, set close together if morris dances are to be presented; if not, then the props may be a little more distant from each other.

When all this has been completed, other beams are placed lengthwise to form the second part of the framework. They should be ½ foot square, well secured and firmly nailed down in such a way that there is no danger of the nails working loose during the morris dances. This is of common occurrence and is very dangerous for the performers.

At the front end a parapet of boards well set together and firmly nailed must then be made, so that the spectators will not see the machines or anything else placed under the stage. This parapet must be removed from the front of the stage almost a foot and should rise higher than the stage by at least ½ a foot. It should not be joined to the stage front but stand by itself, fastened to the floor of the room and to the walls at the side. This is required because of the lamps, as will be described elsewhere. If the lamps are not to be placed there, then the parapet may be joined to the stage front and be made the same height as the stage. Since this chapter describes many things, I deem it necessary to make a plan which will make the explanation clearer.

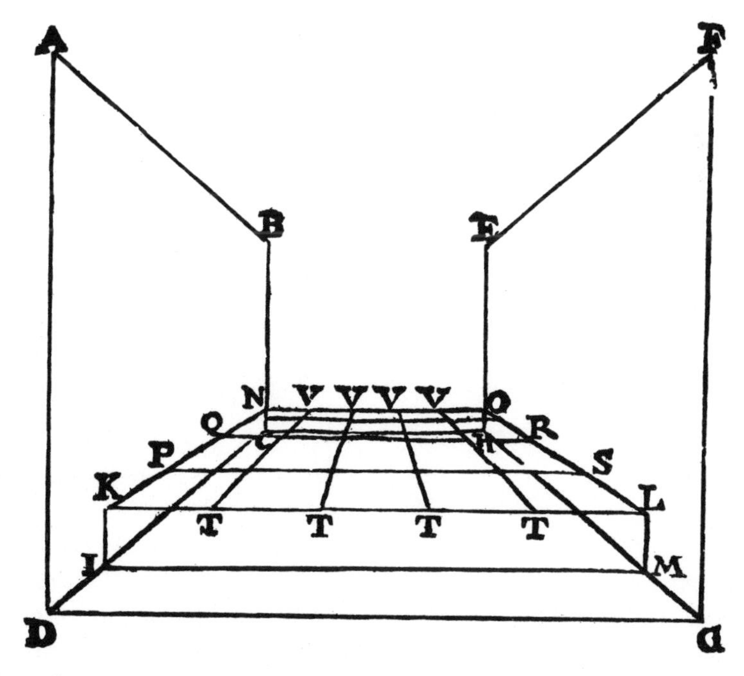


*Figure 1.*

Let ABCD and EFGH be the two walls of the hall which is to be used for the performances, and let DCHG be the floor of the hall. The first height of the stage in front is IK and LM, 4 feet high. The height at the back is CN and HO so much the higher by ½ an inch per foot. If the length of the stage from K to N or L to O is 10 feet, then the height at CN or HO will be 4 feet 5 inches. If the length is 20 feet, then the height at the rear will be 4 feet 10 inches, and so following the same proportion the height at the rear may be determined.

The lines KN and LO represent the slope of the stage, marked by the drawing of a cord against each wall as is said in the preceding chapter. KPQN at one side and ORSL on the other are the holes and the lines KL and PS and QR and NO indicate the first beams, of which there will be more or less according to the length of the stage; the other lines are the planks forming the second part of the structure, marked TV; the space IKLM shows the stage front facing the spectators. To demonstrate clearly the method of making the parapet without joining it to the stage, the plan below will serve, indicating a section of the stage and the parapet.

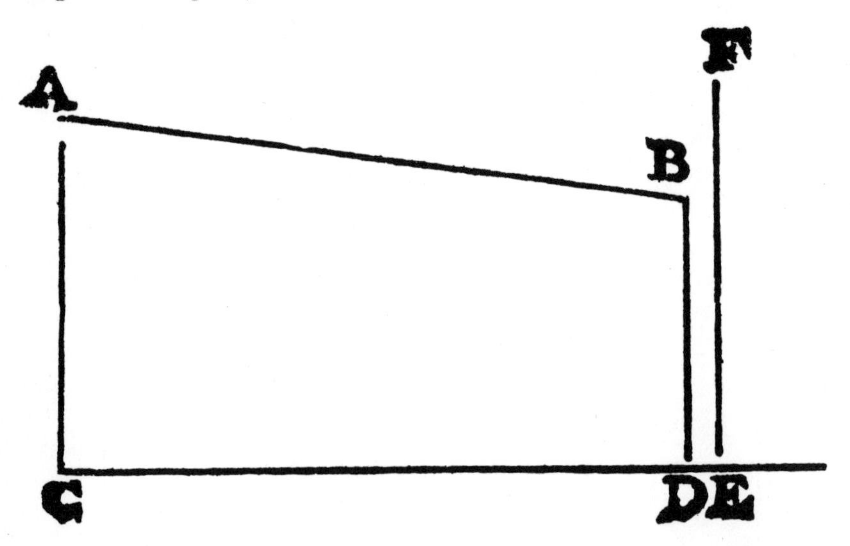


*Figure 2.*

ABCD is the section of the stage and CE is the floor of the room; one foot away from the front of the stage, BD, we have the position at which the parapet stands, EF. It is ½ a foot higher than BD, as is shown.

## 4. *How The Heavens Are Made*

With the plan of the stage fixed, preparations must be made for making the heavens. The heavens may be either whole or divided. The former presents no difficulty, since it can be made with three or four wooden frames or arches made in the shape of a small portion of a circle. When these are put in place, they should be slanted 2 inches per foot, and fixed with good, strong pegs to the roof beams or to another support so as to make them secure.

Then underneath these frames and along their length long thin pieces of lath should be placed and well secured. These laths are commonly called *Ciavaroni*, and in Tuscan *Correnti*. When this second frame is complete, cloth should be stretched over it. This cloth is to be nailed on as tightly as possible to avoid any disagreeable effect. So the whole sky is complete.

But where a divided sky is required, more work is involved, particularly when various machines have to descend or rise. In accordance with these plans, the sections of the heavens must be set, as is provided for in Book Two.

## 5. *How To Paint The Heavens*

The heavens having been made, the architect or someone responsible for this job, must engage some worthy painters, skilled (if possible) in perspective work, for such men will do the painting more easily and with greater honor. Should such men not be available, then take care to get the best there are. A start will then be made by painting the part nearest the spectators with crude colors to represent azure and clouds, gradually softening down both until they melt into each other, taking care to introduce suitable orange color in the clouds. The sky will then display a beautiful perspective.

## 6. *How To Make A Preliminary Plan For The Stage In Front And For The Two First Houses And For The Depth Of The Stage*

When the sky has been painted, the position of the two first houses on the stage at each side must be determined by making two marks at the distance desired, which may be easily seen from afar off. Thus will be indicated the size of the faces of the first two houses, and the space between the two marks will be the width of the scene in front.

Its depth will be determined by the special requirements and it will be the distance from the front of the stage to the back shutter. There one must draw a line parallel to the stage front from one side to the other. Thus will be marked the fronts of the two first houses, the width and the depth of the scene, as is shown in the plan below.

*Figure 3.*

Let the front of the stage be AB between the two walls AE and BF and the size of the two first houses AC on one side and DB on the other. The line EF where the back shutter must go should be parallel to AB, the stage front. From C to D will be the first width of the scene and from C to D to the line EF will be the depth of the scene.

## 7. *How To Locate The Vanishing Point*

The vanishing point must be placed with great care. If it is too high, the houses of the scene will appear to rise in perspective and consequently will not give the proper perspective effect. If it is too low, the houses will seem to go downward. A line is placed at the back shutter parallel to the stage front. At its mid point a small post of wood 1½ feet high is firmly nailed to the floor of the stage. Its top marks the vanishing point. The vanishing point at this height will give good perspective effect only if the depth of the stage is at least 15 feet. If the stage is not so deep as 15 feet, then the vanishing point should be lowered a little, always with particular attention to the depth of the stage.

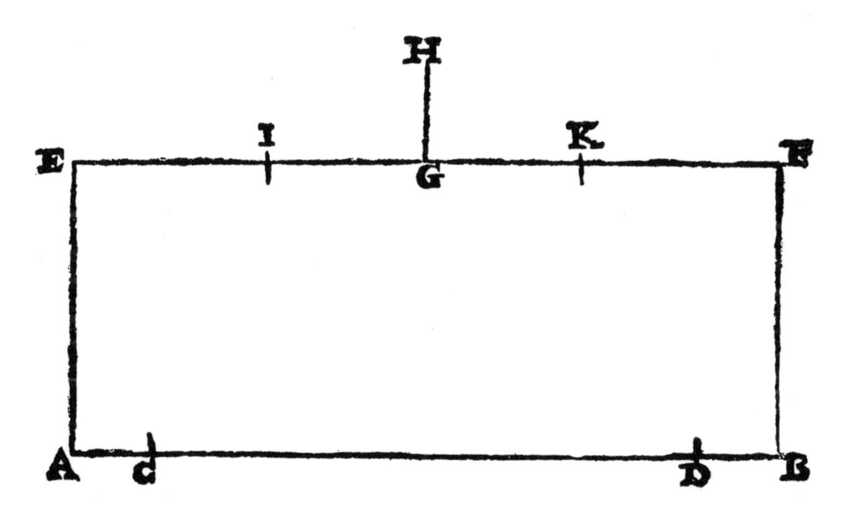


*Figure 4.*

Let AB represent the front of the stage, and the parallel line EF represent the back shutter. At its mid point G, a small piece of wood GH 1½ feet high is firmly nailed to the stage floor, with H representing the vanishing point. You could lay this piece of wood and the vanishing point at one side of the middle at I or K, but the usual (and it seems, the best) position is in the middle.

## 8. *How To Locate The Point Of Distance*

When the vanishing point is established, we should determine the point of distance, which is easily located. A very exact square is needed, such as is used by carpenters and masons. Standing in the middle of the hall or theatre, with the right angle of the square held at the eye, you sight along the two sides of the square and move backwards or forwards until the sight lines along the edges of the square meet the points marked for the first two houses as explained in Chapter 6. Then the point of distance is the point on the floor of the hall directly underneath the angle of the square.

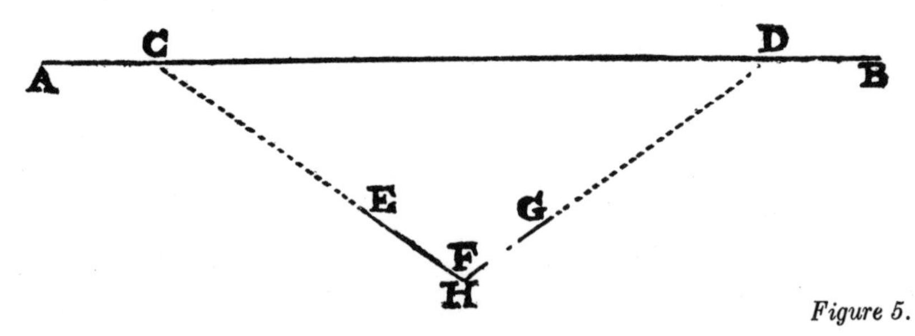


*Figure 5.*

Let AB be the front of the stage, and C and D be the marks for the first two houses. EFG is the square, with the point of sight H. The sight lines determined by the square between the points C and H are HEC; and HGD are those determined between H and D. On the floor of the hall a point is made directly beneath the angle of the square F. This point is the point of distance (and it seems, the best).

## 9. *How To Draw The Cords Between The Points*

When the vanishing point and the point of distance are fixed, a second piece of wood is fixed to the floor of the hall at the point of distance, so that it is a trifle higher than the small piece of wood at the vanishing point. This second piece must be fastened firmly to the floor of the hall and must be perpendicular to the horizon line. From the top of the post at the vanishing point, a brick-layer's cord is tightly drawn horizontally to the top of the other post at the point of distance. In the same horizontal plane of this first cord and making a right angle to it, a second is drawn and fastened to one or other of the walls of the hall.

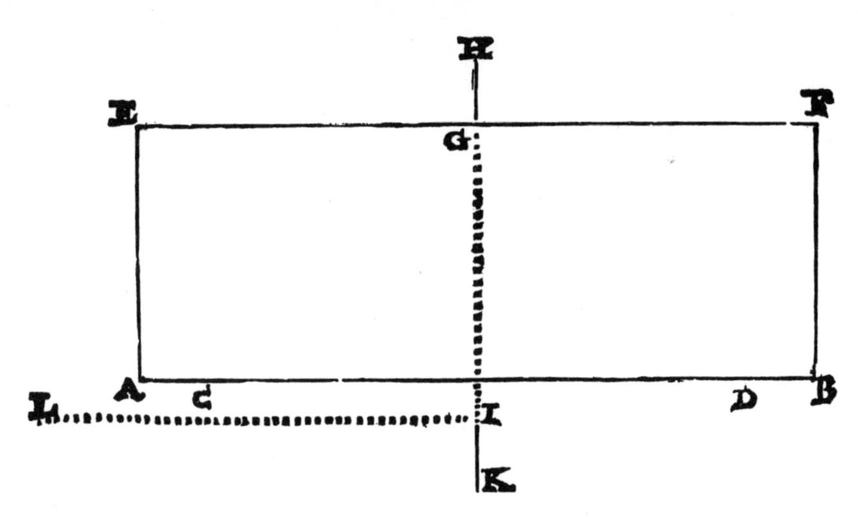


*Figure 6.*

The line where the back shutter is to be placed is EF and the wood 1½ feet high is GH. The vanishing point lies at H and on the floor of the hall is the other piece of wood IK. A cord is drawn equidistant from the horizon line from H, the vanishing point, to the piece of wood IK, which terminates at I, the point of distance. From this same point I the other cord is drawn. It is attached to one of the walls and at L on the same plane as the first, making a right angle with I.

## *10. How To Lay Out The Ground Plan For The Scenery*

When these cords have been stretched and fastened, the plan must be laid out in the following manner. For the houses on the right side, you stand at the left of the scene opening. You adjust your eye level until you see the line marked by the cord coincide with the edge of the first house of the stage floor. Sighting along the cord you will indicate the line which is the ground plan of the houses of the right side, cutting the bottom of the back shutter. The ground plan for the other side will be established in a similar manner.

Instead of sighting, a light may be raised or lowered until a shadow cast by the cord coincides with the edge of the first house. A line can then be drawn with this shadow on the right side of the stage.

On these ground lines the streets are laid out. Their number and size will be determined by the requirements of the action of the play and the *intermezzi*. Let the streets be as narrow as possible, so that the houses can be the wider and consequently give the greater space for doors, windows, archways, and booths: things that give both magnitude and depth to the scene and pleasure to the spectators. But the streets should not be so narrow as to cause any inconvenience to the actors or the dancers, particularly when quick exits and entrances are called for.

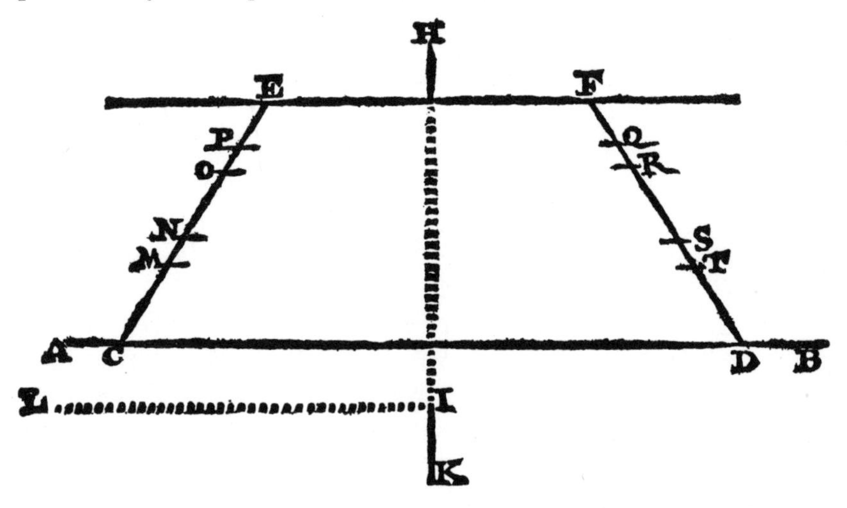


*Figure 7.*

Let H be the vanishing point and I the point of distance, and HI the cord across which the person, responsible for this work, must look. If he stands at D and, looking across this cord, turns to C, then the other part of the cord will come at E and so the line CE is drawn. Then, crossing to C, he will look at D and F, making the line DF. Then the streets will be indicated: these must be opposite one another as MN, ST, OP, and QR.

## 11. *How To Plan The Wings And The Back Shutter*

Next must be determined the width and depth of the frames of the houses from one street to another which are erected on the ground plan marked on the sloping stage. As yet their height at the part nearest the vanishing point has not been determined. First of all will be erected the edges of the perspective face of the first house. The height desired for the edge of the house nearest the audience will be fixed. For the other edge of the frame, the one nearest the vanishing point, you stand at the other side of the stage and sight across the cord, as was done in the other operations,[1] to the height of the first house. Then, where the cord cuts the edges of the frame towards the vanishing point, will be indicated the upper edge of the house representing the roof. The other houses on that side are outlined in the same way. By sighting from the other side of the cord, the houses of the opposite side are outlined.

The frames of all the front faces of the houses must be parallel and equidistant from the stage front. Care must be taken to make the front faces which adjoin the streets wide enough to prevent the audience from seeing behind the scene. The first house at the stage front at either side must be as high as the highest of the houses. There will be no question of seeing behind the scenes here, as the first houses always come up to the side walls of the hall. The back shutter must be made so broad at the sides as to go beyond the faces of the last houses, so that the spectators will not be able to see within the scene through the streets. The back shutter must be as high as the lowest of the two last houses.

When it is necessary to change the scenery or make it disappear, the frames must be made in another way, which is dealt with in the second book concerning the *intermezzi*.

In figure 8 which follows let the floor of the stage be AB and the frame of the first house be CDEF. The part DE is made according to the slope of the stage AB and the upper part C as high as one wishes the house to be and the part F indeterminate. If you go to K and look across the cord GH to C and, following the slope, come to I, then the frame CDEI will be completed.

1. Described in Chapters 9 and 10.

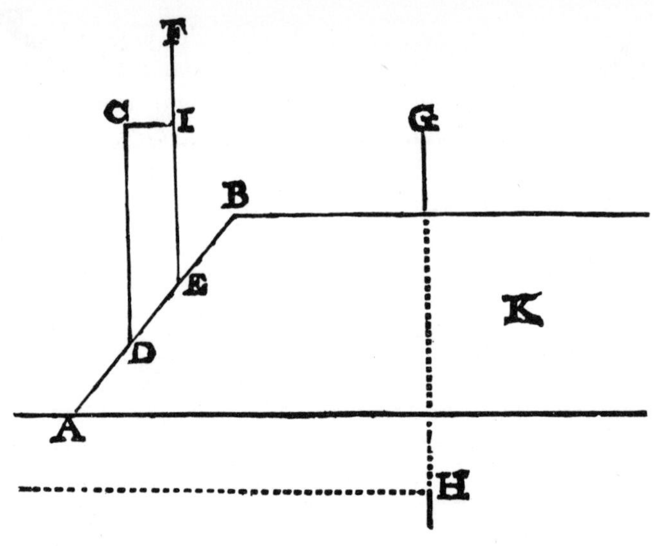


*Figure 8.*

In figure 9 let the slope of the stage be AB and upon it be placed the two houses: LDMCFE of the first house and HGKI of the second. You will make the face of the second house GHNO sufficiently large to prevent the spectators seeing through the street EFGH to the interior of the scene. Nothing need be done with the faces of the first houses since they always come up to the walls.

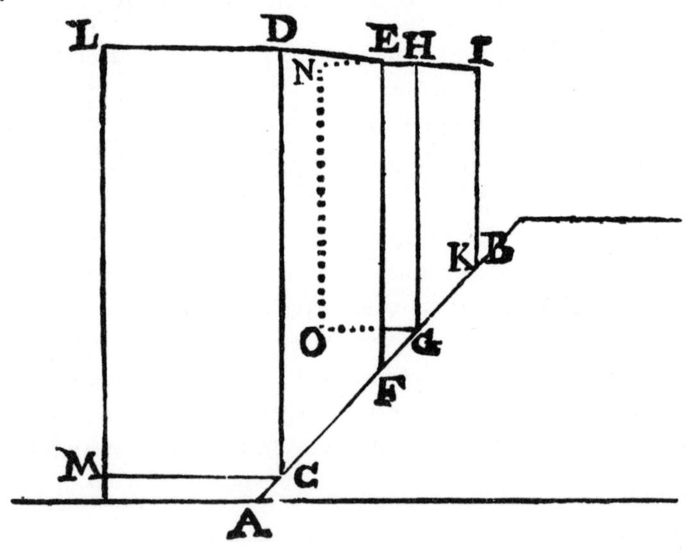


*Figure 9.*

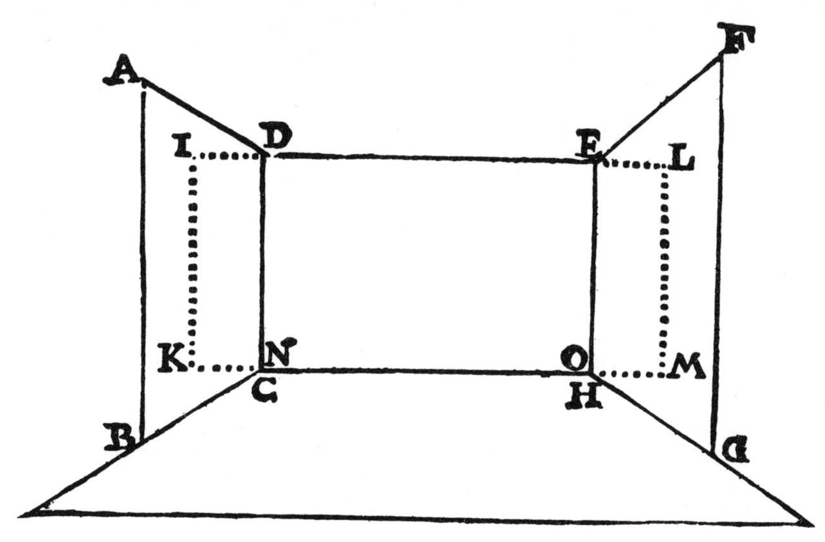


*Figure 10.*

Let the faces of the two last houses be ABCD and EFGH and the frame of the background be IKLM. This background must be so much greater in length than these houses that spectators cannot see within the scene by the streets CN and HO.

## 12. *How To Cover The Frames Of The Houses And The Back Shutter With Cloth If Boards Are Not To Be Used*

When the frames of the houses and the back shutters are firmly secured in position by crossbars, they are covered with cloth. The cloth should first be soaked in the glue that painters use. Then it should be nailed as tightly as possible to the frames so that it will not sag or fold, for that would present a most ugly appearance, particularly under stage lights. Boards, of course, require more time and money, but they are less apt to be damaged by those behind the scene, especially the thick-headed ones. Cloth may be easily torn by carelessness. And assuredly it is a miserable thing and very common to see, at the lowering of the curtain, great tears and gaps in the scenery so that not only those responsible, but the spectators, are amazed and scandalized at such defects.

## 13. *How To Erect The Frames Of The Houses And The Back Shutter On The Stage*

The canvas having been fastened to the frame and dried, the frames must be fixed thus to the stage. Place the frame of the front face of the first house upright and parallel to the stage front and at least 3 feet back from that front. It must be nailed to the floor and braced to the side wall at the top with pieces of wood so that it is firm. Then the perspective face of the house is joined to the first frame and placed on the vanishing line. It, too, must be made firm and braced by a bar to the side wall.

The shutter is set upright and, since it is not to be opened, is secured with strong nails to the stage and braced to the walls by bars.

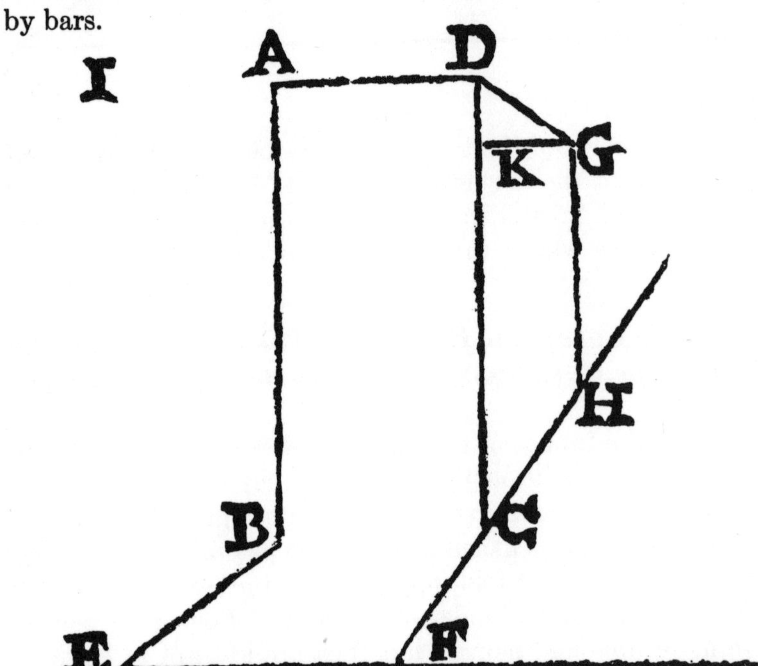


*Figure 11.*

Let the front of the first house be ABCD, fixed to the stage floor, BC, at a distance of at least 3 feet from the stage front EF. It must be well secured to this floor and braced up above by means of bars in the wall as at AI, and similarly the frame CDGH. This is fastened above by the bar GK. And similarly the other frames.

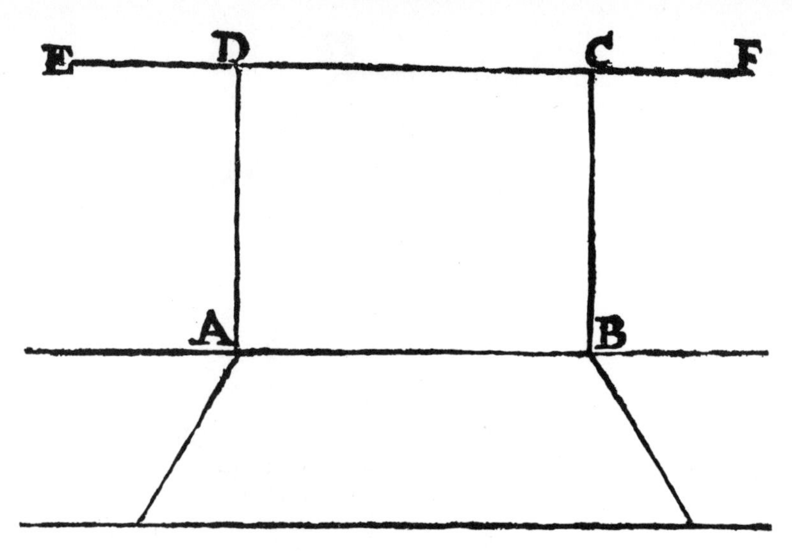


*Figure 12.*

Let the frame of the back shutter be ABCD which is not to open. It is secured with strong nails to the stage AB and with bars in the walls at E and F as the lines ED and CF show.

## 14. *How To Lay Out The Projecting Of The Roofs*

When the frame has been placed and properly secured to the stage, the projections of the roofs must be marked out. A small piece of wood, a trifle longer than the projection desired, is nailed at the highest corner of the house. It must project and slant a trifle to show the slope of the roof. Then at the other corner, towards the vanishing point, i.e. at the lower part of the house, another piece of wood is nailed at the same slant as the first. If the house is on the right side of the stage, you must go to the left and look across the cord from the vanishing point to the point of distance as in the other processes, sighting to the end of the first piece of wood and proceeding to the second at the lower part. Then the line will mark out the projection of the roof. This sighting is done with all the other houses. The projection from the front face is marked out by the line drawn from the extremity of the first piece of wood parallel to the first frame.

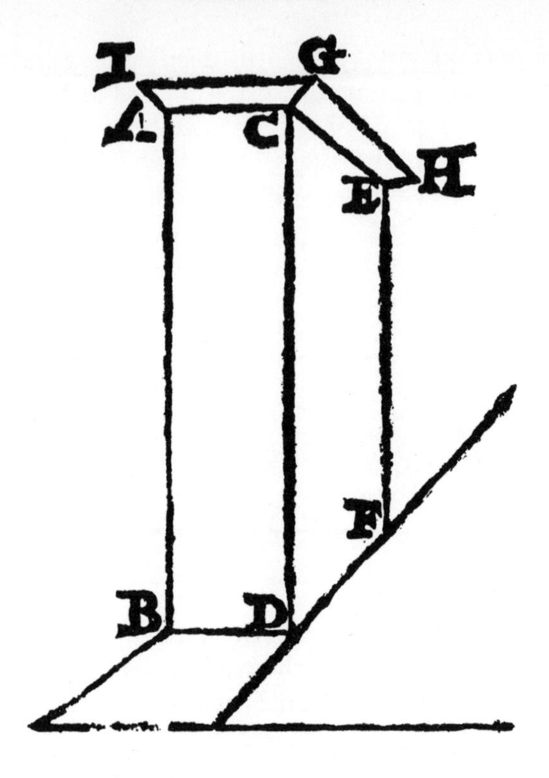


*Figure 13.*

Let the perspective face of the house be CDEF and the first piece of wood be CG at the highest corner. The line of sight over the cord runs from G to H. Therefore, CG and EH will be the roof projection on the perspective face of the house. At the front face, a line must be drawn from the extremity of the piece of wood G, parallel to the frame AC. This line will be GI, showing the projection of the house front.

## 15. *How To Sketch Out The Scene*

After the roof projections have been marked, the entire scene must be sketched out. If the painters are trained in perspective, as noted in Chapter 5, the architect will have little trouble, for the painters themselves will know how to give the effect of distance with the first coloring, or rather with the first sketching, or outlining, as we call it. But if they are not skilled in perspective painting, then the architect will have to see that the nearer portions are painted in deep colors, and the scenery further backstage is gradually made lighter in tone in the same way as the painting of the sky, spoken of in Chapter 5. It is necessary, too, to guard against coloring all the houses in the same tints, otherwise they will seem too artificial. If possible these houses should be painted so that each one presents a different appearance. The back shutter should be painted in lighter tones than the last house, so that it appears to recede into the distance. Care must be taken when painting this back shutter not to place in its centre (as many do) some temple or other building, so large and colored so boldly as to rival the first houses and consequently destroy completely the effect of distance. This is very irritating to the spectators, especially those expert in such matters. It is much better to depict some building that carries on the lines of the last houses, or else to leave the centre open so that the view remains open and unobscured. The open view is most pleasing to the eye and gives the greatest beauty to the scene.

## 16. *How To Place The Highlights and Shadows In Painting The Scene*

When we are ready to begin the painting of the scenery, the first thing to be done is to determine, according to the illumination, where the highlights and shadows are to be.

Here there are many divers opinions. Some believe in having the illumination for determining the highlights and the shadows at the front, *i.e.*, towards the spectators. Others place this illumination behind the scenery, and still others at one side. If the lighting is thought of as being in the front, then the scene will be so light and so insipid that it will not be pleasing. The spectators will not be able to make out any details, as can be realized from the first design below.

If the lighting is thought of as coming from the opposite direction, that is, from behind the scenery, as others devise, the scene will appear so crude and dark that even if a large quantity of lights are placed there, the spectators will experience dissatisfaction since they will always have the impression that they are not seeing clearly, or with pleasure, the various parts of the scenery. This lighting is shown in Figure 15.

*Figure 14.*

But if the illumination is set at one side, left or right, the houses, the back shutter, the stage floor, and the whole scene will have a finer appearance than by any of the other methods. It

*Figure 15.*

will give complete pleasure to the spectators, for the highlights and the shadows are distributed in the way that will give the greatest beauty, as is shown in the third figure. Hence we believe, and this has been commonly demonstrated, that the greatest praise will be gained by this method of painting the scene and placing the light.

*Figure 16.*

## 17. *How To Find The Middle Of Each Perspective Face Of The Houses Or Of Any Other Object*

When the houses and the back shutter have received their first wash of color and the highlights and shadows are properly placed, one must find the middle of every perspective face of the houses in order to locate the place for whatever details are to be painted on that face. Two intersecting lines are drawn between the opposite corners of the face whose center we wish to find. Where these lines intersect, another line, perpendicular to the horizon, is drawn down the face. This line marks the middle of the perspective face, as shown in the diagram.

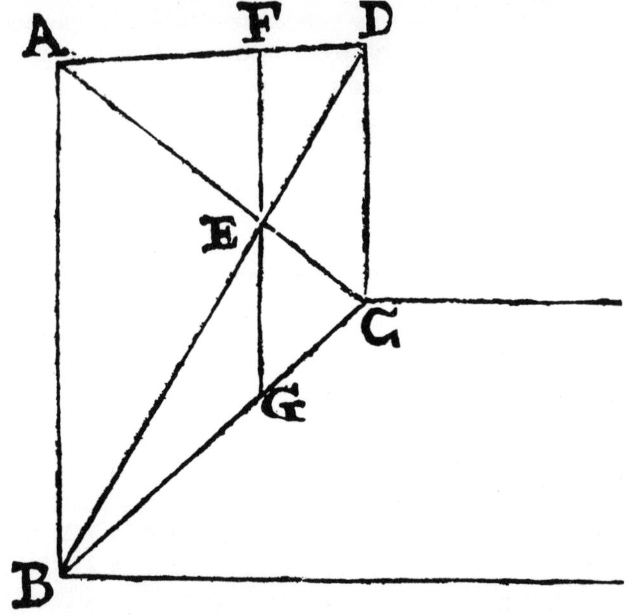


*Figure 17.*

Let the face of the house be ABCD in which you wish to find the middle. The lines AC and BD are drawn and these lines intersect at E. Then the line FEG is drawn perpendicular to the horizon. This will mark the middle of the perspective face ABCD.

## 18. *How To Design The Doors On The Perspective Faces*

Next, if a door is to be marked out in the middle of the perspective face, the height of the house at the angle uniting the two faces[1] is divided into three parts. The first and last parts are to be made equal. The middle part will be as large as you wish the door opening to be. These parts are marked by two points. This done, you will go to the opposite side of the stage and look across the cord from the vanishing point to the point of distance, as was done in the other processes, at each of these points and so draw two lines on the perspective face. Then you will draw a diagonal line across the face cutting the other two lines into two

1. The straight face and the perspective face.

segments. Finally, from the top of the face two perpendicular lines will be drawn so that they pass through these points of intersection. These lines mark the width of the door.

To indicate the height of the door itself, first you will determine how high it should be in actuality and then make a mark on the same line that was used for the points marking the width. From the point taken, by looking across the cord in the same manner as before, you draw the line. Where it cuts the two perpendicular lines is the top of the door.

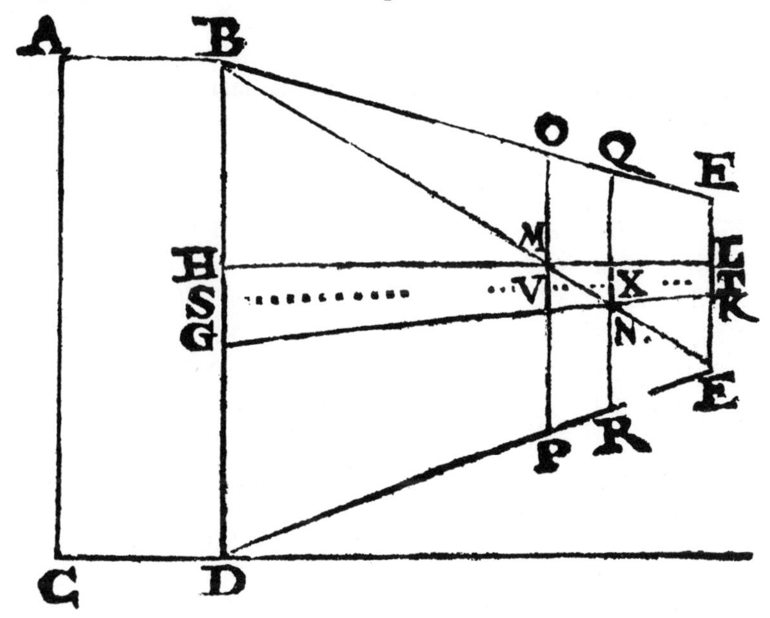


*Figure 18.*

Let BDEF be the perspective face of the house on which the door has to be made. You must divide the height DB into three parts so that the first DG and the last BH are equal, leaving the space GH as large as one wishes the door to be. Then you must look across the cord at the two points GH and draw the lines GK and HL. Then BE is drawn, cutting HL at M and GK at N. Through the points M and N the two lines OP and QR, perpendicular to the horizon, are drawn. These indicate the width of the door. For the height you will take in the line BD another point as high as you wish the door to be, S, and draw from this the line ST, following the same method. This cuts OP and QR at V and X. Then VPRX will be the opening of the door in the middle of the perspective face.

It is not necessary to show here the method of marking the doors on the straight faces of the houses, partly because there will be few of them on account of the narrowness of these faces, and also because the method is the common one which every painter, however inexpert he may be, knows himself how to manage.

## 19. *How To Design Windows On The Perspective Faces*

To design windows on the perspective faces, you divide the height of the house as indicated in the last chapter, but now into several divisions. If, for example, you wish to make three windows with the spaces between them equal to their openings, then you will sight across the cord to all the points precisely as in the other processes, drawing lines on the perspective face as shown by the cord.

Then you will draw a diagonal cutting the six lines at six points, and through these draw perpendiculars to the horizon as before, dividing the perspective faces into six parts. The first part will serve for the space between the angle and the first window, the second will be the window opening, the third another space, the fourth another window, and so on with the rest.

The heights of these windows may be desired. But first you must outline one window on the front face of the house and mark where lines at the top and the bottom of the window cut the angle at the two points. Making use of these points, you will then draw two lines, as in the other processes, cutting the perpendicular lines, to indicate the proportions of the other windows.

If it is desired to make the intermediate space greater than the window openings, then the height of the house must be accordingly divided, *i.e.*, the first part which indicates the intermediate space must be made larger, and the second, which indicates the window opening, smaller, and so on, for the others. Should a greater number of windows be desired, then the height of the front face should be divided into more parts, *i.e.*, if four windows are required, then there will be nine divisions, and so on. Should various rows of windows be wanted, then those which are wanted first should be indicated, whether above or below. The others, however, may be placed wherever we most wish them, keeping them always within the same lines. In fixing the heights of the other rows of windows, then, first will be marked out one for each row on the front face of the house. Then, as indicated above, lines will be drawn to the vanishing point to indicate the heights.

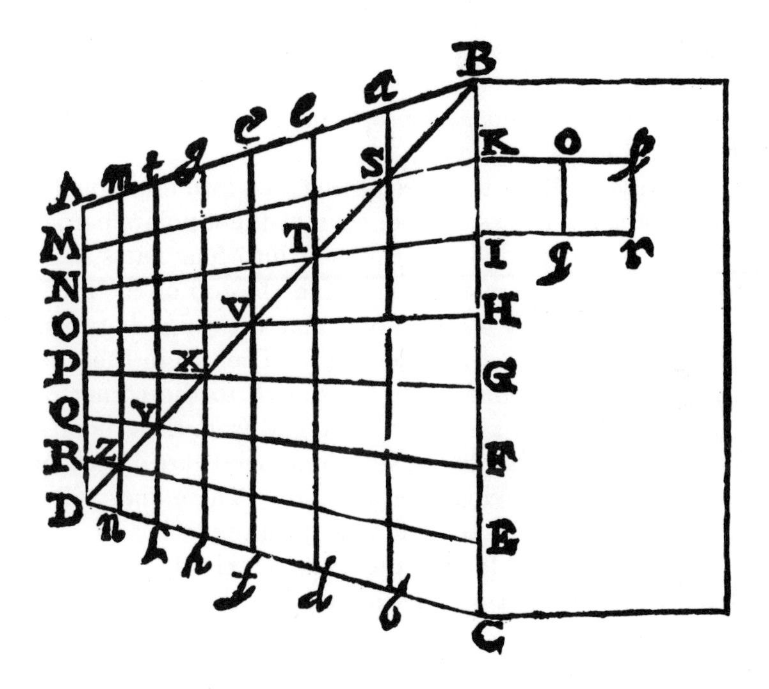

*Figure 19.*

Let ABCD be the perspective face on which there are to be, say, three windows. The height, BC, is divided into seven equal parts CE, EF, FG, GH, HI, IK, and KB. Then, looking along the cord, lines are drawn at ER, FQ, GP, HO, IN, and KM. The diagonal BD is then drawn, cutting these lines at STVXYZ and at the points of intersection perpendiculars are dropped *ab*, *cd*, *ef*, *gh*, *il*, *mn*. From *a* to B will be the space from the corner of the building to the first window, *ac* will be the opening, and *ce* is the intermediate space and *eg* the second window. Should various rows of windows be desired, in the same number as above either at the top or below, the same spaces will be used and the same openings, and the heights may be as desired.

## 20. *How To Lay Out The Arches On The Perspective Faces*

After having designed the windows, as explained in the preceding chapter, you proceed to the planning of the arches. Suppose there are to be two arches on the perspective face, with the openings four times as wide as the columns or pilasters, then an arch with the height and proportions desired is marked out on the front face of the house.

Then you divide the base of this arch into four equal parts by means of three marks. From each of these points perpendicular lines are drawn, dividing the arch into four parts, the first line between the edge of the frame and the top of the arch, the second at the summit of the arch, and the third between the middle of the arch and the other edge. Then from these points and from the cross frame, lines are drawn to the corner of the house, parallel to the base of the arch, and from these points and on the corner, lines going to the vanishing points are drawn on the perspective face by looking over the cord. These lines will serve to indicate the height of the various parts of the arches.

Let the straight face of the scene be ABCD with the arch EFG marked out on it as high as may be desired. Divide the

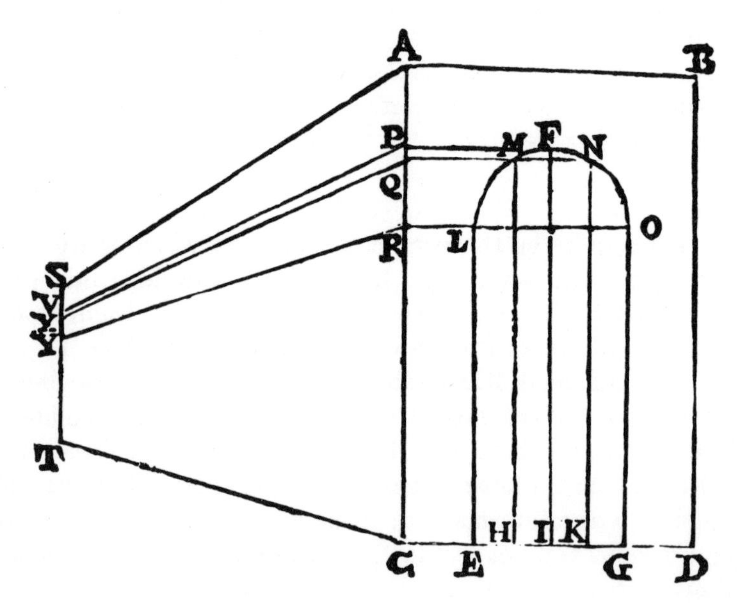


*Figure 20.*

base EG in four equal parts at the points H I K. Through these draw the perpendiculars HM, IF, and KN, and through OL draw OLR terminating at the angle made by the straight face with the perspective face AC at the point R. This line is parallel to the base EG. Draw a similar line NM terminating at Q and FM terminating at P, likewise parallel to EG. Then from PQR draw on the perspective face ASTC the lines PV, QX, and RY which go to the vanishing point.

To mark out the arches on the perspective faces, the space from the point P on the corner of the two faces down to C at the stage level is divided into ten equal parts. Then the space above P[1] makes eleven divisions in all. Of these, the 1st serves to mark the width of the column or the pilaster, the 2nd, 3rd, 4th, and 5th serve to mark the width of the opening of the first arch, the 6th the width of the second column; the 7th, 8th, 9th, 10th the width of the opening of the second arch, and the 11th, the width of the last column. From these points, lines are drawn on the perspective face to the vanishing point by the cord used before. Then, on the perspective face, a diagonal line is drawn from the point X where the last line cuts the other edge. This diagonal cuts all the lines that were drawn to the vanishing point, and from these segments perpendiculars are drawn as was done for the windows in the preceding chapter, dividing the face into eleven parts. This same diagonal also cuts the three heavy lines which were drawn from the divisions of the semicircle of the arch to the corner of the straight face and thence on the perspective face to the vanishing point. On the segments of these three lines the two arches are to be sketched on the perspective face. Where the line from the cross frame of the arch cuts the second perpendicular is marked the first point. Where the second line from the arch cuts the second perpendicular is marked the second point, and where the third line from the summit of the arch cuts the third perpendicular is marked the third point, and so by these three points will be indicated the half of the semicircle of the arch. Further, where the line cuts the fourth perpendicular, a fourth point is marked, and finally where the last line cuts the fifth perpendicular, the last point is located. By joining the five points the first arch is drawn on the perspective face.

By the same operation the second arch can be drawn as

1. EV in the second figure.

shown here in Figure 21. Should a greater number of arches be desired, the same order is kept and more divisions are made, according to the number of arches desired.

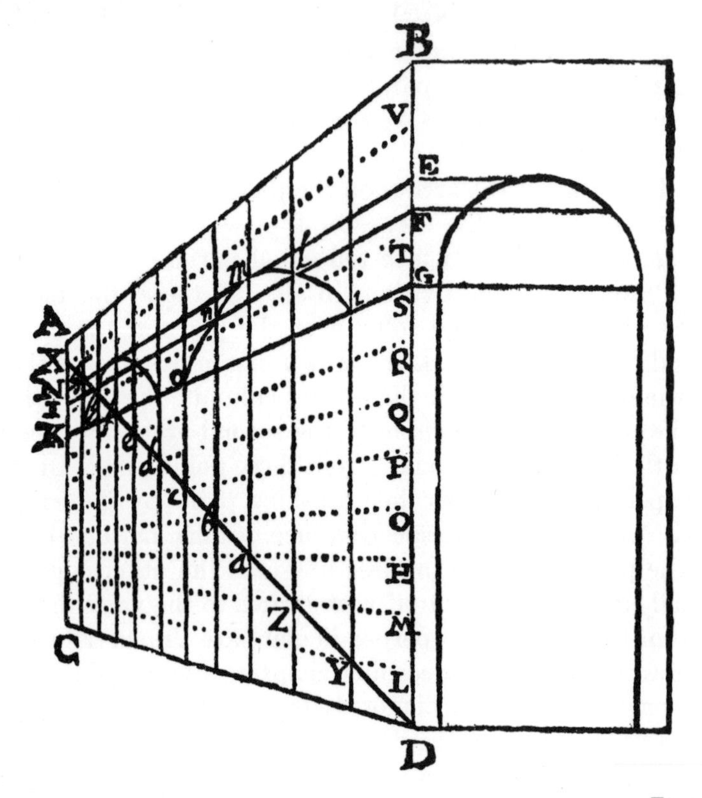


*Figure 21.*

Let ABCD be the perspective face on which two arches are to be drawn, and let their openings be four times the columns or pilasters. The arch is drawn on the straight face and lines EN, FI and GK are drawn to the vanishing point according to the instructions given above. Then the height DE is divided into ten equal parts DL, LM, MH, HO, OP, PQ, QR, RS, ST, TE. Then upon TE is added another part equal to TE, indicated as EV. All these divisions are carried to the vanishing point as shown. Then the diagonal is drawn XD. This line cuts the dotted lines YZ*abc defg* and *h*. Through these segments ten perpendiculars are drawn as described above. In the segment made by the line GK from the cross frame of the arch with the first perpendicular the point *i* is marked. In the next segment FI and the second perpendicular the point *l* is marked. Then where the third perpendicular cuts EN, another point *m* is marked. Then, *n* is marked where the fourth perpendicular makes a segment with FI and lastly where GK cuts the fifth perpendicular another point *o* is added. These points *il, lm, mn, no,* are joined to form the semicircle of the first arch on the perspective face. GI marks the thickness of the first column or pilaster. The same process is used for the second arch and for such others as may be desired.

This chapter and this operation may seem long and intricate to the readers, but they must realize that this matter of arches is perhaps the most difficult process in drawing the scene and could not be presented with fewer words or by the use of fewer lines.

## 21. *How To Draw Shops On The Straight Or On The Perspective Faces*

Now that we have dealt with the method of marking out the arches, let us turn to the means of drawing the booths or shops which commonly embellish the scene. These may be shown either on the straight or on the perspective face. Although only a part of them may be seen on a straight face because of its narrowness, yet some may be shown there. The method is so simple that to deal with it here seems superfluous; the painter will already know for himself. He ought, however, to observe that the counters and the roofs should be drawn in perspective, just as the stage floor.

For shops on the perspective faces, the following method is to be employed. The highest edge of the perspective face is divided into four parts. The first is as high from the bottom as the booth counter is to be above the ground. The next is as high above the first as the opening of the shop is to be, and the third is above the others at the height of the entrance to the shop. From these points the lines are drawn to the vanishing point as in the preceding chapter. Then the diagonal is drawn cutting the three lines, and where it cuts them, perpendiculars are drawn to outline the opening of the shop and the entrance.

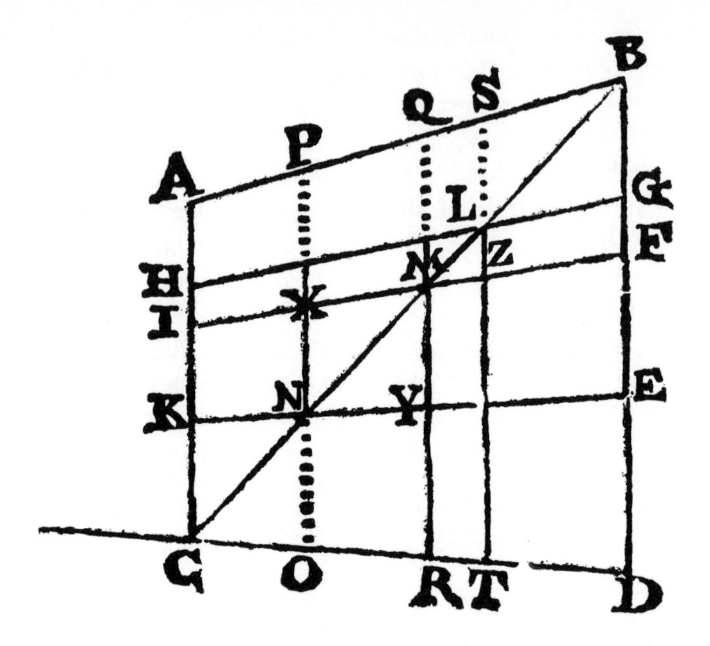


*Figure 22.*

Let ABCD be the perspective face and the height BD be divided into four parts, making DE equal to the height of the booth counter from the ground, EF equal to the window and FG equal to the height of the panel or door. Then lines are drawn from these points to the vanishing point EK, FI and GH. The diagonal BC cuts GH at L, FI at M, and EK at N. Perpendiculars are then drawn PO, QR, and ST. These indicate the proportions of the shop, *i.e.*, MRTZ is the entrance, MYNX is the window. The means of making the counter and roof is demonstrated in Figure 23.

The shop EFGH is shown in the perspective face ABCD. To draw the counter, look over the cord that was drawn from the point of distance to the side wall, sighting to the point H. Then by that cord draw the line ML to the vanishing point, and draw LG from G parallel to HM so as to mark out the counter GHLM.

To draw the roof, the point N is taken on the height BD, as high as the roof is to be. Then another point P is taken as far toward the opening as the roof is to be broad. Through these points then are drawn NO and PQ to the vanishing point. Directly above F on the line NO a point S is marked, and through S is drawn the line SV sloping as much as is necessary to show the

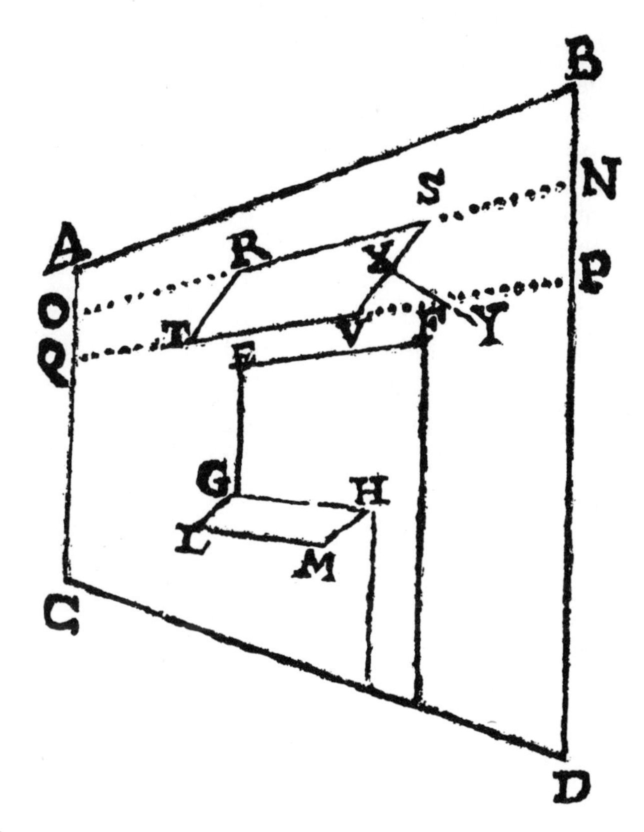


*Figure 23.*

height of the roof directly above E at the other end of the opening of the shop. On the line NO is taken another point R and through it is drawn RT parallel to SV. Thus is drawn out the roof RSTV in height and depth. The supports may also be drawn as at XY.

## 22. *How To Draw The Projections Of The Cornices With Their Separate Parts On The Perspective Faces*

After the doors, the windows, the arches, and the shops, there remain to be designed, among other things, the projections of the cornices and other ornaments above the doors and windows. To do this with accuracy, first are drawn the profiles of the various sections of the cornice. From each of these sections you must sight over the cord drawn at right angles from the point of distance to the side wall as described in Chapter 9, and according to the sighting, the lines are drawn on the upper part of the perspective face to mark the projection of the cornices, or any other thing you desire. Then from these same points on the profile, by sighting over the first cord drawn from the vanishing point to the point of distance, the lines are drawn on the perspective face towards its lower end to mark out the separate parts of the cornice.

In the same way are drawn the steps to a door and the benches or blinds for windows, the iron brackets for holding cloth out from the wall, the signs of taverns, and everything that projects out. The cord from the point of distance to the side wall is used as said above. It is not necessary to speak of cornices on

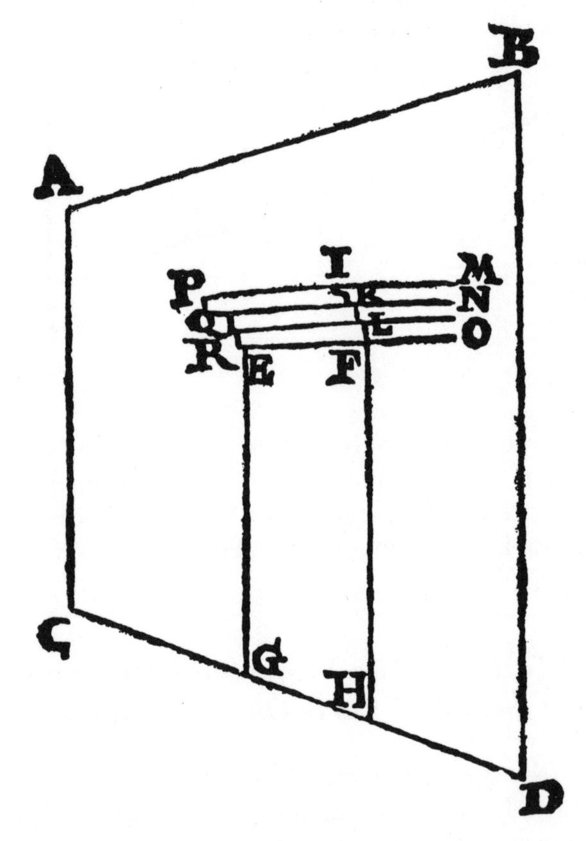

*Figure 24.*

the front faces for they are easy for any craftsman who professes to paint or to design without further instruction.

In figure 24 let the perspective face be ABCD, and the

opening of the door EFGH, on top of which we must draw the projections of the cornice, with its separate parts, as desired. Let us indicate the profile IKL in such a way as we wish it. By means of the same string the tops of the windows, doors, columns, and arches will be indicated. We shall look across the string, which was drawn from the vanishing point to the wall, and according to those points which it will give us, we shall indicate on the highest part of the perspective face, the lines IM, KN, and LO. On this line can be drawn the projection of the cornice. In order to form the separate parts of the cornice, from the points I, K, and L on the forementioned profile, we shall look again across the string from the upper towards the lower part of the perspective face, and according to the points seen we shall indicate the lines IP, KQ, and LR, as long as we wish the cornice to be. Then we shall join the points PQ, QR, and RE, which are parallel to IK, KL, and LF, and by this operation we shall have the projection of the cornice with its separate parts.

## 23. *How To Design Balconies On The Perspective Faces*

Balconies on the perspective faces, if well designed, can add great beauty to the scene. They are drawn in this manner. The profile of the balcony is marked out in the most pleasing and most likely place on the wall. Then by sighting over the cord, drawn between the point of distance and the wall, as in the projection of the cornices to the profile, lines are drawn towards the highest part of the face. Then from the same points by sighting over the other cord from the point of distance to the vanishing point, lines are drawn towards the lower end of the face, and the ends are joined together by another line. These lines, as was said concerning the cornices, will permit the balcony to project further than the first lines.

If it is desired to represent bracing pieces, such as brackets and buttresses, the same process is used, with the outline being designed first and then the details, as shown below.

Let ABCD be the perspective face, and EF the profile of the balcony. With the cord from the point of distance to the wall, we will look across the points E and F, which are the ends of the profile of the balcony, towards the highest part BD. The lines EG and FH are drawn as long as we desire the projection of

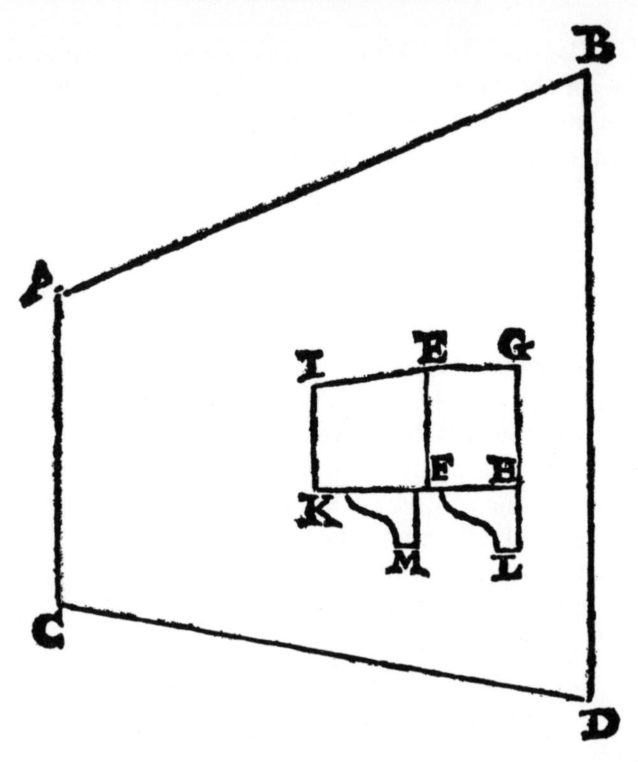


*Figure 25.*

the balcony to be. From the same points of the profile EF we will look across the other cord from the point of distance to the lower part AC and draw accordingly the lines EI and FK indicating the length of the balcony. If we wish to sustain the balcony by brackets or buttresses, L and M, the same process must be carried out.

## 24 *How To Design A Balcony Partly On The Front Face And Partly On The Perspective Face*

Balconies, beside being shown on the perspective faces only, are sometimes designed partly on the front face and partly on the perspective face so that they seem to project beyond the corner of the angle. Although the front of the balcony is composed of two lines, it will appear as one, which will give great delight to the spectators.

We shall indicate on the front face a point on the height of the base of the balcony from the stage floor. From this point we will look across the cord and, accordingly, we shall draw a line partly on the two faces, as long as we desire the length of the front of the balcony. The same is done for the height of the parapet of the balcony. Then we shall indicate the cornices and balustrades by vertical lines part on the front face and part on the perspective face.

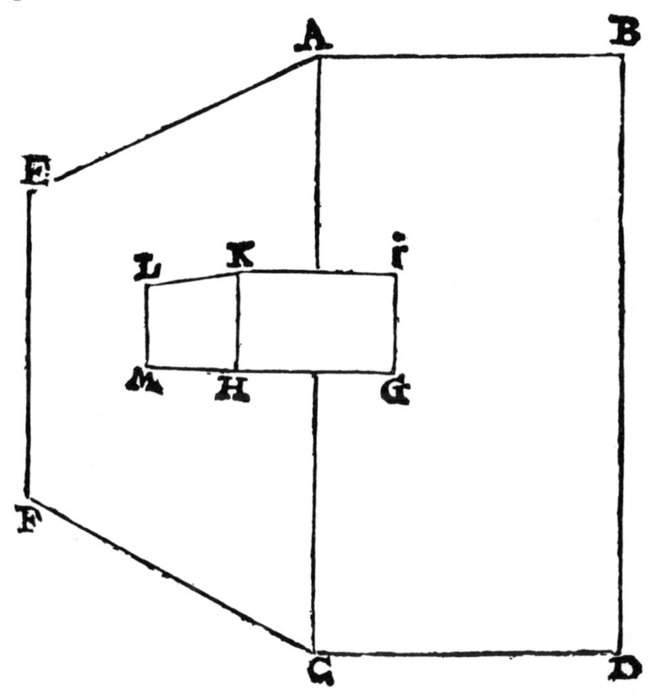


*Figure 26.*

Let ABCD be the front face, and AEFC the perspective face, on which we shall design the balcony. Let us take any point on the front face ABCD and mark it G, as high as we want the balcony to be from the floor of the stage. To this point we shall look across the cord, which was drawn from the point of distance at right angles with the wall, and, according to that line, let us indicate a line which is to be partly on the front face and partly on the perspective face. This line may be as long as the front of the balcony from G to H. Let us indicate above G the point I, as high above G as we want the height of the parapet of the balcony. By the point I we shall look across the same cord, and draw IK as long as GH. The points GI and HK are joined. Thus GIKH will show the front of the balcony to be all in one piece, although it is indicated partly on the front and partly on the perspective face. It still remains to indicate the length of the balcony, which will be most easily done, governing ourselves according to the preceding chapter. From the point H we shall look across the cord and draw HM as long as we want the length of the balcony. We shall do the same from K to L. Let us join LM parallel to HK thus having marked the length and width of the balcony half on each face by means of the figure HKLM.

## 25. *How To Design A Piazza On A Perspective Face*

For beauty and variety there can be added piazzas painted on the perspective faces if these are of sufficient length. On the perspective face, at the highest and lowest point, two houses are indicated as narrow as possible. In the space between these two houses, we may draw the piazza as follows. To mark the outline of the piazza, a point is established at the upper corner of the first house where the piazza is to begin. This point should not be higher than the vanishing point but rather somewhat lower so that the piazza will not seem to be on a hilly place sloping downward, which would put it on a different plane from that of the stage. We shall look across the cord and, accordingly, we shall indicate the line between the two houses. In this manner will be determined the width of the space which is to comprise the piazza.

On the face above the line may be drawn houses, palaces, temples, or other buildings, just as in the case of ordinary wings.

Observe that in the painting of this piazza, no person or any other moving object should be represented here nor in any other part of the scene. It would be scarcely true to nature that an object would remain motionless through the action of the limits of a day, and for other reasons that need not be mentioned here.

Let ABCD be the perspective face on which we are to draw a piazza. At its highest point, let us indicate the house ACEF as narrow as possible and at its lowest point, the house, GHBD. Then, on the corner EF of the first house let us take any point I, which is not higher than the vanishing point, but rather lower and, looking across the cord, accordingly, draw IK, which will show the depth of the piazza. Above this line IK, we shall draw the houses according to the rules for designing all houses.

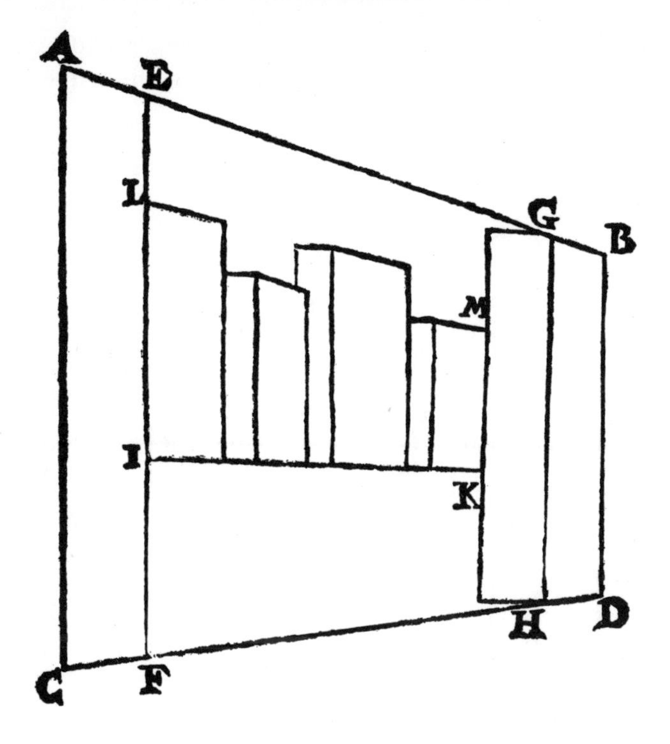


*Figure 27.*

## 26. *How To Design A Street That Seems To Go Directly Off From A Perspective Face*

Besides such a piazza, if there is space enough, a street can be shown that will seem to lead directly off from some other perspective face. This street will make the scene seem larger and more impressive. Here two houses are marked off in their place in the same way on the perspective face, or else instead of the houses, two towers may be drawn according to the rules noted above. Between the two houses a point is established in the middle of the perspective face at the same height as the vanishing point. Then from the point on the stage floor at the upper corner of the first house, and from the point on the lower corner of the second house, lines are drawn to the center point. A line is drawn parallel to the horizon intersecting these two lines and as far from the vanishing point as we wish the length of the street. On these two lines we may complete the houses, and in the remaining space we may draw additional houses to complete the street.

To make the scene still more magnificent a triumphal arch with a street under it may be shown over the whole face instead of the houses or the towers.

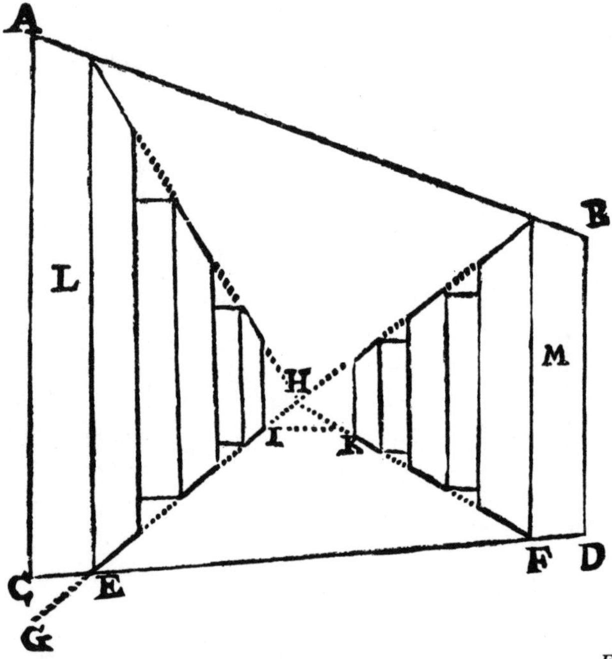


*Figure 28.*

Let ABCD be the perspective face on which we may draw a street which seems to go off straight from it. Let us place two houses at the beginning and end of this perspective face: AE at its highest part and FB at its lowest part. Then, take any point H in the middle of this perspective face, at the same level as the vanishing point, and farther or nearer to the horizon as we wish the length of the street to appear. From the ends of the last angle of the first house E, and from the first corner of the last house F, let us draw two lines to the point H, which are EH and FH. A line IK parallel to the horizon will intersect these two lines not far from point H. On this line palaces or temples may be drawn to indicate the end of the street, or the space may be painted to represent the sky. On the other two lines there will be space, if we wish, to draw the remainder of the first houses, similar to L and M, drawing their roofs toward point H. For the rest you depict what buildings you wish.

## 27. *How To Design The Back Shutter*

After the sides are designed, the shutter in the center is to be laid out. In the middle of the frame there is firmly fastened, at a point equal to the height of the vanishing point, by means of the little stick as indicated in Chapter 7, the end of a cord, at least half as long as the shutter. The other end of the cord is free and movable. After this, the marking off of the perspective can begin. The frame can be carried wherever desired for the convenience of the painter, care being taken, however, to place it in a place having lighting similar to the rest of the stage (so that the frame when returned will be harmonious in color with the rest of the scenery). First there will be marked on the frame the length which was taken on the center line to indicate the length of the perspective, as described in Chapter 10. The same cord is used to design all parts of the frame. First of all the two main lines, where the houses and streets should go, are indicated by bringing the loose end of the cord to the right side of the scene and to the left side allowing as much space as needed to represent the front faces. To mark off the height and base of each house or palace, the loose end of the cord is brought to the lowest or highest point of the buildings to be designed on either side of the frame. Windows, doors, and other details are marked off in the same way. The front faces of the houses are marked off with a line always parallel to the horizon by means of a ruler held always parallel to the horizon, and the sides of the house are marked off by vertical lines, as shown in figure 29.

Let ABCD be the back shutter, CD be the distance between the extremities of the front houses. From each side let us determine the width we desire the two first houses to be, CE and FD. Let us complete the straight faces L and M; G is the center point between them. Above it let us mark point H, perpendicular to G, and as high as the vanishing point, or rather at a height of 1½ feet, as in Chapter 4. At H, the end of a cord is firmly fixed and the other end, R, is drawn to E, the end of the face L and, according to it, a line is drawn as far from H as is desired. The same is done on the other side. These two lines indicate where houses, streets, etc., may be drawn. Roofs, doors, windows, and other things may be drawn in perspective in the same manner.

On the straight faces all the projections may be drawn by

means of a ruler held parallel to the base of the frame, and the same procedure is followed to draw the perspective on the shutter.

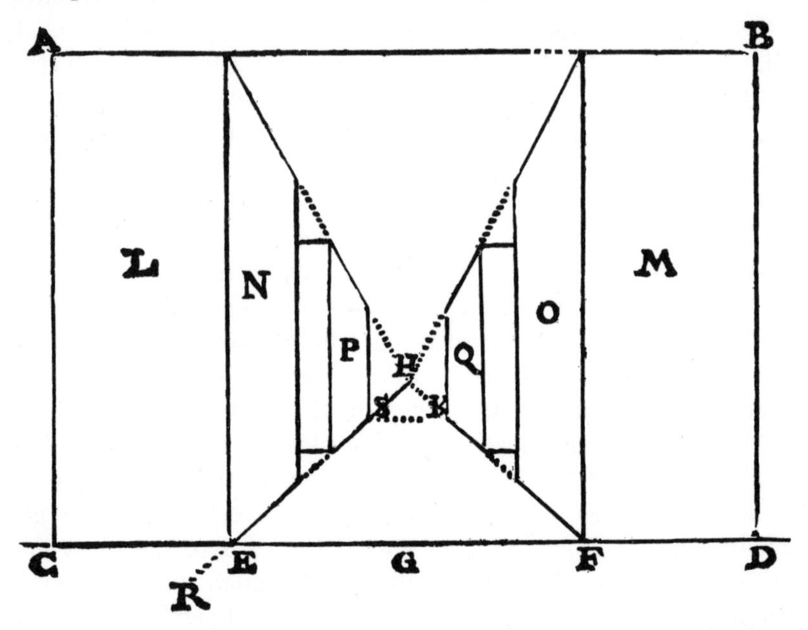


*Figure 29.*

## 28. *How To Show Several Streets On The Back Shutter With One Or With Several Vanishing Points*

Some designers are in the habit of drawing more than one street on the back shutter, either with a single or with several vanishing points. I cannot approve very highly of this treatment because it may make the scene seem larger. It lessens the perspective because the houses and streets become so small that they look like mere specks. However, if you want to do this you can proceed thus: first you mark out the front faces of the first two houses, fasten a cord to the point at the middle of the frame, as in the preceding chapter. To show three streets leading to a single vanishing point in the middle of the frame, the fronts of two other houses are drawn as far apart from each other as the desired width of the center street. Then, with the cord, the details of the street with the houses are laid out as in the preceding chapter.

Let us draw the cord to the right, and mark from the corner of the front of the first house, the line of the second street.

Its length should be such that it terminates on a level with the front face of the first house of the center street. By means of the same cord we shall indicate the houses.

On the left we may proceed in the same manner to indicate the left street.

To make three streets with separate vanishing points, first are marked out the four front faces of the four houses at the head of the three streets. In the side streets the side vanishing points are carefully marked at the same height and level as the center vanishing point. At each vanishing point a cord is fastened similar to the cord from the center point, and the lines for each street are drawn separately in the same manner as above.

Care should be taken not to cause wonder among the spectators that the two houses, which end the two streets, do not almost form a right angle, as did the two houses which ended the three streets going to a single vanishing point. These houses, which will lead to two points, will appear to form an obtuse angle, similar to the houses which end at the straight street in the perspective face in Chapter 26.

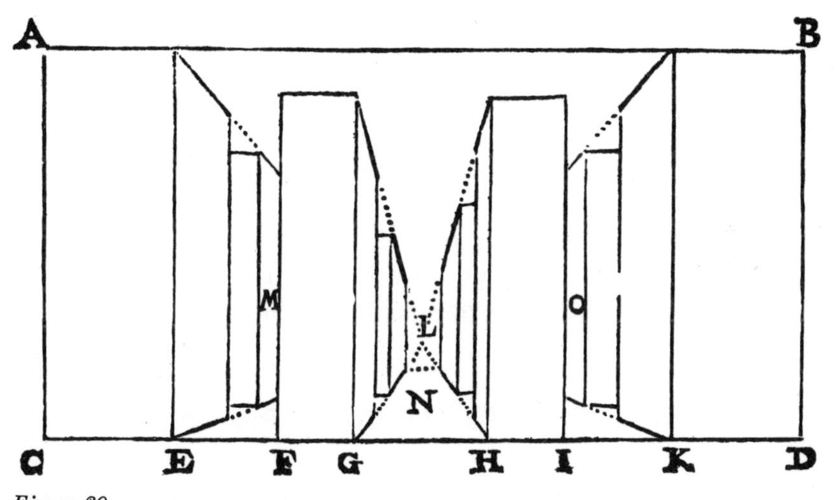


*Figure 30.*

Let ABCD be the back shutter, and CE, FG, HI, and KD be the fronts of the four houses. EF, GH, and IK indicate the spaces for the streets and L the vanishing point. In these spaces three streets are drawn, which lead to the same point L. Let us fix the cord at L, as before. The street N is indicated in the same manner as in the preceding chapter. Using the same cord, a line from E to M and another from K to O are drawn. In this manner three streets with a single vanishing point are drawn on the back shutter.

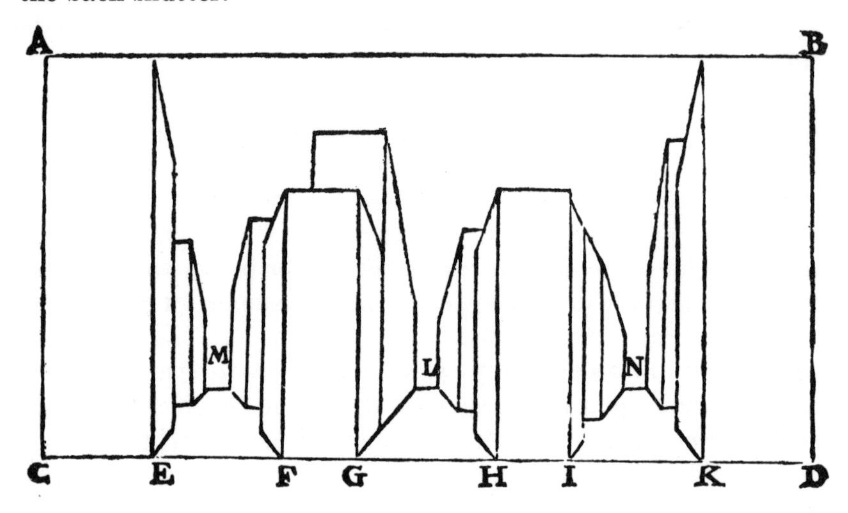


*Figure 31.*

Let ABCD be the back shutter, and CE, FG, HI, and KD be the fronts of the four houses. EF, GH, and IK are the spaces for the streets. Let L be the first vanishing point. Since we want to indicate three streets leading to three separate vanishing points within the spaces which we have marked, let us take two points M and N on the same level and at the same horizon height as our first vanishing point L. At these points M, N, and L let us fix the cords and go through the same operations which we followed to indicate a single center street.

## 29. *How To Make The Roofs And Chimneys*

Now that we have passed the difficulties of the scene and of the back shutter, with the steps for designing them in the easiest and briefest way possible, let us pass on to describe how to complete the roofs and form the chimneys. Possibly this operation may seem trifling and of little importance, nevertheless a careful consideration of these things can give a spirit and ornament to the scene and greatly increase the effect of depth particularly in the case of the chimneys. Care must be taken that these chimneys are not placed without purpose but that they are put where they will seem to belong in reality.

To show roofs, pieces of cardboard are taken and put together with a shape like a jar proportionate to the size of the houses they are to cover. These pieces of cardboard are fastened well on the projections of the roofs. In order that, during the dancing or during other activities that make motion, the chimneys do not fall, frames are made like the large frames. Or two pieces of board are taken at right angles but proportionate to the houses, to which they are fastened tightly. The slant of the roofs is drawn by sighting over the cord, as was done for the large frames of the houses, leaving the front faces parallel to the horizon, or by sighting over the cord that was drawn from the point of distance to the side wall, as was said concerning the projections of the cornices and the balconies, as in Figure 32. On the perspective face ABCD the chimney EFG is fastened with nails to the face at H, I, and K.

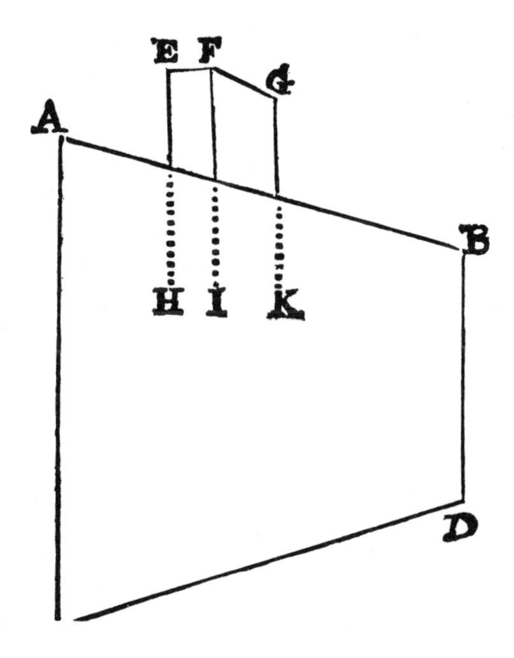


*Figure 32.*

## 30. *How To Paint The Scenes*

When the scene has been fully planned out in detail, the painter, after he has sketched out the main areas as described in Chapter 27, begins to paint it as carefully as he can, both the houses with their embellishments and the back shutter. The same rule is to be followed: the front houses are to be painted in dark colors and as the houses diminish in size, lighter colors are to be used, so that all houses shall not be the same color, but as varied as possible, as in Chapter 15. Take care not to depict any men or women at the windows or in the streets, or birds in cages, monkeys, or other domestic pets. These take away from the impression of reality for the authors make their comedies include action which often goes beyond the period of one entire day, and it is impossible that these men and animals should stand immovable entire days. This is one of the reasons which convinces us that such things should not be painted on the scene. Although this has been said above I deem it necessary of repetition, since it is a matter that much concerns not only the honor of the painter but the reputations of those in charge. Avoid, then, these artificialities and paint on only inanimate things. I cannot help remarking, too, that in mixing his colors the painter should use size or another medium so that the paint may not fall or easily flake off from the scenes as sometimes occurs when pure water is used or when the size is mixed with too little care or too great haste. Accordingly, he who desires good results ought to pay great attention to every process.

## 31. *How To Color The Stage Parapet*

When the scene has been painted, the stage parapet must be colored. This may be done in a variety of ways. Some persons paint it to seem like ordinary red bricks with an edge of simulated marble. The appearance is like that of the battlement of a fortress, as is shown in Figure 33.

Others color it with polygonal shapes, in light and dark tones, and likewise the edge, as shown in Figure 34.

Both of these methods of drawing and painting the parapets are good and praiseworthy and either may be employed as desired according to the taste. I must, however, note that they

*Figure 33.*

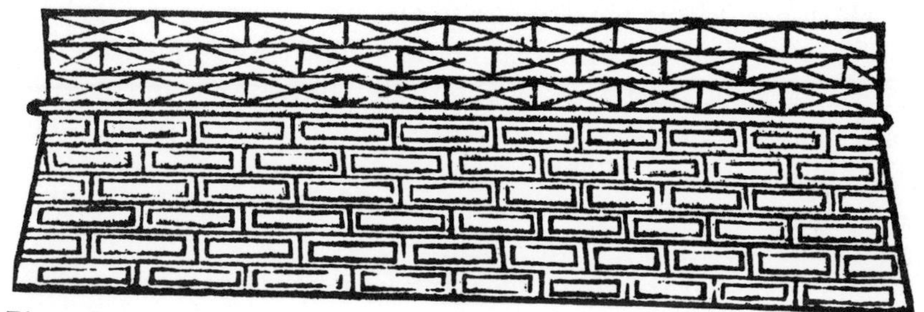

*Figure 34.*

are little enjoyed because of the crowds of people in front of them and also because most of the spectators have thoughts and eyes only for the scene. In fact the parapet can present a fine appearance only on paper.

It, therefore, really matters little how they are painted, although there should not show slits or holes lest the workmen underneath the stage be seen, as noted in Chapter 3.

## 32. *How To Adorn The Beginning Of The Heavens*

From the painting of the stage parapet, which is the lowest part of all, we turn to deal with the method of completing, by means of festoons or other decorations, that part of the sky which is the highest of all, joining the ceiling or vault of the theatre. This may be done by making an artificial festoon of leaves with various fruits with hanging parts. In the middle the coat of arms of the prince or a similar pleasing device may be introduced.

One might also adorn this portion in another way by means of a piece of cloth simulating brocade sprinkled with shining gold, in hanging folds and gold tassels. These, however, must be large and not small and meager so that they not only ornament this part but give distinction to the whole scene. Figures may be painted at the corners according to taste, necessity or appositeness.

## 33. *How To Design And Paint The Stage Floor*

The last thing to be done on the stage is to design and paint the stage floor. This could not be done earlier on account of the rehearsals of dancers and actors and of stage workers all of which necessitate much going to and fro. Because of this both the painting and the principal marks might easily be wiped out. The stage floor, therefore, ought to be marked out and painted only shortly before the time of performance and care taken, when it is finished, not to let anyone walk on it. Should that be impossible then some boards should be laid down which may be walked on without spoiling the work beneath.

To design the stage floor, the front of the stage is marked out in as many parts as may be desired, with or without narrow strips. The same is to be done at the opposite end, that is to say along the line of the back shutter. Lines are then drawn from the two sets of points across the stage floor. After this two diagonals are marked out and where these intersect the others are drawn lines which (if the work has been done accurately) are

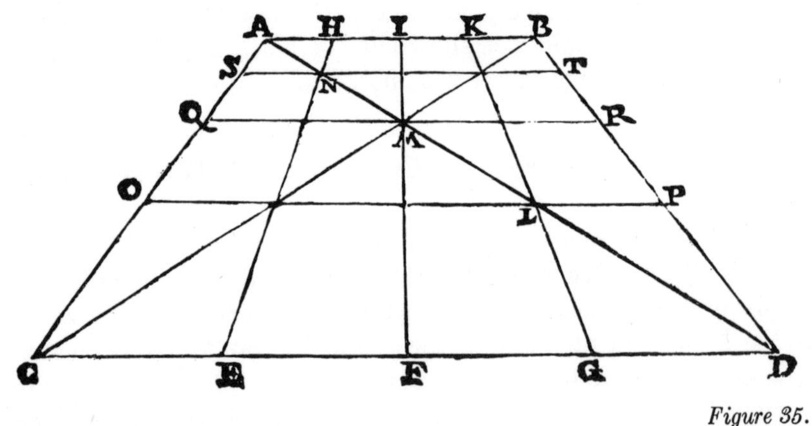


*Figure 35.*

parallel to the stage front. The strips may then be colored white, if desired, and the spaces between with other colors. Thus is completed the designing and painting of the stage floor, as is shown above.

In figure 35 let ABCD be the stage floor with the front at CD. This is divided into 4 equal parts — CE, EF, FG, GD. Similarly the line AB is divided into 4 equal parts, AH, HI, IK, KB. Lines are drawn through EH, FI, and GK. The diagonals AD and BC are then drawn, intersecting the other lines at L, M and N. Then, parallel to the stage front CD other lines are drawn through the points LMN at OP, QR and ST. This is the method when the strips are not used.

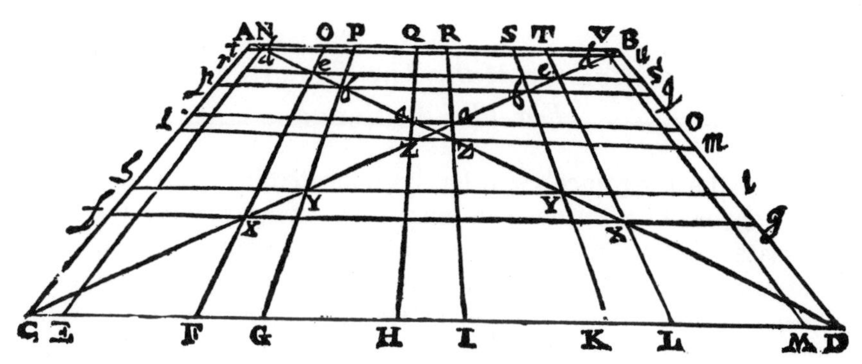


*Figure 36.*

Let ABCD be the stage floor and let the front CD be divided into 9 parts, *i.e.*, CE for the first half strip, EF for the space, FG for the second strip, GH for the second space, HI for the third strip, IK for the third space, KL for the fourth strip, LM for the fourth space and MD for the fifth strip. Similarly the line AB is divided into AN, NO, OP, PQ, QR, RS, ST, TV, and VB. Diagonals are drawn as in the other figure (AD and BC) cutting the lines at *x,y,z,a,b,c* and *d*. The first strip is left out of these segments. The lines *fg, hi, lm, no, pq, rs,* and *tu* are drawn parallel to the stage front. Thus the stage floor is suitably divided with the strips. The method of painting is dealt with above.

## 34. *How To Place The Prince's Seat*

It seems reasonable to me, after having described the stage setting, to discuss how and in what position should be located the seat of the prince or other dignitary who is to witness the performance. You will have to choose a location as near as possible to the point of distance, and elevated sufficiently from the floor of the hall so that when seated his eye will be as high as the vanishing point, for all the objects in the scene appear better from that position than from any other place. You then make a kind of palisade, fixed to the ground with strong beams and secured with stout pegs and nailed, so that the crowd of people, who on these occasions show little discretion, cannot injure it. Around this may be placed seats for the courtiers, or for the soldiers of his guard, as desired.

## 35. *How To Make The Tiers Of Seats For The Audience*

After the prince's seat has been located in an advantageous and convenient position, you must think about making the tiers of seats, so that the spectators may be comfortable, see well, and not interfere with one another. To do this you take good, strong beams. One is placed at the desired height of the tiers upright against the wall, and another is taken which will be as long as the depth of these tiers of seats. They are joined at the ends, the one marking the depth being placed on the floor with its end touching that which stands upright, and great care should be taken to secure them with strong pegs. Then another piece of wood, very strong and solid, is to be selected and stoutly nailed to the ends of the first two pieces. These form a right-angled triangle, or as we shall call it, a *squadro*. Similar structures will be placed around the hall or theatre, so that they are not more than five feet apart. On the longest side of each, smaller triangles of lighter wood 1½ feet high and 1 foot or a trifle more deep will be made to support the seats. They should be well joined together with nails, as very strong boards are to be placed upon them. In this way the tiers of seats are made without injuring the floor or piercing the walls, and yet are rendered very secure. Concerning the accommodation of men and women[1] on the hall floor nothing need be said, for these plank-benches and chairs will serve. This does not require much labor and is done with little trouble.

Let AC be the first piece of wood placed against the wall with its end C on the floor and the other, BC, lying on the floor, joins it at C. Then the third piece of wood AB joins the extremi-

1. Spectators.

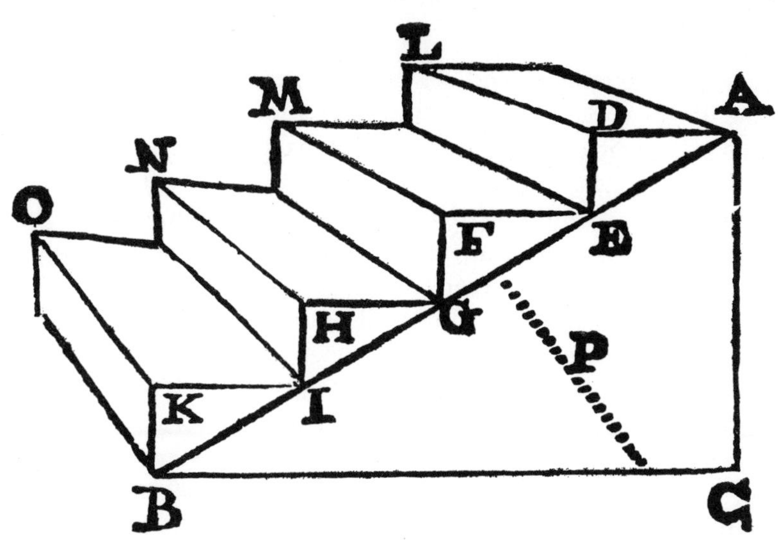


*Figure 37.*

ties of AC and BC and is well pegged. On the piece of wood AB are fastened the triangles ADE, EFG, GHI, and IKB, which are made of lighter wood and securely nailed. On these triangles boards are laid or extended, namely: DL, FM, HN, and KO, which are firmly fixed with nails. If you do not have sufficiently stout beams for AB, then these should be strengthened with another piece of wood, as at the dotted line P.

## 36. *How To Place The Musicians*

When the tiers of spectators' seats have been made, you must give some thought to the placement of the musicians. They should not be set within the scene because they and their various instruments will interfere with the machines.

They may be provided with quarters outside the scene on both sides. To do this two strong wooden balconies are built into the walls, of sufficient size to hold them and their instruments.

The balconies are ornamented with brackets, balustrades, and Venetian blinds. Thus not only will the musicians be comfortable and better able to see everything, but also the instrumental and vocal music will be better heard, and the appearance of the balconies will add to the adornment of the whole. Should it be desired to have the musicians within the scene, the positions they are to occupy are to be fixed in advance on account of the instruments. This is necessary for once the *telari* for the houses have been completed and set in position on the stage floor, it is difficult to work there. Accordingly the position for the musicians and their equipment should be fixed before the *telari* have been set in place. The scaffolds should be built, one on each side of the scene, as large as may be necessary. They should be as long as the distance from the first house to the wall behind the back shutter, *i.e.*, between the perspective and the wall, and should be fixed partly to the wall and partly to the floor of the hall. The beams should pass through holes in the stage floor, so that they make no contact with the stage. Thus the morris dances will not upset the organs and other instruments. These beams should be fixed high enough above the stage floor to provide free passage space below. In this way the musicians may be placed within the scene without being seen by the spectators. Experience shows this to be the best plan.

## 37. *How The Front Curtain Is Raised*

There are two methods for operating the curtain at the beginning of the play. By the first, the curtain is let fall from above to the floor of the hall. By the second, it is raised up to disappear above the heavens, if there is the possibility for this arrangement. The first method involves little trouble. Two simple pulleys, or as we call them, *girelle*, are made fast at each side of the heavens with two cords, two ends of which are tied to the upper part of the curtain and the other ends are held in the hands of two workmen, who, at the instant when the signal is given by the trumpet, or by other means, let the curtain fall free, and the scene is opened. In using several persons in various places in the same operation it is difficult to co-ordinate their actions so that all parts fall evenly. I have seen many times in practice the scene revealed to the audience, first a bit on one side, then a bit on the other, with no little displeasure to the spectators, and the loss of that sense of wonder that comes with the sudden and even fall of the curtain. I, myself, would propose that the ends of the cords be held by one person only. I believe and am very sure that it would be still better to attach two equal weights to the top of the curtain (two little bags of sand will serve) to bring the curtain down the quicker. The weights should be of proper size so that in the rapid fall no harm be done. All this is shown in Figure 38.

The second method, although it involves more expense and more labor, is much better and produces its effect with greater celerity and without confusion and fright, that often occurs w en part of the curtain sometimes falls on the audience.

This is the method. A wooden cylinder is made in the form of a roller, a little longer than the width of the curtain, and within the space available. Its diameter should be one third the height of the curtain, or if there is not space enough for that, whatever size is convenient may be used. This cylinder should be placed above the heavens with its pivot set in two beams built on the side walls, so that it turns easily. The upper part of the curtain is fastened to the roller leaving the lower part hanging down to the floor of the hall. At both ends of the roller, a little distance from the curtain, two ropes are wound with weights so adjusted that by falling they revolve the roller and draw the curtain up. Thus the curtain is lifted in an instant and the scene is disclosed without anyone being aware of what has happened. It is advisable to have the weights fall behind the

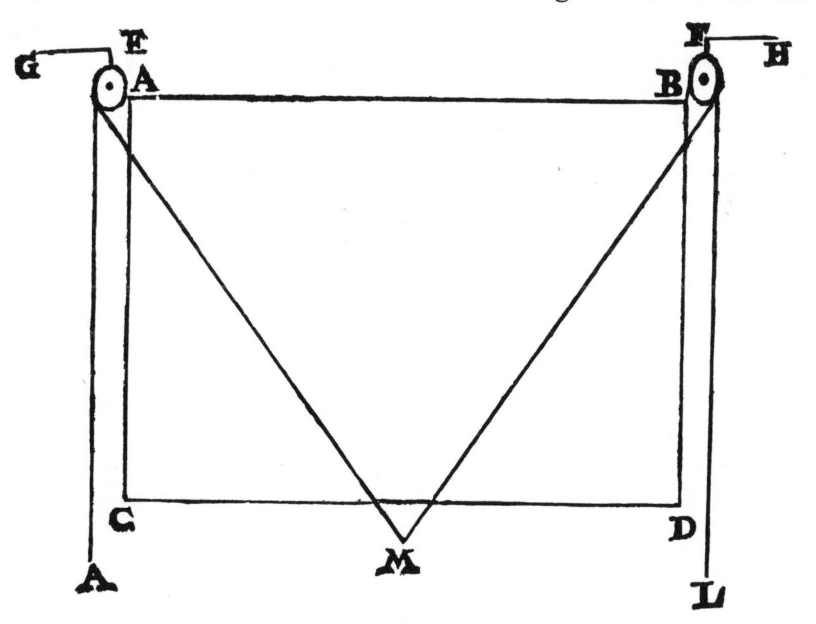


*Figure 38.*[1]

1. In this figure Sabbattini has wrongly marked K as A.

walls where they are not seen and make no noise. Also, a little before the curtain is raised, some faithful persons should be placed in front at the parapet to prevent anyone from coming near the curtain, thus avoiding dangers and confusions, such as sometimes occur because of malice, negligence or lack of discretion of the stage hands who hold the ends of the curtain. The importance of this matter has caused me to give more space than I had originally intended. I beg the readers to pardon me.

Let ABCD be the curtain and the pulleys E and F fastened at the two sides G and H. The cords are AEK and BFL with the ends KL held by two trustworthy stagehands who will let go at the same moment. This is all that is necessary for the first method.

For the second method the ends AEM and BFM are placed in the hands of a single person, and suitable equal weights are placed at A and B. This placing of the two ends in the hands of one person makes the operation safer.

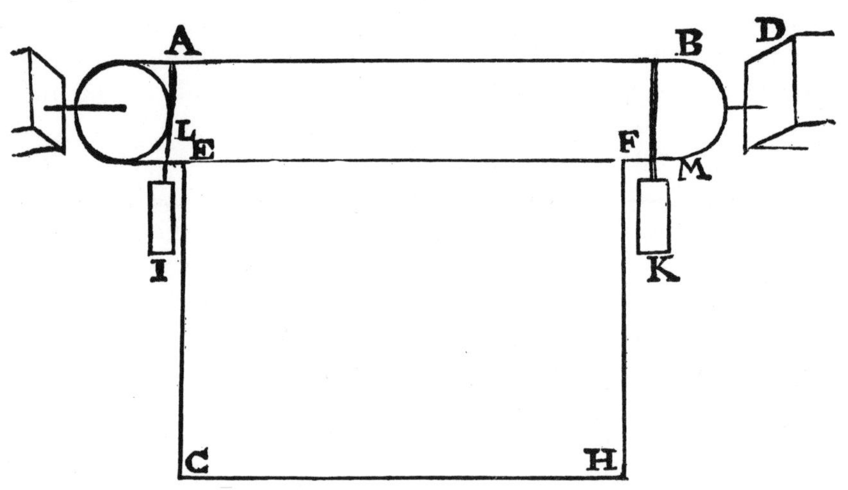


*Figure 39.*[1]

Let AB be the drum the diameter of which, if space permits, is the third part of the height of the curtain EFGH, *i.e.*, from E to G. Its pivots are placed in pieces of wood C and D fastened to the walls and the cords LAI and MBK are wound round the cylinder with weights at I and K. When these are allowed to fall, in an instant the curtain rises, that is to say, as I

1. In this figure G is wrongly marked as C: the block opposite D should be marked C.

and K descend towards G and H, consequently, G and H, at the bottom of the curtain, rise to E and F.

## 38. *How To Place The Lights Outside The Stage*

The lights in the hall or theatre outside the stage should be of different kinds and in diverse places. Some persons use oil lamps, others torches of white wax. As far as the first are concerned, they are less expensive but do not give that splendor which torches do. However, when the illumination is given by good lamps and these are filled, not with bad, but with the best kind of oil, mixed with some pleasing scent to obviate bad odors, they make no poor showing and the spectators are the better assured that the torch wax will not fall on them. But if one lamp starts to go out, as may readily happen when there are so many, it is apt to give out a bad smell very displeasing to the audience.

The torches made of white wax usually give a richer appearance and do not smell badly but it is true that at times they do soil the clothes of those seated beneath them since, being long and of material which in the slightest heat loses its firmness, owing to the breathing of the spectators and to the heat which the candles emit, they become soft and droop over and consequently drip down on the spectators. But if they are made for this special service, *i.e.*, large and short, sufficiently long to last for the time of the performance, there will be no danger of their drooping over or melting down. The better to provide for this, commonly the candle sockets are fashioned with bowls or plates of various kinds. On these the torches are placed and the wax run into them, thus avoiding any danger to those seated below.

The oil lamp should be made of tin, or as we say *banda stagnata*, which has another lamp below so that the oil may not flow over and fall on the spectators. These lamps have an iron hook by means of which they will be suspended to the chandelier, as is shown in the drawing. Quite a number of these lamps are made for each chandelier. None, however, should be larger than ½ foot. These chandeliers may be made in various forms, as eagles or lilies or anything else, as may please the taste of the person responsible.

You will make a chandelier for three torches. It will be constructed on painted wood strengthened with wire as in the

*Figure 40.*

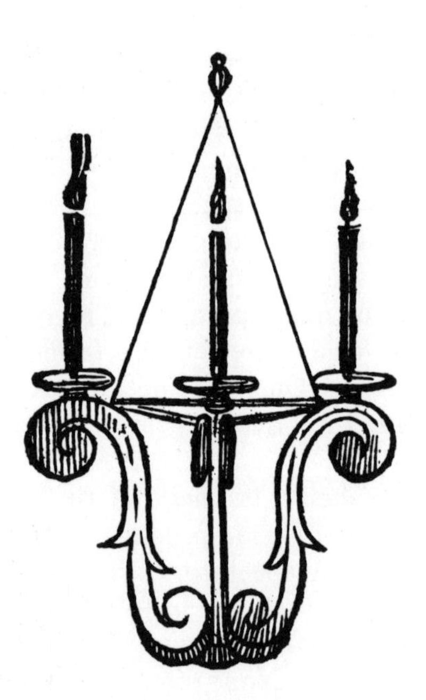

*Figure 41.*

design. Various shapes may be used, such as Harpies, or anything else.

Sufficient has been said above about the nature of these

chandeliers. You must take care to place them as near to the stage as possible, but so that they do not interfere with the view of the machines which may descend from the heavens during the *intermezzi*. They are accordingly to be placed at the sides leaving the center space free and open. Take heed, too, to place very few lamps, or none at all, from the middle of the hall to the back but see that there are plenty near the stage, for thus the houses may be easily discerned.

## 39. *How To Place The Lamps Within The Scene*

In fixing the positions of the lamps within the scene, many things have to be taken into consideration. They must be set so as not to interfere with the changing of scenes and with the machines, and so that, during the dancing, they do not shake and fall down, particularly the oil lamps. This is one of the things that much harms the reputation of a stage director. First of all you must place around the festoon and coat of arms, set at the front of the heavens, as described in Chapter 32, on the inner side towards the stage, a good quantity of oil lamps. These will not be visible to the spectators, will illuminate all the heavens and will produce a very pleasing effect. Then at each street, so far in as not to be seen from the auditorium, other lamps will be placed. These must not interfere with the scene changing, as already remarked, or with the entrances and exits.

Other oil lamps or, better, torches must be distributed over the stage. This will be best accomplished if some suitably sized pieces of wood are used, as long as the distance from the floor of the hall to the lowest part of each house on the street which is to be illuminated. These should be firmly fixed with plaster to the floor of the hall and pass through the stage floor by means of holes sufficiently large that the pieces of wood do not touch the stage at any point. Then their ends are well fixed by means of braces to the walls, and lamps, well secured, set upon them, as many as may be necessary and without any sparing in number. By this means they are firm and steady even when the stage shakes from the dancing and tumbling. You may also place a lamp within each chimney. This is not unsuitable when the scenes do not need to be changed. You generally place, too, a large number of oil lanterns at the stage front behind the parapet which, for this very purpose, was made higher than the stage (see Chapter 3), but, as the saying goes, there is greater harm than gain in this, since the intention is to illuminate the stage better whereas you make it thereby darker and more shadowy. This I have noticed again and again. For it is necessary to have in these lanterns very large wicks in order to secure greater illumination and these give off so much dense smoke that it seems as if a mist had risen between the eyes of the spectators and the scene, preventing the details of the scene from being seen. Besides which there is the bad smell arising from the oil lamps, especially when these are placed in this low position. True, one can see better the costumes of the actors and the dancers, but it is also true that their faces seem so pale and wan that they look as though they had just had a bad fever. In addition is to be noted the impediment experienced by actors and dancers because of the glare of these lamps. Sufficient has been now said about this matter. Let each man have liberty to do as he pleases.

## 40. *How And In What Order To Accommodate The Audience*

The accommodating of an audience is a matter of much importance and trouble. Yet, at these performances there is never a lack of willing helpers, especially those who seek the job of showing the ladies to their seats. Were the performances given daily, there would still be plenty of those. You must take care, however, to select for this purpose, persons of years of discretion, so that no suspicion or scandal arise. The ladies are to be placed in the orchestra, or as we say, in the third of the hall nearest the stage, taking care to place the least important in the first rows nearest the parapet and proceeding in the other rows according to rank. Care should be taken always to place the most beautiful ladies in the middle so that those who are acting and striving to please, gaining inspiration from this lovely prospect, perform more gaily, with greater assurance, and with greater zest.

The more elderly ladies should be seated in the last rows on account of the proximity of the men, so that every shadow of scandal may be avoided. Those who are responsible for seating the men should be persons of authority and, if possible, should be acquainted with all or at least part of them. In giving them the seats, it will be necessary to see that the common or less cultivated persons are set on the tiers and at the sides, since the machines give a less perfect appearance in these places, and because such people do not observe them minutely. The persons of culture and taste should be seated on the floor of the hall, as near the middle as possible, in the second or third rows. They will have the greatest pleasure there, since in such a position all the parts of the scenery and the machines are displayed in their perfection, and they will not be able to see the defects which are sometimes discerned by those on the steps or at the sides.

## 41. *How To Light The Lamps*

When all the spectators are seated and the time has come for the performance to begin, the lamps must be lighted, first those of the hall, then those of the stage. Every care must be taken to get this done as quickly as possible to avoid restlessness in the spectators who think this business is endless. But the method must be practical and safe lest the haste cause disorder, harm and still greater delay. You must consider well the methods for doing this in order to choose the best. As far as the lights within the scene are concerned there is no difficulty. They are easily reached and quickly lighted by the many people working behind the scenes. For lighting the auditorium, you must choose from two ways. The first is to make a fuse, or as we would say, a braid,[1] with a flaxen wick on an iron wire dipped in coal oil or *aqua vitae* or similar liquid easy to light. This wire should begin at one side of the chandeliers and follow round the tops of all the candles. It ought to be fixed in at least three places to the master wire holding the chandeliers lest the continuous heat of the candles cause the wax to drip to the danger and injury of those below. This danger is avoided if the wire is fastened all around at the same height. If all the chandeliers are arranged this way they can all be lighted quickly by having experienced men at given signal set fire to the end of each candle-taper.

Although I include this method, it never appealed to me because of the trouble it is likely to cause. For often the flames go out before they reach the candles. At other times as the fire

1. *trina*

follows the flaxen wicks, these sometimes divide and burning pieces of flax fall down causing damage and general confusion.

By using the second method it is possible to avoid such inconvenience and be on the safe side, though the spectator may have to have a little patience. By this method you soak the top of each candle in coal oil before fixing it firmly on the chandelier. Near each chandelier have a reliable and experienced man with two thin poles long enough to reach easily to the top of the candles. On one of the poles is a little candle for lighting. On the other is a sponge soaked in water to use in case any candle, burning more on one side than on the other, begins to drip on those below.

I should remark here that plenty of water should be ready above the beams or the heavens and below the stage. This may be kept in small tubs, jars or other containers ready for any emergency. For where there are so many lamps, and the other lights that are used in the *intermezzi*, accidents occur easily. If there is a quick remedy at hand no one will be harmed and there will be little disturbance.

If oil lamps are to be used three persons must attend to each chandelier. Here the same device of the poles may be used as for the candles. Or the whole chandelier may be let down, lighted, and raised again to its place.

# BOOK TWO

## 1. *Concerning The Disappearance And Changing Of Scenes*

In the first book we dealt with the method of making scenes and stage devices: now in the second, we shall deal with the *intermezzi*, for today it seems that no good show can be presented without complete or partial change of scenery. Indeed, discussion of this subject is essential because in practice the disappearance and changing of scenes is a thing which ordinarily arouses great delight and wonder among the spectators, particularly when the change is made so quickly that no one notices it. As this is difficult to accomplish, we ordinarily use various tricks to distract attention. For example, some confidential person is sent to the rear of the hall, who, watching for the time when the scene should be changed, feigns to make a noise with another person also in the know, or else (although, this might occasion much disturbance) pretends that some of the beams supporting the seats are in danger of breaking, or with the sounding of a trumpet, a drum, or some other instrument draws attention from the stage. At that very moment the change of scene is made without anyone seeing it. Obviously care must be taken not to reveal this stratagem to any save those responsible for carrying it out.

Of such devices the best in my opinion is that of the trumpet or other instrument since the pretense of a brawl or the collapse of the tiers brings many dangers resulting in great confusion not easily calmed down. When there is merely the sound of an instrument, the audience turns back toward the stage, as undisturbed as they were at first, ready to admire with wonder and pleasure the new scene set before their eyes.

## 2. *What Is To Be Done With The Two Houses Nearest The Stage Front*

When it is desired to construct the scenes so that they may be changed during the *intermezzi*, the front faces of the two first houses should not be joined to the perspective faces, as in the case of the ordinary scenes described in Chapter 13 of Book I. They must be disjoined and immovable, so that during the change of the others no one in front can see behind the scenes.[1]

Care must be taken that the front faces of these two houses are well nailed to the stage and secured to the walls with braces, so that they will stay firm in spite of the movements of the machines or anything else introduced into the *intermezzi*.

## 3. *How To Treat The Scene Front*

While the method described in the preceding chapter for making the first houses at the stage front is the most practical,

1. When the first house at each side is permanent, the house masks the scene shift and also serves as a partial proscenium arch.

and the most usual, yet it seems to have this defect. Sometimes, when the scene of the houses has been changed to woods, mountains, and so on, these two house fronts remain alone unchanged, and do not give either a pleasing or realistic impression. To obviate this difficulty, you may place at the front of the stage an arch with columns or statues, and build the scene within it. Beside the assurance that the part behind the scenes will not be seen, this arch will give a very grand splendor to the setting, and at the same time give a greater sense of depth to the perspective. Behind the arch a large number of lamps may be concealed for the purpose of illuminating not only the stage houses but the entire heavens as well. In constructing this arch, you must take care not to join it to the stage, but separate it as in the case of the front parapet. (See Chapter 3, Book I)

## 4. *How To Cover The Rest Of The Scenes So As To Make Them Changeable According To The First Method*

When the fronts of the two first houses have been completed or the arch has been made, as mentioned above, the rest of the houses must be constructed in such a way that they may be changed when occasion arises. At the top of the houses, where the roofs are represented, the tiles and chimneys are not shown in relief. Instead a rounded edge is made, well polished and glossy, so that the change may be easily made, as will be described at full length.

At each side of the scene is made a small scaffolding the length of all the houses, well secured to the walls about 4 feet lower than the tops of the houses, yet not coming so near the stage floor as to hinder easy passage underneath. Here the architect should exercise his own judgment so that no disorder occurs in the work.

## 5. *How To Change The Scenes By The First Method*

After making all the houses in this manner, some light, fine pieces of cloth are taken, cut to correspond with the height of the houses, so that they may easily cover the front and perspective faces of each one. The cloths are then painted to represent whatever is desired. Instructions should be given to the painter to make the size and other distemper as soft as possible so that the cloths may be easily gathered and spread in covering and uncovering the houses. This done, two sticks, 2½ feet long and 1½ inches thick, made of good, hard, polished wood are taken and at the end of one of these pieces is nailed the top corner of the short edge of the cloth intended to cover the perspective face of the house. Then the other end of this cloth is taken at its highest point and is nailed to the further corner of the straight face of the house. Then the entire cloth is gathered at the edge of the straight face, in such a way that it is concealed from the front. The same is done for all the houses.

When the time comes for changing the scene, at least two men are put in charge of each piece of cloth, holding the nailed stick. These sticks have been soaped, *i.e.*, that part near the cloth and also the rounded edge at the top of the house. To make the change, the men slide the stick over the edge of the house around to the end, and this in turn pulls the cloth around and covers the houses in a second. The same is done in a reverse direction to uncover them.

If, however, the perspective faces of the houses are very long, then another piece of stick will be placed in the middle of the cloth with additional men, so that the first man can unroll it to the edge of the straight face of the house and the second to the middle of the perspective face. The same method may be used to uncover them.

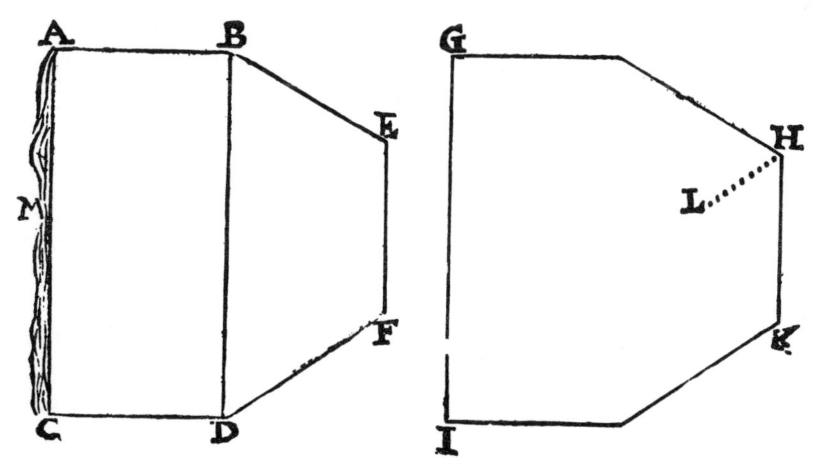


*Figure 42.*

Let ABCD be the straight face, and BEDF the perspective face and let ABE be the top of the roof where the smooth, soaped rounded edge is. GHIK is the piece of cloth which has to cover the house ABCDEF. The piece of stick HL is nailed to the cloth GHIK at the point H at the lesser side HK, and the top G of the greater side is nailed to the extremity A of the house. This completed, all the cloth is gathered at the edge of the straight face AC at M. At the time of operation, you turn the end of the stick H over ABE so that when H of the second figure comes to E in the first, and K comes to F, the house will be covered. The same is done for uncovering them in the reverse direction.

## 6. *How To Change The Scenes By The Second Method*

To change the scenes by the second method, the houses are set on the stage in this way: the second 3 inches behind the first, and the third 3 inches behind the second, and so on.

This done, a frame[1] is made of the same length, width, and height as the second house. This is covered with cloth painted to represent whatever you wish to appear in the change of scene. Then, a groove 2 inches wide, 3 inches deep, and the length of the first and second houses is made in the stage floor behind the first house. A second groove is made to hold them at the top.[2] The same is done for the other houses, *i.e.*, behind the second to cover the third, and behind the third for the fourth and so for all the others.

When all the frames are finished and painted, the first is placed in the groove behind the first house and is adjusted so that it will run freely in this groove to cover the second house and so with the others. It is necessary to take into consideration, that if the first or second house has doors or windows which are used in the play, the frame behind the first house must have apertures with simple edges in the cloth corresponding to these doors and windows, so that they may be used in acting. Likewise, for the other houses.

The method of operating this is to have two men appointed to each frame, who ought to be, if possible, familiar with sound and time cues, so that during the playing of the music, they cause

1. *telaro.*
2. Literally: "The same is done above at the roofs of the houses."

the frames to be run to their positions all at one time. Before doing so they must soap well the edges of the frames and the groove. This method will provide for the changes in the second and other houses. As far as the first house is concerned, the first method may be employed as described above in Chapter 5.

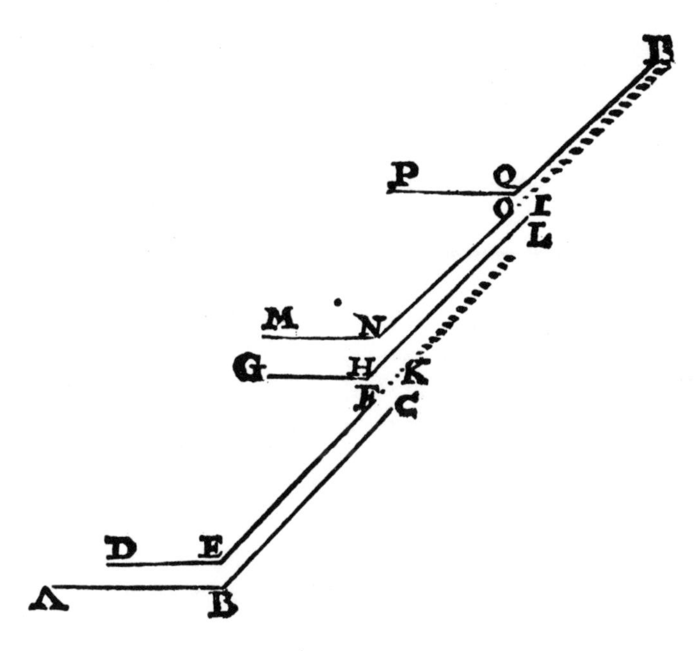


*Figure 43.*

Let ABC be the first house and DEF the frame behind it, which has to cover the second house GHI. Let EFKL be the groove. When the time comes for changing the scenes, the frame DEF is run on the groove KL so that when E is at K, similarly, F is at L. The same will occur in the parts above in the grooves of the roofs, and so the second house GHI is covered. In the same manner, the third house PQR is covered by making the frame MNO run in the grooves, and so with the others.

## 7. *How To Change The Scenes By The Third Method*

This method of changing the scenes seems to be better than either of the others mentioned above, if it is executed with swiftness, otherwise there is much danger of showing what is behind the scenes, which does not happen with the others. You must take care to use the greatest diligence in this procedure in order to avoid mistakes.

To employ this third method some frames are made with strips of wood having the bases and tops in the form of equilateral triangles, as shown below. These frames are of what height, length, and width, and in whatever number you wish the houses to be. The slope of the tops of the roofs is determined by looking across the cord, as described in the first Book, Chapter 11, but the bases of the triangles must be placed parallel to the horizon and not on the slope of the stage, so that they turn easily on their pivots.

When these frames have been covered with painted cloth and have been in their appointed positions, a pivot is set in each one, and it must be secured in the middle of the triangle at the top. This pivot comes down through the bottom triangle and passes through a hole in the stage floor, sufficiently large for this purpose, and rests at the base on a die placed on the floor of the hall, so that it stands poised and can turn easily. The same is done with the other triangles.

After this has been completed, two windlasses are placed under the stage floor, in the middle, one towards the back shutter, and the other towards the stage front, so wide that by a half turn, it is possible to wrap and unwrap the cords, which are twisted around the pivots. These cords must be adjusted so that by a half turn of the windlasses they are wound and unwound on them and the pivots, and so make the other faces of the houses appear.

When it is wished to make the triangles turn to indicate a change of scene, say a wood or some similar thing, the first windlass is turned and consequently the first end of the cord wound around the pivot is unwound, and is taken onto the first windlass. At the same time the other end winds itself about the pivot, and is unwound from the second windlass. In this way the face of the house formed by the triangle is changed.

To make the triangle return to its former position, the second windlass, placed under the stage near the front, is given a half turn. This will unwind the cord from the pivot and will wind it on the windlass, and at the same instant the other cord will be wound on the pivot and unwound from the first windlass. Immediately, the house will be brought back to its former position.

On the same windlasses and on the other pivots of each triangle, other cords will be fixed so that by one half a turn all the triangles are revolved in a single motion of the windlasses, and by another half turn returned to their places.

In this operation great care must be taken to have worthy and sincere men, since there is danger of the many cords getting entangled and interfering with the smooth action.

To avoid such mistakes, I should recommend that trustworthy men, who can understand time and sound cues, carry out these duties, as mentioned in a previous chapter. One man should attend each triangle, which may easily be turned and reversed without any complications of cords and windlasses. It is, however, somewhat difficult, when the men are scattered in different places, to get proper coordination, as we saw in the raising of the curtain in Book I, Chapter 37. However, this is not impossible of achievement.

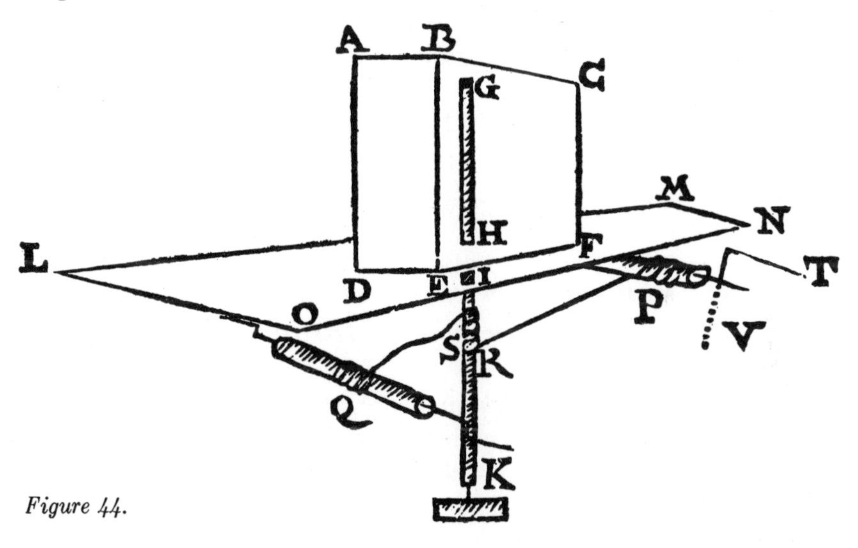


*Figure 44.*

Let ABC be the upper triangle and DEF the lower, so that the face of the house ABDE shows the straight face, and BEFC the perspective. Let the face ACDF behind show woods or other scenes for the *intermezzi*. Let GHIK be the pivot with the extremity coming to the center of the upper triangle at G, and the lower triangle at H, and passing through the hole I made in the stage floor LMNO, and poised on the floor of the hall at K. The first windlass is at P under the stage in the center towards the back shutter and the second at Q towards the stage front. The first end of the cord is tied to the first windlass at P, and the other end wound round the pivot at R. The second end is tied to the pivot at S and the other end wound round the second windlass at Q.

When it is desired to turn the triangles, as described above, the first windlass is given a half turn; hence, the first end of the cord is made to wind on the first windlass P and the other end unwinds from the pivot R. At the same time the second end of the other cord winds on the pivot S and the other end unwinds from the second windlass Q. At this instant the triangle is made to turn, and the other side of the house, painted for the *intermezzi*, is caused to appear, for when the handle T of the first windlass turns to V, the point moves to F, and F to E of the lower triangle, while in the upper triangle A moves to C, and C to B. When it is desired to return the house to the former position, the second windlass Q is turned as was the first windlass P and, in an instant, the house is returned to its place. By this means all the triangles of the houses can be turned by attaching cords to each pivot and to the two windlasses, and they will disappear and return, as described, in one movement.

A single windlass might be employed by tying to it all the cords in a contrary direction, but this causes difficulty and brings danger of mishaps.

## 8. *How To Increase The Stage Space When The Scenes Disappear*

When in an *intermezzo* many persons have to be introduced and the stage space is not sufficiently large to permit free, unencumbered movement without confusion, and, also, because of the narrowness of the place and the crowd of morris or ballet dancers, there is no opportunity of seeing with pleasure the actions of the play, it is possible, in changing the scenes, to provide greater space for the performer, and lessen the danger of confusion. To do this another three holes are made for each house, beside those already described in the last chapter, one in the stage floor, the other in the lower triangle, and a third in the upper triangle, all set in line with the first holes but nearer the back of the scene by as much as you wish to enlarge the stage place. The same is done with all the triangles of each side of the stage.

Just before the change is made, gently and noiselessly, the

pivots are raised from the first holes made in the middle of the triangles, and are placed in the new holes mentioned above. The pivots are then fixed to the floor of the hall and the cords are adjusted to the windlasses, so that when the first windlass is revolved (as described in the previous chapter) all the houses will be turned back leaving a larger space than before.[1] The turning of the second windlass will bring them forward again to their former positions.

Let ABC be the upper triangle and DEF the lower, with G and H holes in these and the pivot GHI poised on the hall

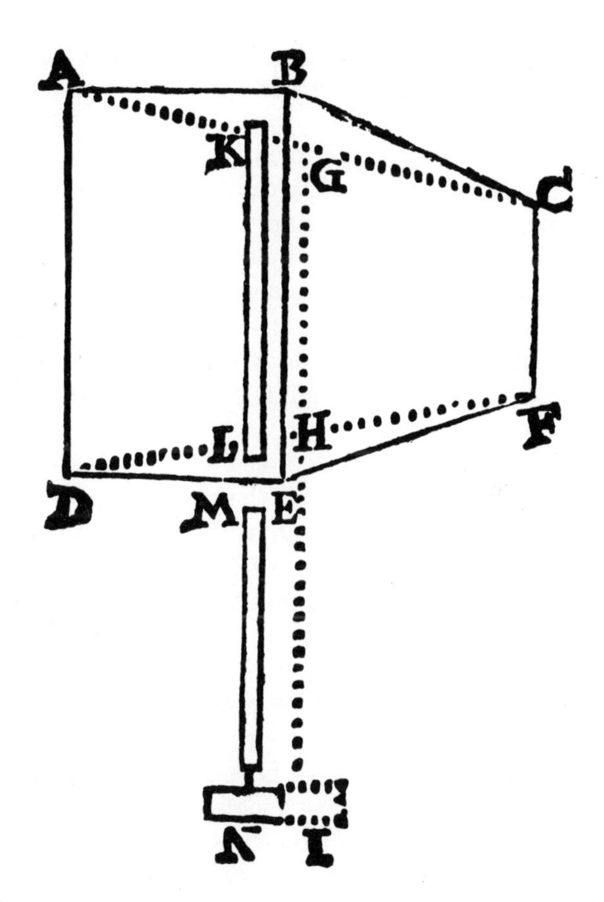


*Figure 45.*

---

1. From the title of this chapter it would seem that Sabbattini intended the houses to disappear entirely. However, the text indicates that they are pushed back far enough to permit the action, which in some cases might be out of sight, to be seen. Cf. Book II, Chapter 9.

floor at I. In the upper triangle another hole (marked K) is made as far from G towards the back face as you wish to increase the stage space. Similarly in the lower triangle the hole L is made immediately below K, and a third M in the stage floor, while directly below on the floor of the hall is located the die N for the pivot. When the time comes, the pivot GHI is raised and placed in KLMN and the cords are adjusted to the windlasses, as described. This is done for all the triangles, and the windlasses are turned as before.

## 9. *How To Lessen The Stage Space During Change Of Scene*

Sometimes during a performance of a play you have to put on an *intermezzo* in which few characters are required, or one for which few actors are available. In such a large space this small number does not appear to advantage, and not wishing that the spectators search them out with a lantern (as the saying goes), the stage space, in these cases, may be diminished with artifice. By this means everything is proportioned and the actions are made harmonious and intelligible so as to arouse greater pleasure among the spectators.

To do this another three holes, besides those described in the previous chapter, are made in the upper and lower triangles and in the stage floor, with the die in the floor of the hall, all set in line with the first holes. These holes are nearer the perspective face of the scene so that when the first windlass is turned the stage space is diminished. The cords will be adjusted again, as in the enlargement described in the preceding chapter, making everything move evenly, and bringing fame and reputation to the director.

In this operation there is no necessity for showing anything but the plan of the upper triangle. The lower triangle corresponds with this, as also the stage and hall floors, so far as the number of holes, their position, the position of the die, the pivots and pivot points are concerned.

Let ABC be the triangle and the hole in the middle of that be D, used for the disappearance of the scene, when the scene is to appear in the same position.

Let the second hole be E towards the back face of the

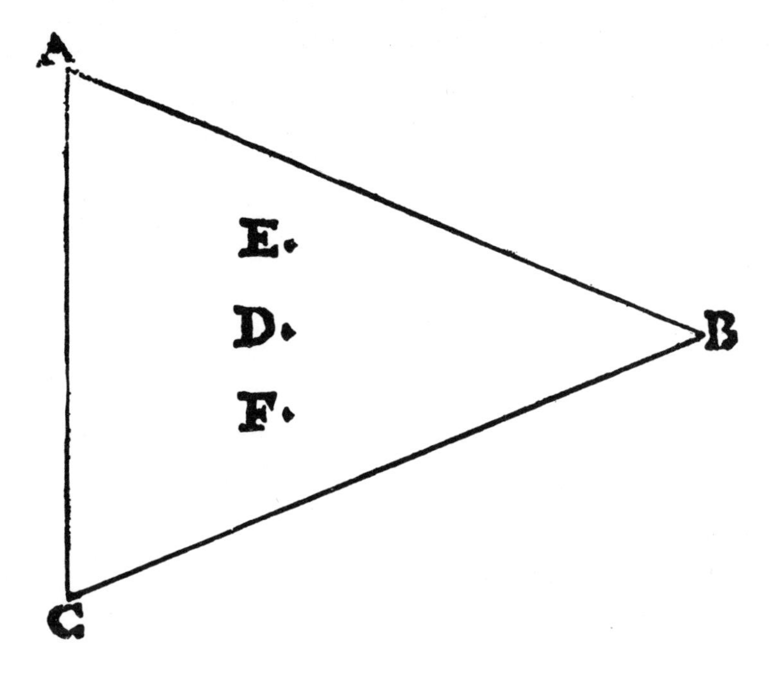


*Figure 46.*

scene, used when the stage space is to be enlarged, and the other hole be F, near the perspective face, used to diminish the stage. Vertical to these three will come the other holes and the die for the poised pivots. The scenes could be made to disappear in another manner: namely, placing the houses in sectional angles,[1] but since this is a common practice, I need say no more than this: instead of triangles, quadrangles[9] can be used.

## 10. *How To Stage The Total Destruction Of The Scene*

When in an *intermezzo*, it is necessary to show all or some of the houses demolished, then it is well that the scene be made of boards, since the operation may be carried through more easily and with less toil and risk. By this means, the straight and per-

---

1. Sectional angles may refer to the two wedge-shaped prisms used by Joseph Furttenbach at Ulm. The points of the prisms met to form a two-sided house. Quadrangles may refer to four-sided houses (possibly made by joining the long faces of two prisms). A design for revolving quadrangles is included in Jean Dubreuil, *La Perspective pratique* (Paris, 1642–1649), 3 vols.

spective faces may be split into as many portions as are wished and joined together with iron plates or hinges,[1] as we call them, and held together with bars. The reverse side may be painted to represent ruins, or whatever you wish.

When the time arrives to present the ruins, all the bars at one instant are caused to slide down towards the stage floor, so that immediately all the pieces of houses are overturned and represent ruins. To bring them back to position, each piece must have attached to it a small cord to draw it back into place. It is difficult to do this without being seen, but if it must be done, then the greatest swiftness is necessary. It is best to place this *intermezzo* at the end of the play so as to avoid this last operation.

If the scene is made of frames covered with cloths, they are demolished in the same way, but the bars are placed against the wooden uprights and the reverse side must be covered with cloth, *i.e.*, those parts which have to come to pieces, so that they may be painted on the other side as well.

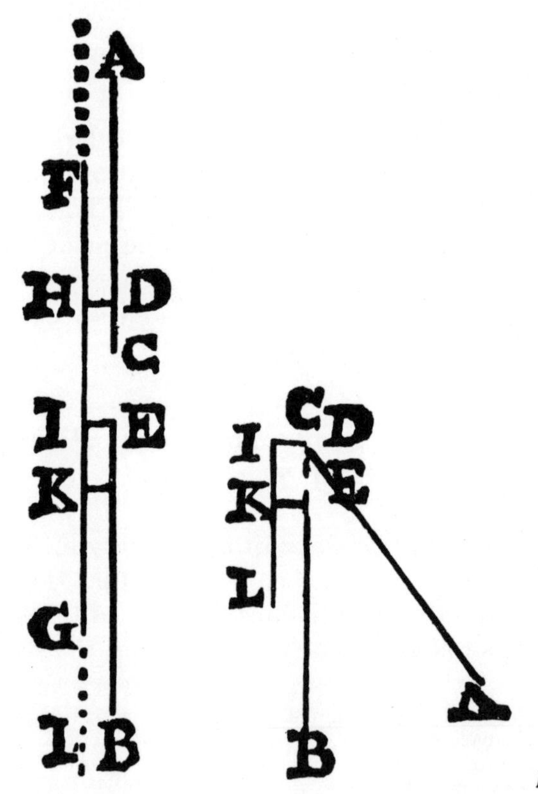


*Figure 47.*

1. *barduelle.*

Let AB be the cross section of the house which has to come to pieces from A to D. Let D and E be the thin iron plates or hinges, and F and G the bar, which holds together the two pieces of the house AD and EB by means of three eyes placed one at H in the upper part, and the other two at I and K in the lower part, as in the first figure. (Figure 47.)

When you wish the house to come to pieces, the bar FG is drawn downward towards L and immediately the piece DA is overturned, as is shown in the second figure. (Figure 47.) The same will be done for the other faces of the houses, and thus the destruction of the scene will be accomplished.

## 11. *How To Show The Whole Scene In Flames*

This device of making use of fire in the *intermezzi* should be avoided as much as possible on account of the danger sometimes attendant on it. Even when the least dangerous method is used, still there is always a certain risk.

If in some *intermezzo*, there is need to show all or part of the scene in flames, it is done in this way: as many pieces of cloth are taken as needed for the number and size of the houses you wish to show burning. A little before the appointed time, the pieces of cloth are soaked in *aquavitae*, prepared for this purpose, and quickly fixed upon the faces of the houses which are to be changed. When the time arrives one man is deputed to each house. With a taper he sets fire to the face, and the turning of the triangles sets fire to all the houses and completes the operation.

For this chapter there is no need of further demonstration, as in itself the process is very clear.

## 12. *How To Darken The Whole Scene In A Moment*

When it is desired to darken the whole stage in a moment, this method is used: as many cylinders of soldered tin are made as there are lamps to be darkened. These are at least ½ a foot high, a little less in diameter, and at the top they are open. This done, you adjust each cylinder over its lamp, as in the figure below, in such a manner that by one motion at the side of the stage, the cords with the cylinders descend over the lamps and so darken them. When the cords are again raised to their places, the stage is illuminated. It is necessary to take care in placing these lamps, so that they offer no impediment to scene changes, as explained in Book I, Chapter 39.

When the stage is to be darkened in the *intermezzi*, few lamps should be placed outside the stage,[1] and those few rather far away, because if too many lamps should be near the stage they would interfere with the darkening effect and the effort would be vain.

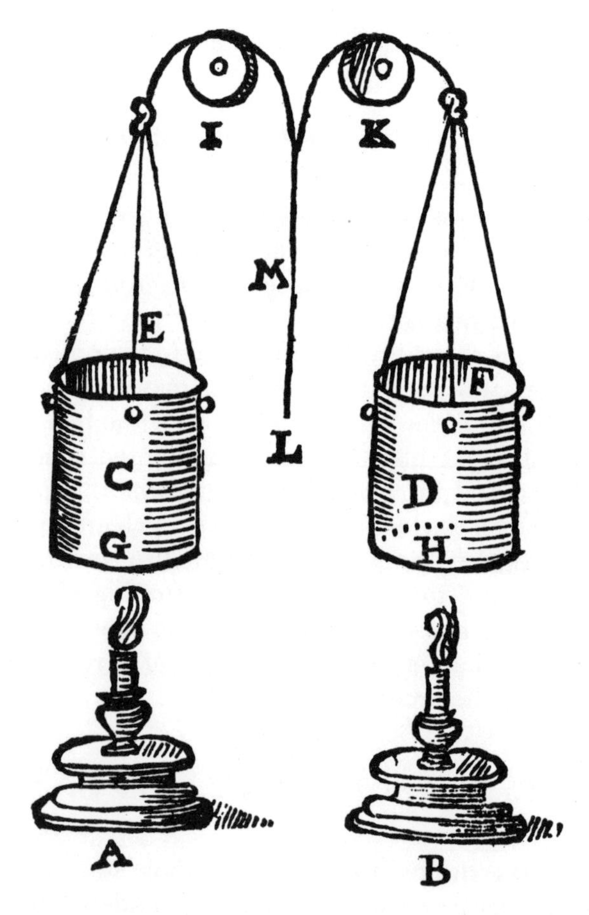

*Figure 48.*

Let A and B represent the lamps to be darkened, and C and D the cylinders, with the small holes at the top at E and F and open below at G and H. The cords supporting the cylinders

1. In the auditorium.

pass over the pulleys I and K and are adjusted to hang perpendicularly above the lamps to be darkened, A and B. The cords are joined at L.

To darken the lamps, the end of the cord is raised from L to M, and consequently the cylinders C and D will cover the lamps A and B. To uncover the lamps, the cord is then drawn from M to L, where it was at first, and in an instant the lamps are revealed. The same is done for the others by joining the various cords into one, if that is possible, and in this manner the effect will be successful.

## 13. *How To Open The Back Shutter*

Various devices may be employed to open and close the back shutter during the *intermezzi*. For the first method, a frame divided into two equal parts must be made and the parts must be placed on the line marked out for the back shutter, as described in Book I, Chapter 6. Along the line a groove is made of two strips of board not more than 1½ inches high running from one end of the back shutter to the other. On the inner side, this groove must be well polished, smoothed, and soaped, and nailed to the stage floor in such a manner that the nails do not offer any impediment to the free running of the back shutter. In width this groove should agree exactly with the width of the boards used for the frame.

This completed, the frame is fixed in the groove so that the two pieces join in the middle of the stage. In the middle of the uprights is placed a bolt or iron hook holding the two parts of the frame together. Behind, at the line of junction, a wooden prop is placed to prevent the back shutter from toppling over backwards.

Over the groove, above the floor at about three-fourths the height of the frame, you should place for each shutter two wooden guides fixed to the walls. These support the parts of the frame preventing them from falling forward. They should not, however, be carried out so far as to be visible to the spectators.

When the back shutter is to be opened, first the bolt is slid back or the hook lifted, and at the same time the wooden prop is raised. Then at one time two men at each side run the parts of the back shutter to the sides of the stage, thus concealing them behind the perspective faces of the last houses of the scene.

To make the shutter return, the same men run the parts in till they meet, replace the bolt or hook, and set the wooden prop as at first.

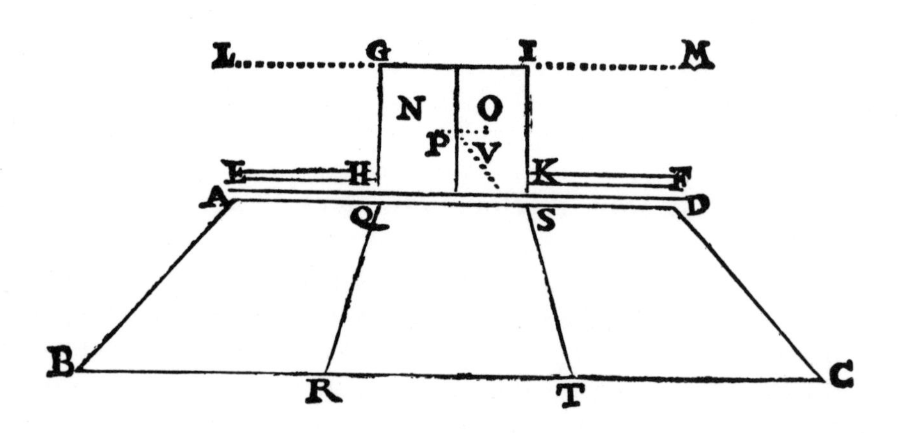


*Figure 49.*

Let ABCD be the stage floor from one wall to the other. EF is the groove and GHIK the frame for the back shutter placed in the groove. The wooden guides LN and MO[1] are fixed in the walls at L and M, so that the parts of the shutter do not fall forward. The bolt or hook is placed behind at P to hold them together and the wooden prop V is in the same place.

When you wish to open the back shutter, first the prop V is raised and the bolt or hook P is undone, and at one time the two parts of the frames are run aside, until the side GH is at LE and IK at MD.[2] Thus, the back shutter is opened.

To make it return, the parts of the frame are run till they meet, and are quickly secured by the bolt or hook P, and the wooden prop V.

---

1. The lettering in the text is incorrect; to correspond with that in the figure it should read LG and IM.
2. To correspond with the figure MD should be MF.

## 14. *The Second Method Of Opening The Back Shutter*

The second method of opening the back shutter is this: the frame is divided into two parts, as described in the preceding chapter, and is then divided into two other sections so that the division is a little in front of the perspective faces of the two last houses of the scene. These sections are united by hinges, similar to those used at doors, so that they may open and close easily. The reverse sides are painted to conform with the faces of the triangles which are used in the *intermezzi*. The central parts of each shutter are joined with a hook at the back, as described above in the preceding chapter. At the top of these parts at the side a thin cord is placed in such a manner that one end is nailed to the top of the frame and the other suspended over the highest point of the roof of the last house towards this back shutter. Similarly two other pieces of thin cord are nailed to the same tops of the frames where the first cords are fastened. These must be as long as the distance of each part of the back shutter when it is opened towards the face of the last house. The other ends of these thin cords are stretched within the sections of heavens at each side, passing through a small hole made in the heavens for this purpose.

This done, two men are placed at each side behind the two last houses, who hold in their hands the ends of the two cords, and similarly behind the heavens two other men are placed, who hold the other ends of the cords, as described above. At the moment of opening the back shutter, those men behind the last houses, after the hook is raised, draw the cords at the same time so that the parts of the back shutter open out towards the two perspective faces of the last houses. Likewise, to shut the back shutter, these men behind the houses, upon receiving a sign, slacken their cords, and those behind the heavens draw theirs so that the parts of the back shutter are united as at first, and the hook is quickly replaced, as described above for the first method. At the bottom of each part of the frame is left a piece of cloth painted similar to the faces so as to cover the portions of the houses revealed by the slope of the stage.

Let AB be the back shutter which has to be opened, divided in the middle at C. On the part A are the hinges EF and on B the hinges GH, with the hook D holding the two sections AB

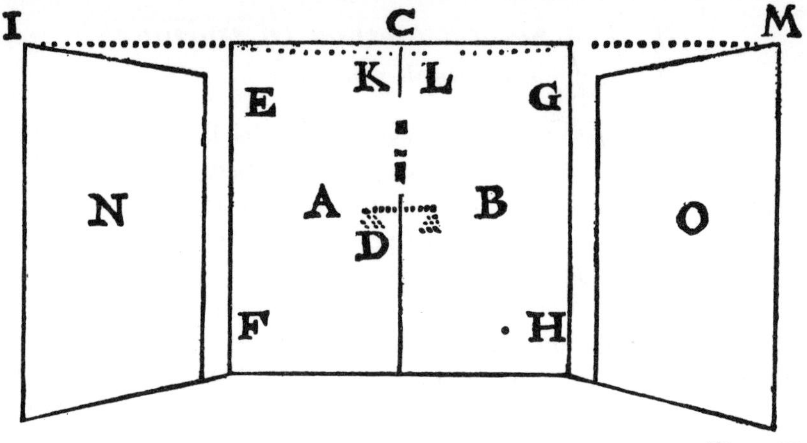


*Figure 50.*

together. The thin cords IK are placed so that the first end is nailed to the extremity of the piece A at K and the other end over the roof of the last house N at I. Similarly the end L is at the extremity of the frame B and over the house O at M.

At the moment of opening the back shutter, the hook D is raised, the men placed behind the houses draw the thin cords to each side so that K comes to I and L to M, placing A on N and B on O, and thus is the scene opened.

To close it, those men placed behind the heavens draw the thin cords mentioned above, while the other men behind the houses slacken theirs, as described above.

The cords are drawn until K and L return to C, where they were at first. In this manner the back shutter is closed and is quickly secured with the hook.

## 15. *The Third Method Of Opening The Back Shutter*

To open and shut the back shutter by the third method, this procedure is used: the frame is constructed in two parts, with the groove below, as described for the first method in Chapter 13. At the bottom of each part two wheels of quite hard wood are placed, of a diameter not more than half a foot, and of a width corresponding to the width of the groove, so that they will run easily in it and not be visible. This done, a piece of wood is nailed across the top edge in line with the wheels, which is as long as the distance from the top of the frame to the heavens.

There a groove, at least 3 inches in depth, is made double the length[1] of the lower groove. It should be wide enough to fit conveniently the wheels which are to be secured to the top of these pieces of wood, and serve as an axis for them. Then this groove is painted the color of the heavens, so that when the back shutter opens the groove and the space above are not visible.

The method of operation: the hook is raised as before. With only one man at each side the parts of the back shutter are run off, the upper and lower grooves and the wheels having first been soaped. Thus, the back shutter is easily opened, and the desired effect secured.

To close the back shutter, the same men run the parts back to their places, and to make them meet in the middle, a small wooden peg is nailed to the lower groove, not so high or wide as the groove. It should be an inch wide so that the wheels cannot run from their appointed places. In this manner everything will be successful.

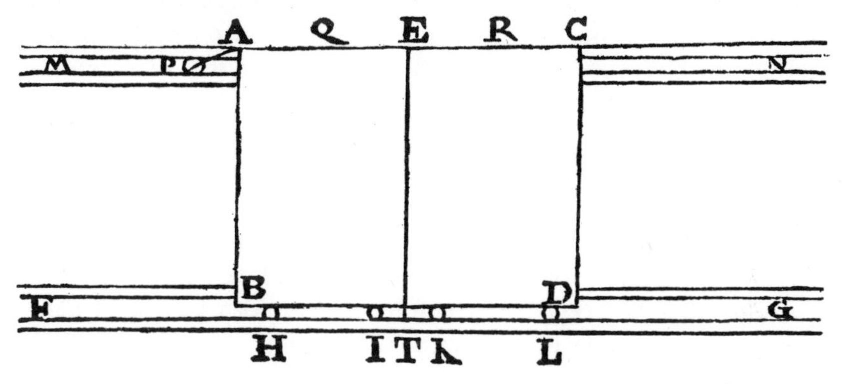


*Figure 51.*

Let ABCD be the back shutter which is to be opened, with the division at E. The groove placed on the stage floor is FG and the wheels H, I, K, L, are so placed that, while invisible, they run in this groove.

Let MN be the upper groove, made double and wide enough to permit the end of the piece of wood AP to pass, which is to serve as axis for the wheel P, and deep enough to allow the

---

1. This is probably required in order that the ends of the upper groove may be attached to the walls of the hall. Otherwise, Sabbattini may mean "double the strength." Below the illustration he refers to the groove made "double."

wheels to run easily in it, both in front and behind. The other three pieces of wood with their wheels are at Q, R, and S.[1]

When the back shutter is to be opened, one man is placed at each side, as described above. At a signal each makes his part run so that A goes to M and C to N. This will open the back shutter easily and quickly. To bring it back into place, the parts are run to meet at E. They cannot go farther because of the small wooden peg T set in the middle.

## *16. The Fourth Method Of Opening The Back Shutter*

In the fourth method of opening the back shutter, the particulars given in Book I, Chapter 37, relating to the raising of the curtain may be followed. A cylinder, similar to that shown in Figure 39 of that chapter, will be used but with this difference, that while the former was placed in the front of the heavens, this must be situated on the line with the back shutter and in a section of the heavens. The way this can be done will be explained when we deal with the sectional heavens. On the cloth serving for the back shutter, houses are to be painted and the space above them is painted in the same tones as that section of the heavens immediately behind, so that when the cloth of the back shutter rises above the heavens by the revolving of the cylinder, that part of the heavens which is uncovered will not remain out of harmony with the rest. At the foot of this cloth you must place a piece of rod which is the length of the cloth. This is sewn on so as not to be visible, holding the cloth well stretched, and when the back shutter is lowered, causing it to remain at the same place without crumpling. When you wish to make it disappear, the weights are slackened, as for the raising of the curtain (Book I, Chapter 37), but to make it fall the weights are quickly raised and suddenly it falls into place. Some consider it improper to see the houses rising into the heavens, but if this movement is done quickly, both in the raising and in the lowering, the method will not be discernible.

No figure is needed here since everything is fully demonstrated in Figure 39 in Chapter 37 of Book I. This method could

1. S has been omitted from the figure. It should be on the right, corresponding to P.

also be used with a single frame only, this being made to descend under the stage like a portcullis. But the space under the stage is usually not sufficiently large for this operation, and, consequently, no more need be said about it.

## 17. *How To Open And Close The Stage Traps*

Sometimes in the *intermezzi* to be shown, the necessity arises for making characters rise from under the stage. In such instances it is necessary that the traps be quickly opened and shut, especially when the dancers have to move over them immediately afterwards. These traps are either small, allowing only one person at a time to rise, or large, admitting several.

The small traps will cause little trouble in opening and closing, if they are well constructed; *i.e.*, if the traps on the side next to the back shutter are joined with two iron hinges, similar to those used in cupboards, and firmly secured. These hinges are so placed that on opening the trap falls of itself, and the parts under the stage are not seen due to the slope. Then, under the stage must be placed transversely two staples, one at each side, 4 inches square, made of very good wood and well nailed underneath. Through these staples is to be passed a well-polished wooden bar, a little longer than the width of the trap, and the distance between the staples. This piece of wood is to be made in such a way that it can move easily through the staples, and, in order to prevent the trap shaking when it is closed, one or two wooden wedges are inserted in the tiny space between the trap and the bar. Thus it is held firmly and securely, even while dancers tread upon it. To the tops of these wedges small cords are nailed, and the other ends are fastened below the stage. They should be sufficiently long to leave the wedges entirely free. This is done so that when the trap is being closed and opened, you do not have to look for wedges, for often enough in the necessary haste you may easily make mistakes and forget where they were placed. When the time comes to open the trap, one man should remove the wedges, and pull out the bar, and thus the trap drops. When the characters have ascended, the same man will place the trap in position and replace the bar and wedges, all without noise. Thus, the operation is safe.

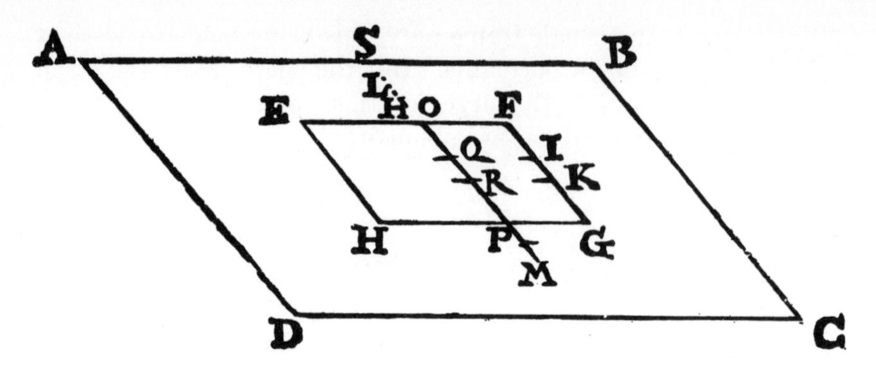


*Figure 52.*

Let ABCD be the stage floor, and EFGH the trap door. IK are the hinges set towards the back shutter BC. The bar is LM which passes through the staples NO[1] on one side and PM on the other. The wedges QR keep the bar and the trap door secure.

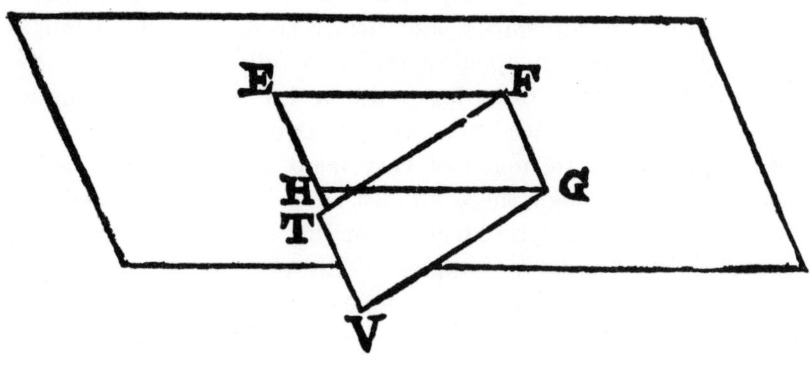


*Figure 53.*

When the trap door is to be opened, first remove the wedges QR, run the bar LM to OS, as in Figure 52, so making the trap door quickly fall to TV, as in Figure 53. To reverse it, raise the door until TV, in Figure 53, comes evenly to EH, run the bar from OS to LM, and reinsert the wedges as in Figure 52. So the trap door is closed in an instant.

When the traps are large, allowing passage for many characters together, great care and judgment must be used because of the difficulties both of opening and of closing on account of

1. The N in the figure is defective.

their weight and size. The following method should be employed: after making the trap door the size desired, and after fitting a sufficient number of strong hinges on the side towards the back shutter, just as used for the small trap doors, you fit on the other side a strong wooden bar in length corresponding to the width of the trap door and 5 inches square, which is nailed to the underside of the door. To it are fastened two or three or more pieces of wood similar in size to the bar but sufficiently long to serve as a prop, *i.e.*, from the bar to the floor of the hall when the trap is closed. The top of each one of these pieces of wood is joined to the bar by a hinge, fastened on the side towards the back shutter. When the trap is opened, one man takes charge of each prop. At the same moment, everyone must incline his prop in the direction of the back shutter and, thus, the trap door is opened and falls down towards the back. Care must be taken to have other men ready to aid in lowering it on account of its great weight and size. To close it, the men in charge of the props raise them to their positions by the help of the other men, just as in the former operation. Care should be taken to have persons experienced in this business and trustworthy, so that the movements go smoothly.

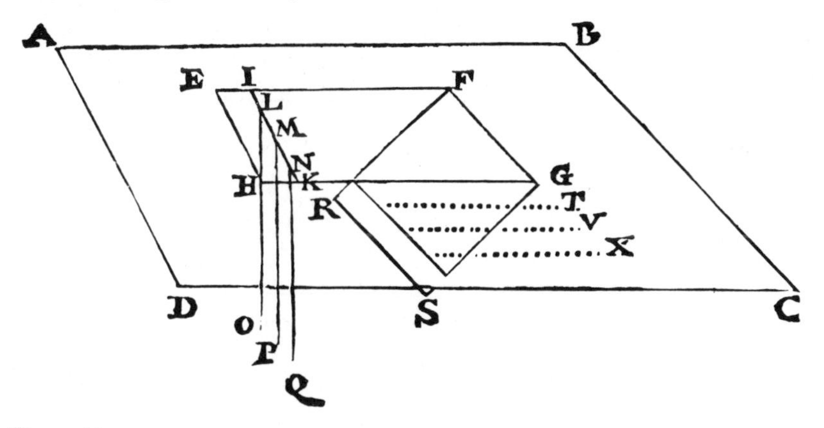


*Figure 54.*

Let ABCD be the stage floor, and EFGH the trap door. The bar IK is placed on the door towards the stage front AD, and the props on this bar are hinged at L, M, and N. These props go to the floor of the hall at O, P, and Q. To open the trap the props are inclined so that O goes to T, P to V, and Q to X, and the part of the trap EH falls to RS. To close it then, the part RS of the trap is brought back to EH, and, consequently, the props TVX return to LMN. Thus the trap is closed as required.

## 18. *How To Bring Men From The Stage Trap Quickly By The First Method*

In the preceding chapter instructions were given for the opening and closing of the traps. Now, we must deal with the method of bringing characters from the stage trap rapidly. Most certainly this action, if well done, provides the very greatest delight and wonderment, especially when the spectators do not see how and when these characters have ascended. The following means may be employed: a small ladder is made with as many steps as are necessary, reaching from the floor of the hall to the opening of the trap, one end being on the floor of the hall and the other set under the trap so as not to interfere with the falling door. When the time arrives, the person who is to get on the stage must stand ready on the first step, leaning in such a way as not to get into the way of the falling trap. As soon as it is open, he straightens himself, places his foot on the second step and ascends quickly to the stage. Thus the operation is completed.

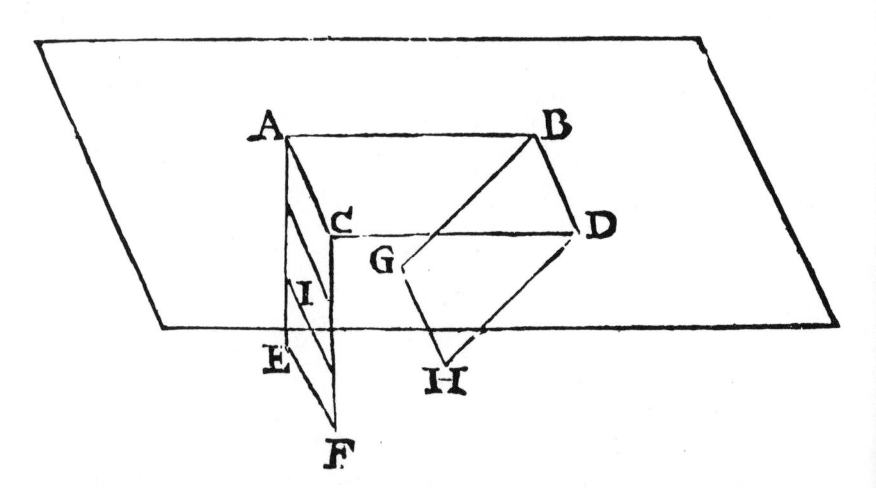


*Figure 55.*

Let ABCD be the trap door, and ACEF the ladder with the top AC fixed under the stage floor, and the lower end EF on the floor of the hall. Let I be the point where the person stands who must ascend the ladder. The person is bent in such a manner that he will not be in the way when the edge of the trap AC opens to GH. When the trap is open, the person who was bent over at I must rapidly straighten up, and, putting the other foot on the next step, he must mount rapidly onto the stage as the trap is quickly closed.

## 19. *The Second Method*

Characters may rise quickly to the stage in another manner, as follows: a handbarrow of suitable size is made and placed a little higher than the floor of the hall on a line with the trap door. In the middle of it is placed the character who is to ascend. He stands leaning, as said above, and at each side of him are two men, strong and sturdy. When the trap door is opened, these men suddenly raise the handbarrow with the character on it up to the stage level, and with one movement he then rises rapidly.[1] The men lower the handbarrow immediately, while the others close the trap.

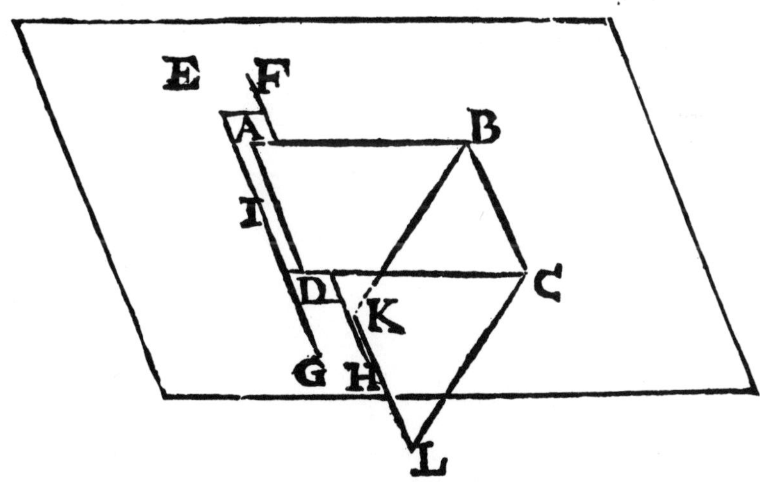


*Figure 56.*

Let ABCD be the opening, and EFGH the handbarrow. Let I be the person who must ascend, and the four men who must lift the barrow be at EFGH. When the trap is open from points

1. On to the stage.

AD to KL, at the proper time, the men stationed at EFGH will lift the barrow up to just under the floor of the stage. At the same instant, he who is at the point I will rise with a single rapid step onto the stage. Quickly the barrow is lowered, and the trap is closed.

## *20. The Third Method*

To cause the characters to rise rapidly to the level of the stage, there is a third method: a lever, of length proportionate to the force and weight, is set in position. It has its fulcrum a short distance from the trap door from which the person is to ascend, and is worked from the right or the left or elsewhere under the stage, wherever may be most convenient and cause least impediment to the other machines. The shorter arm of the lever is directly under the trap, and the longer arm on the other side. When the time comes, the man who has to ascend gets on this arm of the lever, stands leaning, as said above, while one or more men are at the longer end. As soon as the trap is opened, immediately these men bring down the greater end of the lever so that at the same time, he who was placed on the lesser end is raised and may at one step get out on the stage. The lever is then

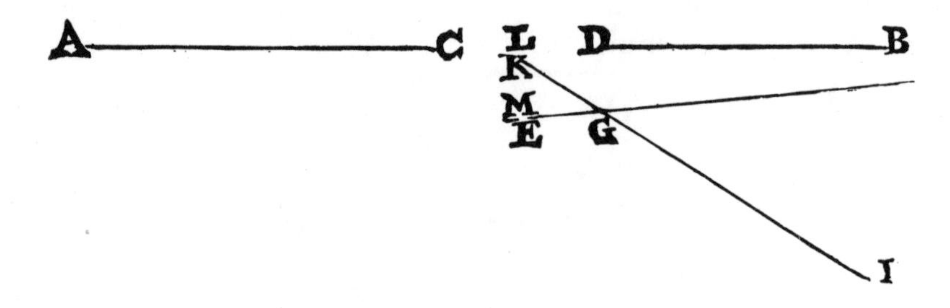


*Figure 57.*

returned to its position and the trap door is closed.

Let AB be the stage floor, CD the opening of the trap, and EF[1] the lever under the stage with its fulcrum at G. At its shorter end E, in line with the opening CD, place the person who must ascend at M. Then, at the longer end F we may place one or two men, as said before, who will lower the longer end from F

1. F is not marked in the figure. Its position is immediately below B.

to I. Thus, the shorter end E will rise to K, and the person who is placed at the point M will come to the point L, and by a single step will easily come onto the stage.

## 21. *The Fourth Method*

Truly it is a fine thing to get characters to rise from under the stage without anyone noticing it, but this action cannot be accomplished unless first a dance is performed by other people on the stage. The dancers must be well acquainted with the locations of the traps, so that at the time the persons rise from them they may get into double rows in front of these traps, *i.e.*, towards the spectators, and in that instant the characters rise. As soon as they have done so, the traps are closed hurriedly, and the dancers immediately change their groupings so that the spectators cannot see how or where the others have risen. But in using this method, great cleverness and care are needed both from the director and the actors.

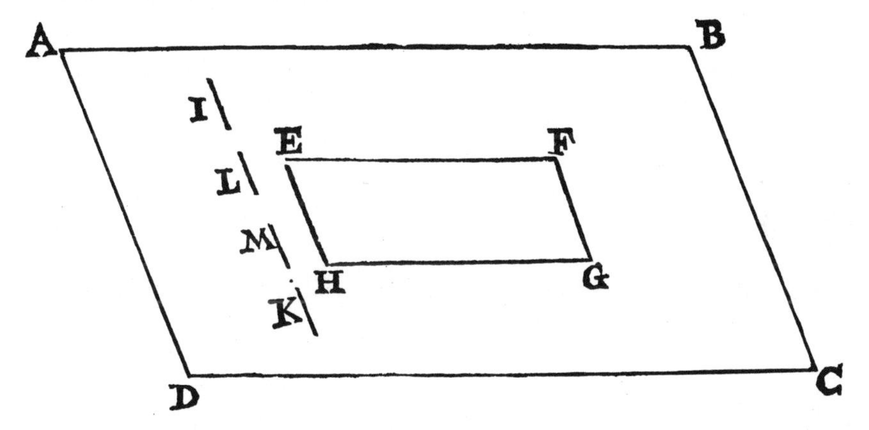


*Figure 58.*

Let ABCD be the level of the stage, EFGH the trap and IK the dancers. At the time that the person must come up, the dancers IK must group themselves at LM. Immediately after, the trap EFGH must open and the person rise. As soon as the trap is shut, the dancers at LM will return to IK, or to another grouping, without the audience being able to imagine how it was done. However, in all these things, great rapidity is necessary.

## 22. *How To Make A Hell Appear*

In representing a Hell, if there is behind the back shutter a space or inner stage which may be exposed, then you may proceed thus: two fires are lighted, one at the front of this inner stage and the other some distance from the first but in line with it, so that between the two those who are to take part in the scene may move and dance without danger. All spectators get the impression that the persons are right in the middle of the flames, for they see the flames are real, and distance does not permit them to see how it is done. This is a method which gives security to the actors. No demonstration is demanded here, since the process is self-evident.

## 23. *Another Method Of Showing A Hell*

A Hell may be shown in another way. This method is to make a very large opening in the middle of the stage floor. When the time comes to show a Hell, this opening or trap is opened, as described in Chapter 17. Underneath the stage, four men are placed one at each side of the trap. They should be worthy, zealous, honor-seeking persons. Each of them holds in his hands an earthen pot or small bowl with a hole in the bottom, sufficiently large to permit the passage of a torch. A piece of torch at least a foot in length is put through each pot so that the top projects out of the mouth of the pot, and the remainder, extending below, will serve as a handle in the hand of the man responsible. Then, the pot is filled with finely ground Greek resin and the mouth of the pot is covered with thick paper in which many small holes are made, but the hole through which the torch passes must be neither larger nor smaller than the torch itself. The hole underneath, through which the torch passes, is sealed with wax so that the resin does not fall out. The same is done for all the other pots.

At the time of opening the Hell, these men must be at their places, each with his torch lighted, and now and again must throw flames of fire through the trap to the stage by raising the pots violently, but in such a way that the lighted torches are not visible, and do not injure the dancers or whoever has to enter or leave the Hell. It is necessary in these actions to take great care

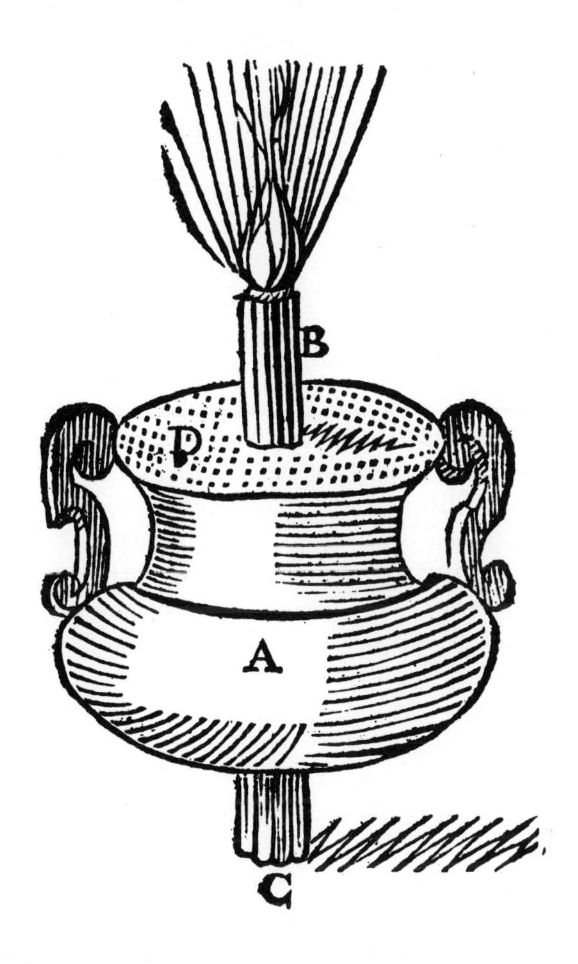


*Figure 59.*

since very often mishaps result, and fools and thick-witted persons should not be allowed to participate.

Let A be the pot in which we pass the piece of torch BC, long enough to let B come out of the top and C remain below the pot. When the time comes to use it, some one must hold part C in his hands, the torch having been lighted at B. When we want the flame to be thrown on the stage, the pot will be rapidly lifted, and the resin will come out of the holes which were made in the paper D, and catching fire will result in a big flame. Thus, the other men will do the same thing from time to time while the trap is opened.

## 24. *How To Make Mountains And Other Objects Rise From Under The Stage*

Should you wish to make mountains rise from under the stage, it may be done this way. Take a piece of wood of the right thickness and in length double the height of the mountain. Then make a vertical groove from the floor of the hall up to a trifle below the stage floor so that the piece of wood can move along it. This supporting bar for the mountain should be notched like the gear which brings the oil to the lamps of brass formed like candles. Then, in the groove is placed a windlass with cogs to raise the piece of wood. Should there not be sufficient room under the stage for this purpose, an excavation of sufficient size under the flooring must be made to accommodate the groove, the supporting beam and the windlass. This done, a piece of cloth, the length and width of the mountain with the top representing the summit, is nailed to the top of the notched piece of wood, the cloth being stretched by crossbars of unequal length to give a mountain-like form. The bars should be of good strong wood and the last one serving as a base of the mountain must be longer and thicker so that when the wood is raised it will hold the cloth stretched out at the bottom. This done, the mountain is painted on the cloth, and even though the cloth is flat, the painter may, by the judicious use of light and shade, make it seem round. Then, an opening is made in the stage floor sufficiently large to admit not only the piece of wood which sustains the mountain, but also the cross bars and the cloth itself.

When it is desired to raise the mountain, two or more men are used according to the weight to turn the windlass until the machine becomes visible to the audience. To make it descend, the windlass is reversed until the mountain returns to its place and the trap door is closed.

A figure is not given here because the device is a common one; there is no one who has not lamps of this kind at home.

## 25. *How To Transform A Man Into A Rock Or A Similar Object*

Should you wish to transform an actor into a rock or stone, the following method is employed: a piece of cloth of the desired size is painted in the form of a stone or rock. Then the lower part of the cloth, the base of the stone or rock, is nailed to the stage floor and to its top is attached a smooth, round piece of wood, like a spear handle, about 2 fingers thick and 6 feet long. In the stage floor a round hole is bored immediately beneath the cloth, sufficiently wide to admit easily this piece of wood which must remain concealed under the stage floor. The cloth is lying crumpled on the stage invisible to those in front. When the time arrives, a man is sent beneath the stage who, at a signal that the actor to be transformed has arrived at his appointed place, raises the cloth little by little. Gradually, as the actor bends down, the cloth rises, and it seems that he has been transformed.

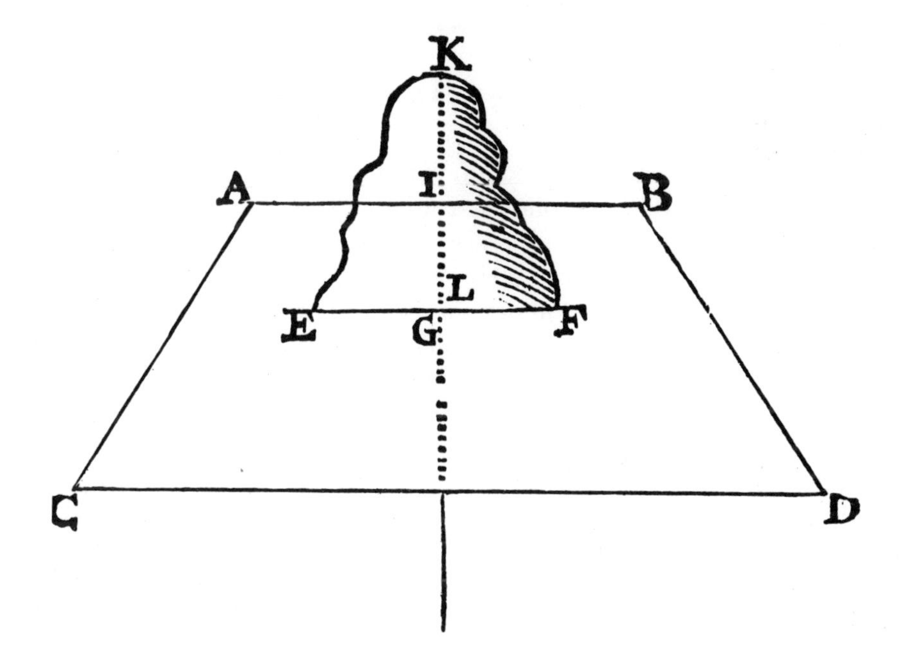


*Figure 60.*

Let ABCD be the stage floor, and EF the cloth attached to the floor of the stage at EF. The end of the stick GH is attached to the middle of the cloth at G, where it passes through the floor at G. To produce this transformation, a person under the stage holds the lower end of the piece of wood at H. He lifts the piece of wood GH little by little, so that the extremity G comes to K at the same time that the person I, who is undergoing the transformation, may be seen stooping at L.

## 26. *How To Transform Rocks Or Stones Into Men*

In the last chapter was described the method of changing men into stones or rocks. Now the reverse process is described. To do this the same procedure is employed, but the man under the stage holds up the piece of wood and cloth painted like stone, and the actor to be transformed stands behind the cloth, bending down a little so that he is not seen. When the time arrives, the man under the stage begins to lower the piece of wood little by little, and the actor straightens up, so that it seems as though the rock or stone had been changed into a man.

No figure is needed here.

## 27. *First Method Of Showing A Sea*

Seas are represented in various ways during *intermezzi*. The first method is as follows: a wooden frame is made in length and depth according to the size of the sea desired. Upon it a cloth is fastened not too tightly stretched, and is painted to represent a sea. This done, under the cloth are placed various pieces of cord, about 1½ feet apart, which are sewed on below, with the ends brought outside of the frame about a foot at each side. When the time comes men must be placed at each side to hold the ends of the cords, and now and again alternately to tighten and slacken them, starting from the farthest part towards the horizon and coming down to the front which represents the shore. Thus it seems as though there are sea waves, as shown in Figure 61.

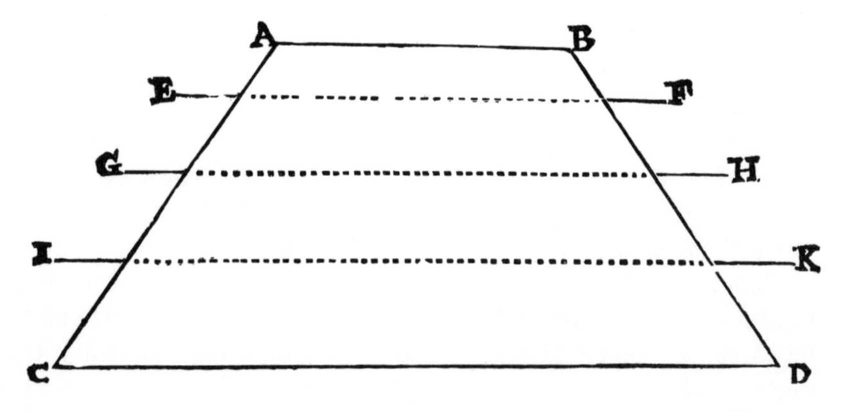


*Figure 61.*

Let ABCD be the frame on which the loose cloth is fastened. Let EF, GH, IK, be the ends of the cords sewn under the cloth. Having placed the frame, put on either side as many men as there are ends of cord with a man holding each end. When we want to give the impression of the sea in motion, let the two men stationed at E and F pull the ends of their cord, letting them slowly come back to place. As the cords return to place they will make the cloth billow. Then have the men stationed at G and H repeat the process of the first men. The same is done at I and K. Thus each one will follow after the other and, in this manner, the waves will be shown rising and falling, and coming in to the shore.

## 28. *Second Method Of Showing A Sea*

For the second method of showing a sea, strips of plain wood are cut in length corresponding to the sea and at least 4 inches thick. On one side these are profiled in the form of waves. Then the cloth is attached to each strip on the side cut to indicate waves, and hangs down below in the other side. The depth should be 1½ feet and the color azure with silver tops. There should be made as many of these as are sufficient for the size of the sea. The waves should be 1½ feet apart so that there is space for a man or any other object to pass between one wave and another.[1] For the depth of the sea there are placed underneath two light pieces of wood stretching from the back of the sea to the front with at least 1 foot projecting at the rear for each piece. To these long pieces of wood each wave is secured by a small piece of wood 1 foot long. The waves are then arranged so that their plane goes to the vanishing point. Then, at the front of this sea, towards the spectators, is placed a wave nailed to the stage floor, and in the middle of it the ends of the pieces of wood are fixed with a loose hinge so that each may move easily. To one of these pieces of wood are nailed the small pieces which sustain the second, fourth, and sixth wave, and to the other those for the third and fifth, the distance between them being that given above. The same order is followed if more waves are used. When it is desired to set these waves in motion, two persons are

1. From here onwards the translator has changed the sequence of the sentences.

placed under the stage directly in line with the ends of the pieces of wood, each of them holding in his hands the end of the piece of wood and, at a given signal, they lower and raise them, so that the waves will be raised and lowered, as shown below.

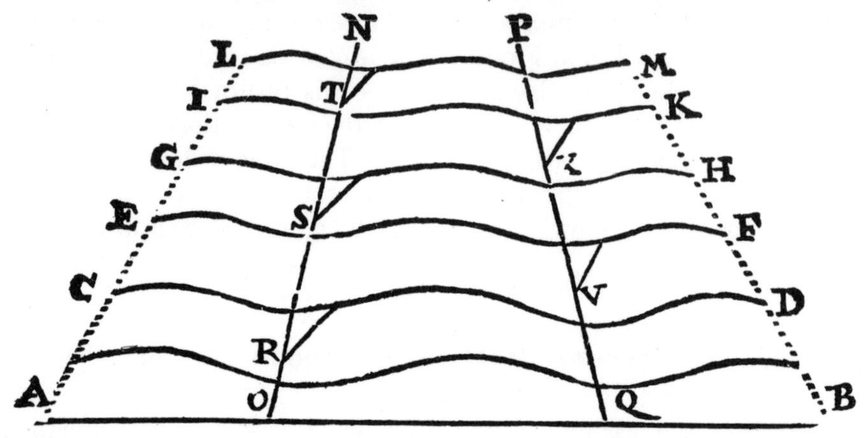


*Figure 62.*

Let the waves be AB, CD, EF, GH, IK, LM. The first AB is immovable, being nailed to the stage floor. The pieces of wood PQ is nailed the small piece V sustaining the third wave AB at O and Q in such a way that they may be easily raised or lowered. On the wood NO is nailed the small piece of wood R sustaining the second wave CD, and S sustaining the fourth wave GH, and T sustaining the sixth wave LM. On the other wood PQ is nailed the small piece V sustaining the third wave EF, and X the fifth wave IK. To set the waves in motion, the ends of the sticks at N and P are raised and lowered successively.

## 29. *Third Method Of Showing A Sea*

This third method of showing a sea is, in my opinion, better than the others. To carry it out, some cylinders made of strips of board not broader than 4 inches and as wide as the sea are shaped like waves. The ends of the cylinders should be of the very best 1½ foot board, with a small iron crank 1 foot long attached to each. Then the cylinders are covered with cloth, colored blue and black with a touch of silver at the top of each board. As many such cylinders are made as needed, and are placed on two pieces of wood as long as the depth of the sea in a manner that the cranks turn easily. They are generally about a foot apart but, when men pretending to arise from the sea will have to come from between them, they may be set as far apart as necessary. Care must be taken to place these pieces of wood on which the cylinders are suspended a little above the slope of the stage. One man is placed at each crank behind the scenery invisible to the audience who, slowly turning the cylinder, sets the sea in motion.

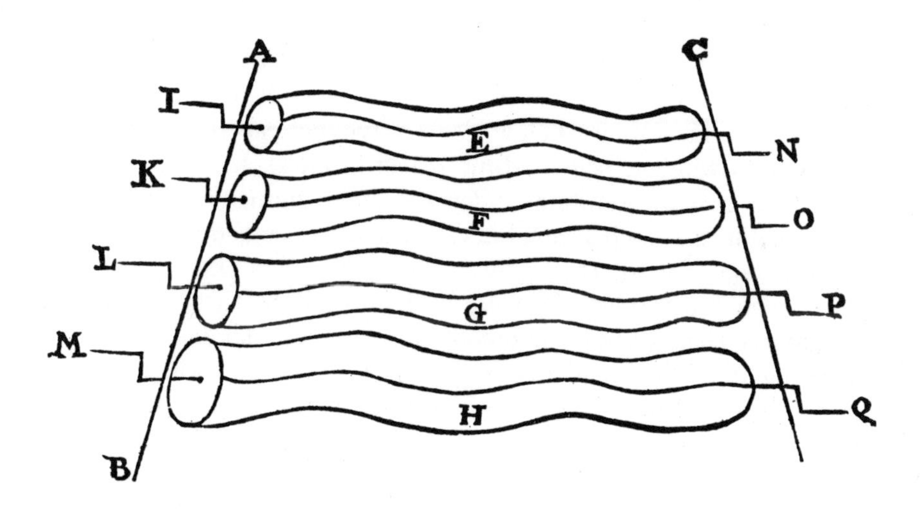


*Figure 63.*

Let AB be the piece of wood on one side, and CD[1] that on the other, placed a little above the slope of the stage. Let E, F, G, and H be the cylinders made in the shape of waves, at whose ends the cranks I, K, L, and M are well nailed, on which the cylinders may easily rotate. These are placed as far apart as necessary. To operate these you will place a man for each cylinder, holding the crank in his hand. When the time comes, he will turn the cylinder, and thus the sea will move as desired. We must, however, consider that if the cylinders are too long for a single man to turn with ease, we may add to the other ends of the cylinders the other cranks N, O, P, and Q, which may be turned by a similar number of men.

1. The letter D is missing in the figure.

## 30. *How To Make The Sea Rise, Swell, Get Tempestuous And Change Color*

If the sea is made as described in the preceding chapter, and if you wish to make it seem to rise, grow tempestuous and change color, then the following method is to be employed: between one cylinder and the next is placed a piece of board shaped like a wave and covered with cloth as described for the second method in Chapter 28. It is painted entirely black with a silver top. Then it is adjusted so that it is lower than the cylinders without interfering with their movement. The number of these cloth-covered boards will correspond to that of the cylinders. This done, below each wave behind the cloth are nailed two wooden pegs distant 3 feet from each other and so long that a man standing under the stage immediately underneath holding one with each hand can easily raise and lower them. This is done for all the other waves. For this effect, each of these men must raise his wave and lower it in turn but more frequently than the movement of the first cylinder and without lowering it so far as to make visible the cylinders which must stand firm and motionless, *i.e.*, so long as you do not wish the sea to show itself quiet and calm. When you do, the darkened waves may be lowered all at once and returned to their places, while the cylinders may be moved in their former manner. You might also by this means simulate a flood by raising the dark waves so far as it seems suitable to whoever has this in charge.

Let A and B be the cylinders. Between those are the waves made of pieces of board covered with colored cloth as said above, CEGD. Let the two pegs be EF and GH of the length

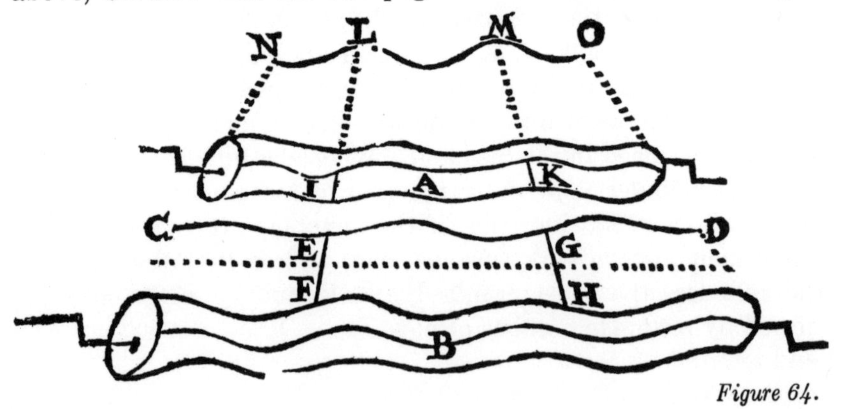


*Figure 64.*

described above and nailed to the waves behind the cloth at E and G three feet apart. The said wave is placed lower than the cylinders so that the top CD is not seen by the spectators. When you wish to change the color of the sea the men who hold the pegs F and H raise the wave so that F and H come to I and K and, consequently, the top of the wave CEGD arrives at LMNO. By lowering and raising it with greater frequency than the cylinders, as said above, the result will be certain. The same is done with the other waves placed between the other cylinders. To make the sea seem calm again the waves are returned to their former position and the cylinders are revolved. The same is done with the other waves placed between the other cylinders.

## 31. *How To Make Ships Or Galleys Or Other Vessels Seem To Move Over The Sea*

To make ships or galleys or other vessels seem to move over the sea, they must be made to appear to progress by the use of sail or oar. If by sail, this method is used: the profile of a ship is cut out upon a piece of board of such size as desired. When this board is cut according to this pattern, the ship is completed by means of painting, shading it out so that it seems in the round with masts, ropes, sails, and other gear such as these vessels are commonly furnished with. Then between two waves of the sea a groove is made of wood like a swallow's tail and in this groove the base of the ship is fitted, as it is also fashioned in the same shape. The base and the groove should be well soaped. When you wish to move the ship, one or more men make it pass forward on this groove with a slow motion. Thus it seems to move under sail. If the ship is a galley, the same procedure is followed except that you put in a bank of oars on one side in such a way that on the side where these oars would be held by the hands of slaves, they are joined and nailed onto one strip of wood. In the middle of this strip another piece of wood is fastened so long that a man standing immediately underneath the ship below the stage can hold it and, while the other men make the ship move on the groove, he can move it up and down in a rowing motion. All the oars are fastened loosely to the wood and in the loop-holes so that they may move easily, and, while the piece of wood is raised and lowered by the man, these oars seem to dip into and rise out of the water.

Let A be the ship seeming to sail over the sea, and BC the groove placed between the two waves DE and FG, and in it the swallow's tail is marked by HI, made under the base of the ship. Let the bottom of the ship be placed low enough so that it will

*Figure 65.*

not be seen by the spectators on the floor of the hall. When it is desired to show the ship in motion, one or more men under the stage move the ship, as said above, so that it will glide on the groove with a slow motion.

In figure 66 let A be the galley, and B and C be the ends of the oars within the galley, which are fixed in the loop-holes, and let BC be the piece of wood to which they are nailed. Let DE[1] be the other piece nailed to it in the center D. To make the galley seem to advance by means of oars, the man placed under the stage for such a purpose will lift DE so that the point E will rise to F and, consequently, the extremity of the oars G and H will lower to IK. In this manner the oars will seem to plunge into the waves of the sea. By returning F to E as before, the oars will lift out of the water.

1. The letter D is missing in the figure, and the letter E is that below F.

*Figure 66.*

## 32. *How To Make Ships, Galleys And Other Vessels Move Across The Sea By Sail Or Oar, Turn And Move Back*

When it is desired to make believe that ships, galleys, or other vessels come from far off over the sea by means of sails or oars and turn around and go back, this procedure is followed: the cylinders are made to represent waves, as described in Chapter 29. They are divided into two parts with the gap in the middle for the ship to pass. Care must be taken to set them so that they can be easily turned by handles placed at the other ends of the cylinders. This done, a ship, galley, or other vessel is made in the round, without a bottom, and around it is secured a piece of cloth at least 2 feet wide. Wooden masts bearing the sails and other necessary equipment for seaworthy boats will be added and the cloth and all the rest colored in an appropriate way. Then one board or several, as long as the distance to be covered, is cut in the shape of waves, and is nailed along the length of the gap projecting above the wave so as not to interfere with the action of the cylinders. A small roller ½ a foot long is fixed at the prow and poop of the ship in such a manner that it will turn easily on its pivot. When it is desired to move this vessel, the following method is employed: four men are placed directly underneath the stage, that is, under the prow and poop of the ship. They slide the ship with the rollers over the top of the board, which is cut like waves, so that it rises and falls like ships at sea. Care must be taken that under the cylinders serving as waves and immediately below the gap there must be an opening in the stage floor, so that the men operating the ship can work without impediment.

The following is done to represent a boat in full sail. Pieces of thin cloth are fastened to the yards with iron wires to give the bulging effect. Then the yard arm is tied to the mast with a small cord running through the pulley. To let out the sails within the ship, so that they appear to unfold, one or more men are employed. They draw the end of the small cord and immediately the sails will be seen to come up. Likewise for striking the sails, they may loosen the cords. This is all you can do in order to represent sailing.

To represent a galley moved by oars, the body of the vessel is made similar to the above mentioned ship. Oars are placed on both sides in number and length according to the size of the ship. Both sets of oars are attached to a single bar of wood within the ship and to the middle of this bar of wood is attached a handle, as described for the galley in the preceding chapter. To give the rowing action, the galley is made to move on its rollers over the board placed in the gap as described above. From time to time the man in charge raises and lowers the handle giving the effect of rowing. To make the ship go back, it is swung around, and the rollers having been adjusted on the board, it will be moved back to its starting place.

*Figure 67.*

Let A be the ship made in the round but without a bottom. Let BC be the cylinder placed under the prow and DE under the poop. Let FGHI be the hanging cloth which surrounds the ship, attached at the bottom FH, and the other end GI free. Let KL be the board cut in the shape of waves, and let BC and DE be the cylinders placed on the said board. In order to make the ship advance as far as desired, the men mentioned above slide the ship to the end of the board. To make the ship turn around you must turn the ship or galley, placing the rollers on the board, and making it go back to its place.

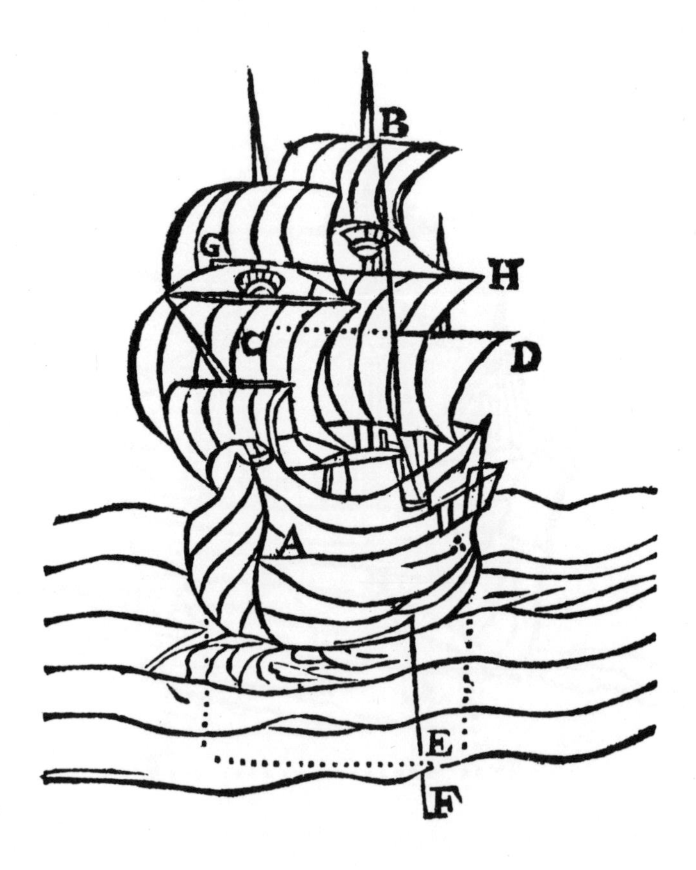


*Figure 68.*

Let A be the ship, and B be the top of the mast with the pulley, and CD the yard with the sail, which can be lowered into the ship. The piece of cord, BE, with one end attached to the center of the yard CD, passes through the pulley B, and the other end should come to E. When you wish the sail to unfold you pull the end E of the cord until it comes to F and, consequently, the yard which is at CD will come to GH. The sail will be lowered in the same manner by letting the end of the cord F up to E, lowering the sail from GH to CD. The same process may be followed with the other sails.

## 33. *How To Make A Ship Or Other Vessel Appear To Anchor In The Middle Of The Sea*

When it is wished to make a ship or other vessel appear to stop, or as we say anchor, while at sea,[1] this is the method: first a beam is erected perpendicular to the floor of the hall long enough to reach the ship when it is at anchor. At its top is fastened a

*Figure 69.*

pivot pin of iron of a suitable thickness and ½ foot long. In the bottom of the ship at the center is nailed another board with a hole large enough to allow the pivot pin to enter easily. This done, to make it appear that the ship has finished its course on the board track previously indicated, the same men who are moving it will raise the ship slowly and fasten the pivot pin into the hole, then raise and lower the poop and prow very slowly in such a manner that the ship appears to ride with the waves that surround it in relation to the cloth attached round about the vessel.

Then with the weighing of the anchors, which should have been thrown out when the vessel first paused, the vessel is put back on the board track and made to continue its course.

Let A be the ship and BC the board placed in the bottom. In the center of the board is the hole D. Let the piece of wood placed on the floor of the hall be EF with its iron pivot G. Let this piece of wood be as long as from the floor of the hall F to the bottom of the ship when it is in place. To operate, let us place the hole D on top of the pivot G, moving the poop and prow of the ship as has already been shown.

## 34. *How To Make Dolphins And Other Marine Monsters Appear To Spout Water While They Swim*

Dolphins or other marine monsters are made to glide along the sea and to spout water from time to time from their heads in this manner: a dolphin or other monster is made of a piece of painted board, and on the dolphin's stomach is nailed a 2 foot piece of wood which will be held by the person who is to move it. From underneath the stage the dolphin is moved by this handle in the space between two waves, the head and tail being raised and lowered in imitation of nature.

To make it seem to spout water from its head, underneath the dolphin's head is placed another man who holds in his hand a cardboard cornucopia fully half a foot across, with a tube at the bottom. In it is put a large quantity of pieces of beaten silver or pounded and pulverized talc. When the dolphin is to spout water, this cornucopia is put behind its head out of sight of the spectators.

1. "While at sea" is not in Sabbattini.

The man below blows through the end of the cornucopia. In an instant those little pieces of silver will come out of the larger end of the cornucopia and, by means of the reflection of the light, it will truly seem that water comes out of the head of the dolphin. By having a sufficient quantity of pieces of silver, the man below can repeat this operation from time to time.

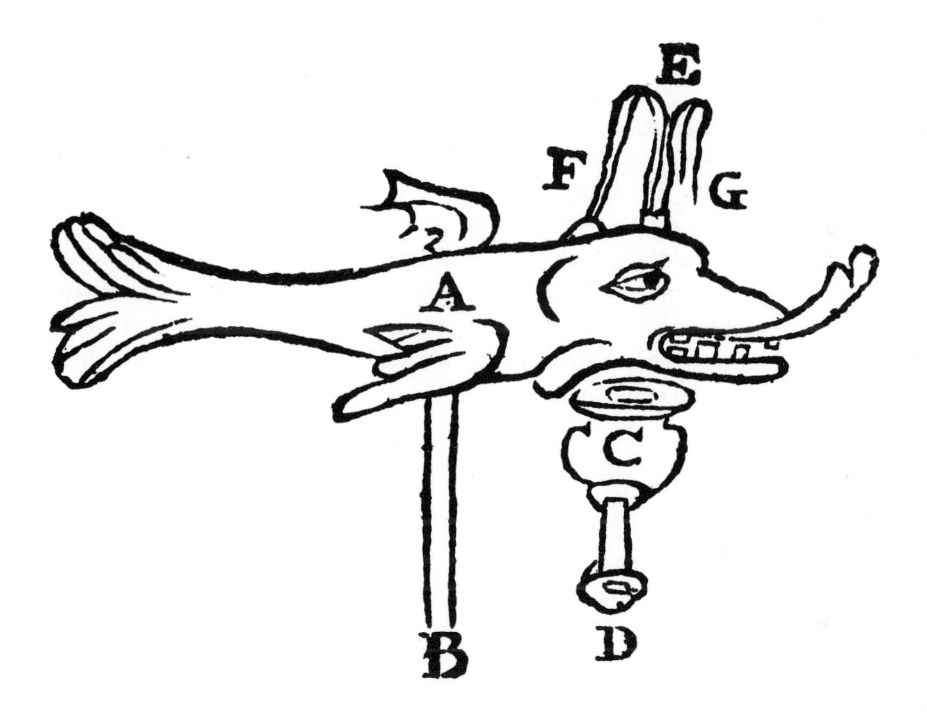


*Figure 70.*

Let A be the dolphin, and AB be the piece of wood nailed to the stomach of the fish. Let CD be the cornucopia, and the pieces of silver placed in the wider part of C. To do this, he holds the piece of wood AB at B which will raise and lower the dolphin, in imitation of its natural motion. From time to time the man who holds the cornucopia CD directly under the head of the dolphin will blow in the smaller end D and immediately the little pieces of silver will come out at E, F, and G, making the spectators believe that it is water.

## 35. *How To Represent A River That Seems To Flow Constantly*

Sometimes the action calls for one or more rivers with or without figures carrying urns from which it seems water continuously flows to form the course of the river. To represent such an urn, a piece of thin cloth is used which is twice as long as the distance from the urn to the end of the course of the river and as wide as the greatest breadth of the river. It is painted blue and touched with silver. Let us pass one end of this cloth into the mouth of the urn, and the other end under the stage floor through a small slit made for that purpose under the figure.[1] The first end will be passed through a slit in the stage floor as far away from the urn as we wish the course of the river to be. This opening must correspond to the width of the cloth the ends of which come forth together. To make the river flow, a man will be under the stage floor directly beneath the opening, pulling the cloth continuously and holding it always at its widest part. If there is no figure represented, a river may be shown to flow between mountains, or from any other place desired.

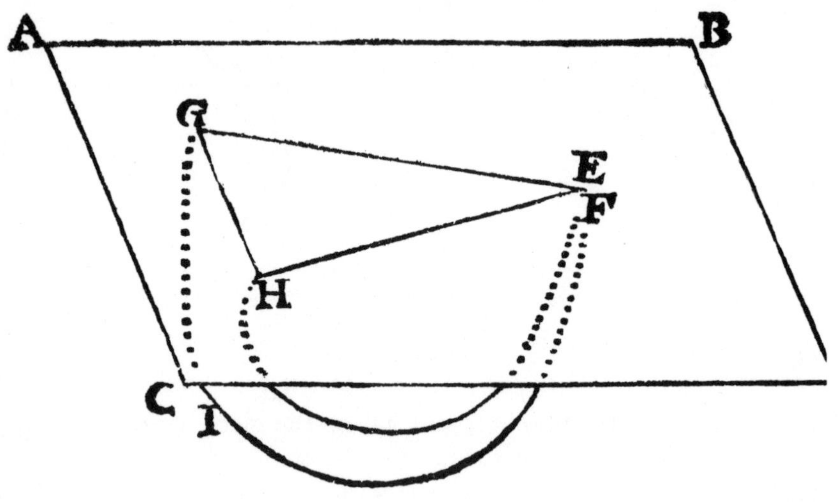


*Figure 71.*

Let ABCD be the stage floor, and E the urn with the figure, and slit at F. Let GH be the narrow opening and I the person who is to make the cloth EFGH move. At the proper

1. In Chapter 36, the cloth is referred to as an endless belt.

time the person will pull the end of the cloth GH at its widest part and thus the part F will flow, coming out of the urn E, widening constantly, and it will seem that the river is flowing continuously.

## 36. *How To Make A Fountain That Seems To Throw Forth Water Continually*

To represent a fountain spouting water continually, we shall proceed as follows: into the middle of the basin of the fountain is placed a small tube 2 inches in diameter so that a piece of

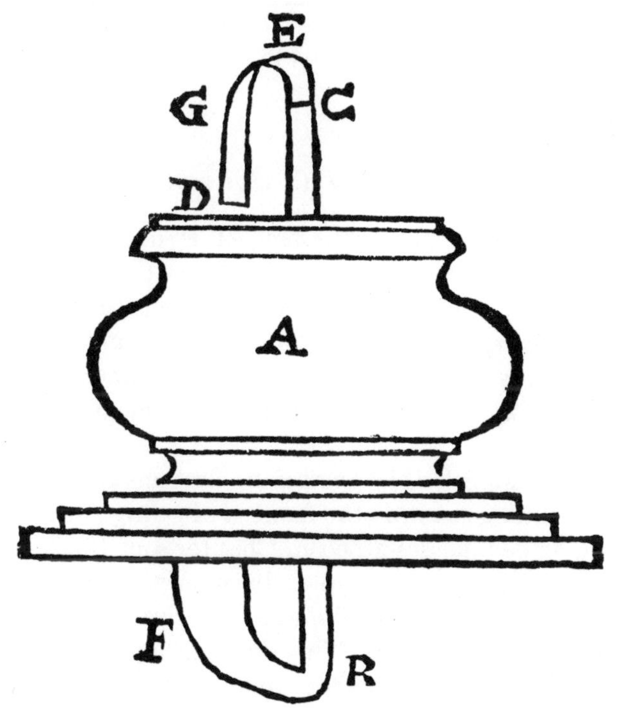


*Figure 72.*

cloth, when bunched together, can pass through it easily. Onto this cloth about ½ foot apart are sewed several rods the thickness of a finger and about ½ foot in length. The cloth and the rods are painted as the river was and, just as in the preceding chapter, one end of this cloth is made to come out of the tube on the side toward the audience and down through a large fissure in the basin out of sight of the audience. The ends of the cloth are sewed together, as was done in the operation of the river. The fountain is operated by two men underneath the stage. One must continually push the little rods and the cloth up through the small tube, and the other must be beneath the fissure to pull and spread the cloth, keeping it as wide as possible.

Let A be the basin, and BC the small tube placed in it, and let the opening within the basin be D. The cloth is BCEF, and the little rod CE. Place the operator at B, who is to make the little rods rise towards the top of the tube C. Let another man be placed at F under the opening. When this man hears the little rod CE falling outside of the tube as at CG, then he must pull the cloth through the opening, holding it as wide as possible, to show the spread of the water as it falls to earth. He must pull it constantly towards F, while the person at B continually pushes up the little rods.

## 37. *How To Make The Heavens In Sections*

When, during the *intermezzi*, it is desired to make the machines rise into the heavens or descend to the stage, it is necessary to have the heavens divided into sections for the ease of the operator. This spectacle will arouse delight and wonder among the spectators who cannot see how the machines are hidden as they rise from the earth or how they come out and descend from the heavens.

To accomplish this operation, first make a piece of the heavens beginning towards the front of the stage at a convenient height and sloped, as described in Chapter 4 of Book I. It must be wide enough to cover the space between the front of the stage and the space where the machines are to rise. This piece marks the end of the first section. This done, in line with this piece, a second section is made with the upper edge enough higher than the lower edge so that the gap between the sections cannot be seen by the spectators seated on the first rows near the front of the stage. This gap should be as large as is required so that the machines may easily rise and enter without any impediment. In the same fashion, the other sections are made according to the need.

The painter should exercise most exquisite diligence in coloring these sections in order that the bottom of one will blend with the upper part of the next.

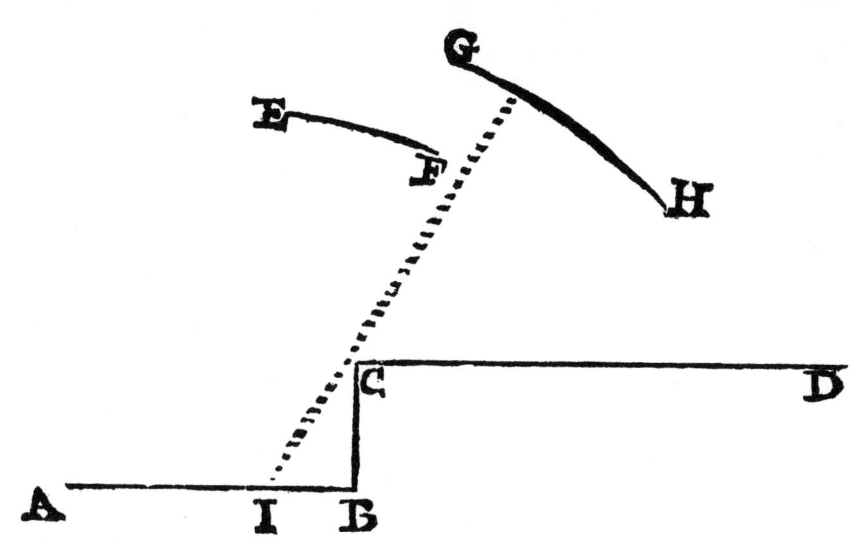


*Figure 73.*

Let AB be the floor of the hall or the theatre, and CD the stage floor. Let EF be the first section of the heavens, and GH the second. Let there be as great a distance from the end of F to the beginning of the second piece, G, as is necessary for the machines. Let the part G be high enough above F so that the people in the first row I will not see the gap FG, but instead will see K,[1] following the sightline IK. These four lines have been made in profile so that the demonstration will be more intelligible.

## *38. How To Make Part Of The Heavens Grow Slowly Clouded*

Sometimes we want the heavens to grow clouded gradually. To do this the heavens are first made in several sections, as described in the preceding chapter. At one side of the stage back of the houses and in line with the gaps between the sections is placed a framed piece[2] for each gap, made of thin boards as broad as the cloud desired and covered with cloth painted in cloud forms. The clouds of the first space are made brighter than the others just as in painting the scenes. At the back of each frame, behind the houses and low enough not to be seen by the spectators, are placed one or two supports of tie beams of strong, thin wood

1. The letter K is missing in the figure.
2. It is apparent from what follows that this is painted with clouds.

to pass between the sections. To make the heavens grow clouded, one or two men are placed above the heavens, holding in their hands the supports of the frame. Upon a given signal they must run the frames under the heavens, stopping them where it is necessary. Care should be taken that the upper or convex part of the frame accosts as much as possible the lower or concave part of the heavens as is shown in Figure 74.

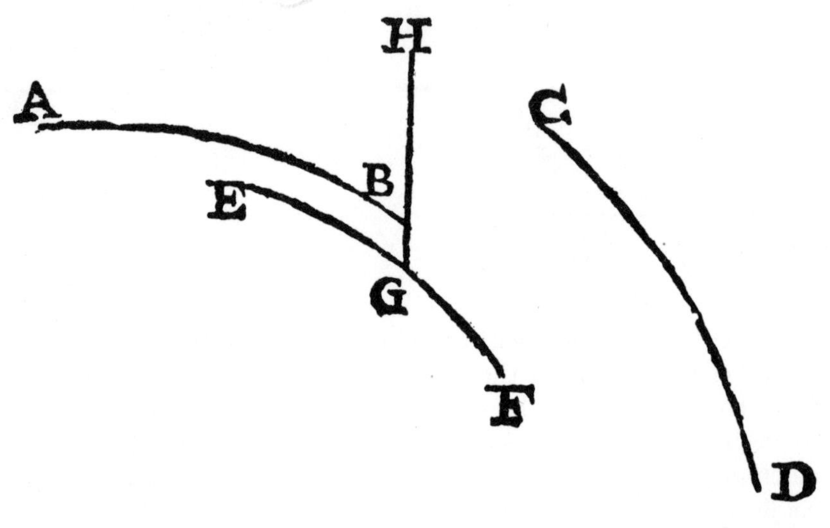


*Figure 74.*

Let AB be the cross section of the first section of the heavens, and CD the second, and EF a frame as a cloud, placed behind the houses at one side in a convenient position. GH is the support. The person who has to stand above the end of the first section is at B holding the support GH at H. When the time arrives, the person placed at H must walk slowly above the last section of the heavens holding the support in his nands and drawing the frame with it to its appointed place, thus achieving the effect. If the frames are large, two or three persons with two or three supports may be employed.

## *39. How To Cover The Heavens With Clouds Instantaneously*

If you have to cover the sky with clouds instantaneously, although this is not a natural thing, yet supposing it to be desired, then the following method is employed: the heavens are made in sections as described above. Then frames are made corresponding to the number of the sections and of the length and breadth desired for the clouds. These frames are painted as described. They are then placed in line with the beginning of the sections so that they are not seen by the audience. They are placed in grooves which must be made first and set at each side so that they can be run in like a shutter. These grooves are to run from the beginning of the frames through the whole depth of the section of the heavens to be covered, and must be painted sky color. This done and the frames set, each in its place, two or three men are appointed to every frame and when the time comes they all run the frames along the grooves so that in an instant that section of the heavens becomes clouded. The first section will have to remain as it was since it cannot be changed. There is, however, another device for this, described in Chapter 40.

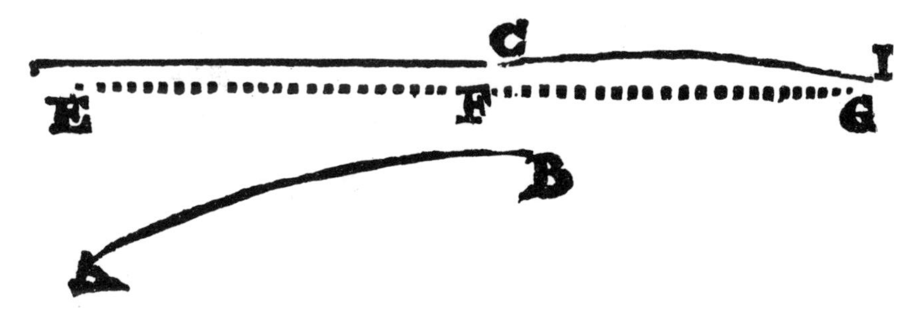


*Figure 75.*

Let AB be the profile of the first section, CD the second which has to become covered with clouds, and EF the frame placed above the first section AB in line with CD and adjusted in the groove EFG so that it can run easily in it. To cover the section CD with clouds the men at E cause the frame EF to be run in an instant so that when E is at F, F is at G. In the same manner the other sections are covered with clouds except the first, as said above.

## 40. *Another Method Of Covering The Heavens With Clouds Instantaneously*

This second method of covering the heavens with clouds is almost the same as the first, with this difference that in the first method the frames were placed at the beginnings of the sections of the heavens. In this method cloths painted in cloud forms which correspond in length and breadth to the sections of the heavens they are to cover must be placed in the same positions. One part of each cloth is fastened to the beginning of the section. On the other parts are sewn two or three ends of small cords (or more if the cloth is large). These small cords ought to be double the length of the cloth, passing on pulleys which are placed in the extreme end of the parts of each section of the heavens which is to be clouded. The cloths are then folded or drawn to the places described above so that they are not seen by the spectators. When all things are arranged, men are assigned to their positions, to hold each an end of cord. At a given signal they all draw the cords together so that in an instant the heavens are immediately covered with cloths painted as clouds. Should you desire to make the heavens return to its former state, the cords are redoubled to draw the other ends so that the sections of the heavens are uncovered again. The first section may be clouded by this method: a piece of cloth is simply fastened to its edge.

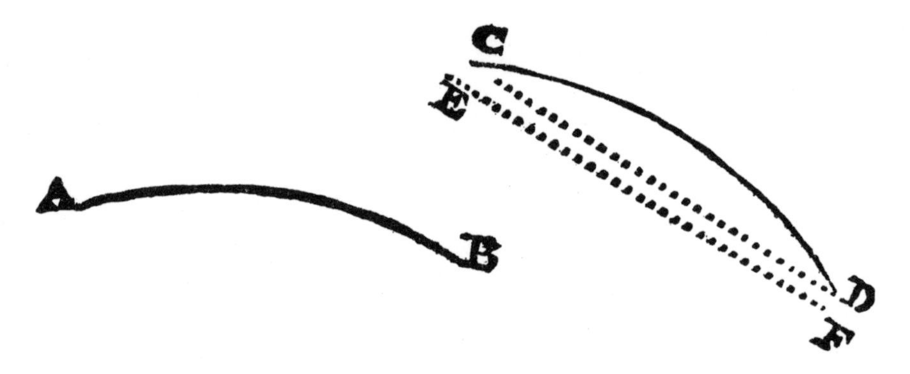


*Figure 76.*

Let AB be the first section of the heavens, CD the second, which is to be clouded in an instant. Let EF be the piece of cloth painted as a cloud, folded and gathered up at E. Let E, F, and C be the small cord with its end E sewed onto the cloth at E and passing through the pulley at F and returning with the other end at C. The operator must hold the end of the cord C in his hands. At a given signal he will rapidly pull the cord, bring the end of the cloth E to F, and thus the section of the heavens CD will be clouded. The same process may be followed for the other sections. The other end of the small cord, which is placed above the cloth and as long as from E to the beginning of the cloth, may be pulled, and its end which was at F will return to E, as it was in the beginning.

## 41. *How To Make A Rainbow Or Arch Appear In The Sky*

Should it be necessary to introduce a rainbow in the *intermezzi*, first of all the method described in Chapter 40 is followed: on one of the sections of heavens where it is most appropriate a piece of cloth is placed on which a rainbow is painted. This is made to appear or disappear like the clouds. No demonstration is required, for that has been given in connection with the clouds.

## 42. *How To Cover Part Of The Heavens With Clouds, Starting With A Small Cloud Which Becomes Increasingly Larger And Changes Constantly In Color*

This last method of covering part of the heavens with clouds, although it may appear difficult, seems to me the most beautiful, and arouses more wonder than the others. It can be done only in one part, in the center, because of the concavity of the heavens. Eight or ten lathed cylinders are made at least 1 foot in diameter and in length corresponding to the opening of that part of the heavens in which the clouds are to appear. At each end of the cylinders is fixed an indented wheel 2 inches thick and of the same diameter. The cylinders are covered with cloth and are arranged on the floor touching each other exactly as they are to appear in the heavens in order to paint them. A highly skilled painter should be employed, for not only should he color one side of them to match the rest of the heavens where they are to be fitted, but also on the other side there should be painted clouds, starting with the beginning of a small cloud painted on the first cylinder at the back of the heavens and proceeding with larger clouds on the following cylinders. The color constantly changes in a natural manner. The cylinders are then adjusted in the opening of the heavens so that they turn easily on their pivots, which are placed upon two beams located one at each side at the convex of the heavens. At the other side lengthways a firm, smooth, wooden groove, a little wider than the thickness of the wheels and at least 4 inches deep, in which there is a wooden beam having indentations corresponding to the wheels, is placed so that when the beam slides the wheels will turn. This beam is longer than the groove and long enough to permit the cylinders to make a complete revolution. Thus that part of the heavens may be clouded, and the clouds made to disappear in order to make the heavens appear as it was at first.

To put this into effect, four men are stationed above the heavens, two of them towards the sections, and two at the opposite side.[1] They must hold in their hands the ends of the indented beams. When we wish the heavens to be clouded, those two men placed towards the spectators will gradually pull the ends of their beams towards them. Consequently, the parts of the cylinders painted with clouds may be seen revolving. These men must pull the beams to the indications which will be made on the beams, corresponding to the revolvings of the cylinders. In this manner that part of the heavens will be clouded as desired.

In order to make the heavens return to its former state, the men who are at the opposite side will make the indented beam return. But if it is desired to have the clouds move forward and vanish, this may be done by the persons[2] who may continue pulling the beams until the cylinders have made a complete revolution. The indented beam, however, will have to be made proportionately long.

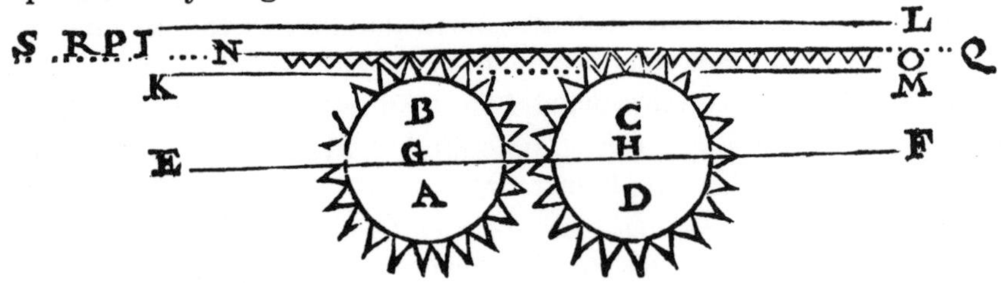


*Figure 77.*

Let AD and CD be the indented wheels placed at the ends of the cylinders, and EF the piece of wood on which the pivot G of the wheel AB and the pivot H of the wheel CD are placed. Let IKLM be the groove 4 inches deep in order to accommodate the wheels. Let NO be the indented beam placed so in the

1. Two towards the audience and two at the farther ends of the beams.

2. Those near the audience.

groove that its teeth unite with the teeth of the wheels. Let P be the men placed above the heavens near the spectators and Q those on the opposite end. At the desired time, the man at P will pull the indented beam slowly towards him. At the same time the wheels will revolve and, consequently, the cylinders. Thus, when N is at R, the end of the beam O will be at N, and the half of the cylinders A and D will be at B and C, and clouds will be seen. A similar process will be followed for the clouds to return backwards. But if it is desired for the clouds to vanish, the person at P will not stop pulling the indented beam at R, as was said above, but will continue pulling it to S. Thus the halves of the cylinders B and C will return to the positions occupied by A and D, as they were in the beginning. Thus the clouds will have vanished and the heavens will be as at the beginning. The same process may be followed for the other cylinders, two having been indicated in the drawing to avoid confusion, but in the same way you can make as many as you like.

## 43. *How To Make A Cloud With People In It Descend Directly On To The Stage From The Heavens*

When it is desired to lower a cloud with people in it from the heavens directly on to the stage, this method is used: two beams of sufficient size, preferably 9 inches but at least 4, are set up, stretching from the heavens to beneath the stage floor, so that there is formed between them a very smooth swallow-tailed groove ½ foot deep and wide. It is properly erected behind a partition wall in a vertical position secured with braces to the rear wall. Another piece of wood, 6 or 7 feet in length and of the same thickness or a little less, is set into the groove in such a way as to move easily on it. This done, a horizontal piece of wood of the same thickness is securely fastened with strong tenons on to the end of the vertical piece in the groove. Its length is determined by the extent that the cloud is to hang over the stage. A brace is then firmly nailed 2½ feet from the end to which the cloud is attached and 1½ times as long as the horizontal arm, reaching to the bottom of the piece of wood in the groove, where it is well nailed. These three pieces of wood form a right angle triangle. At each end of the piece of wood in the groove is attached an iron ring, of sufficient strength to sustain the weights of both the cloud and the people in it when the cloud is lowered and raised. A piece of strong rope is tied to each of the rings. The upper piece is passed through a pulley, securely fastened above the heavens directly over the groove, and the end is brought down and wound around a windlass which is beneath the stage at the lower end of the groove. The other end of the rope will be fastened to the lower ring and brought down and wound around the windlass in a contrary direction to the first, so that when one is being wound the other unwinds in the same proportion. A cloud of sufficient size is made and secured by wooden crossbars and circles, so as to hold the people within it as safely and comfortably as possible. The framework, covered with cloth which is painted to appear as natural as possible, is nailed securely to the end of the arm. This done, a cut is made in the heavens in line with the groove to provide easy passage for the arm to which the cloud is attached and the cut should reach down to the level of the stage. To prevent the cut being seen, a piece of cloth, equal to the length and width of the cut and painted like the heavens, is attached to the bottom of the arm. Similarly, another piece is made for the upper part of the cut, one end of which is fastened to the heavens, and the other to the upper part of the arm. When

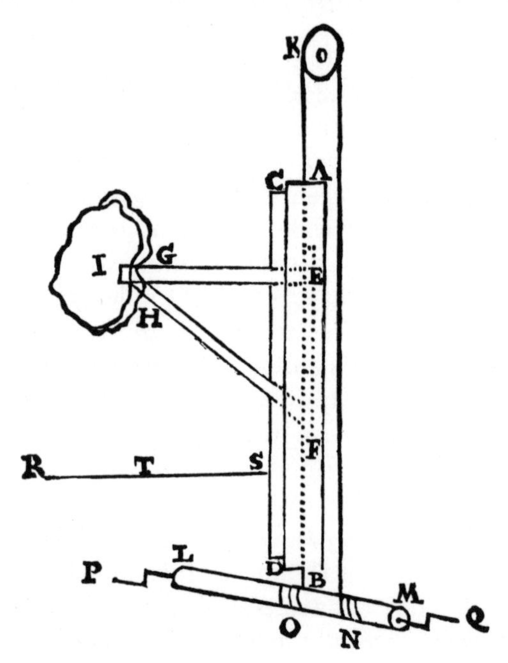


*Figure 78.*

the cloud is lowered both the upper and lower cloth will also come down covering the cut, so that it always remains closed. The contrary happens when it is raised, so that in this manner no opening is seen. Care must be taken, however, that the cloud is hidden between the sections of the heavens. Two or four men are placed at the windlass to raise or lower the cloud.

Let AB and CD be the two pieces forming the groove, and EF be the piece of wood placed in it. Let GE be the piece of wood sustaining the cloud, and HF the other piece sustaining the weight. These are nailed at H, E, and F forming a right angle within the groove at E. Let the cloud I be placed on the end of the piece EF at E, to which is attached[1] one end of the rope. It passes through the pulley K and comes down to the windlass LM at N, where it is wound sufficiently so as to permit the cloud to move from above the heavens to the stage floor.

The second ring is placed at the other end of the piece of wood at F, to which is fastened another rope which is brought down to the windlass at O. The men are placed at the handles of the windlass PQ. When the time comes to lower the cloud, they will turn the windlass winding the rope FO and unwinding the other rope EKN at the same rate, so when F is at B, the cloud will be above the stage floor RS at T. To raise the cloud to its place, the windlass is reversed.

## 44. *Another Method For Making A Cloud Descend With One Or More Persons In It*

If we wish to have a cloud descend with people in it by means of another method, we shall proceed in this fashion: two vertical grooves are made, as in Chapter 43, but with this difference, that instead of the swallow-tail groove, there are smooth, evenly cut parallel grooves. These extend from the floor of the hall through the heavens. These will be put one on each side directly under the sections of the heavens made for that purpose, but out of sight of the spectators. They are fastened securely to the walls perpendicular to the horizon. Then a beam is adjusted as long as the distance between the two grooves plus 1 foot at each side. In this manner the ends of the beam will move easily within the grooves. Directly under each end will be fastened to

1. By a metal ring.

the beam another piece of wood of the same thickness and 2 feet long. This piece is pegged at the lower part so that the main beam will not revolve, which might easily happen with the weight of the people which sometimes is not quite balanced. When all this has been adjusted, we shall place above the heavens directly over the grooves a pulley on each side through which a rope of the proper thickness will be passed. One of the ends[1] will be attached to the main beam near the grooves. Let the other end pass through the pulley and, coming down, let it be twisted around a windlass which should be 1½ feet in diameter, and a little longer than the distance between the grooves. Place it under the stage, and adjust it so that the ropes which pass through the pulleys are perpendicular to the windlass. Adjust it with its pivots so that it may be easily turned. Directly in the center of this windlass we shall place a capstan far enough away so that its handles may be turned. This capstan must make the windlass turn by means of a rope of the proper thickness, whose half will be twisted around the center of the windlass with as many turns as are sufficient to uncoil the ropes which were tied to the beam placed in the grooves. The other end of the rope should pass around the capstan. The cloud will be made in the center of the two pieces of wood. It must be long so that the ends of the wood will not be seen. At the time that the cloud will be lowered by four or more men, according to necessity, let the capstan be turned, because in the same proportion to the unwinding of the rope from the capstan, the ropes wound about the ends of the windlass will unwind. Consequently, the cloud will be lowered with the people in it. But if there are many people, more men will have to be added to the capstan. One of them, however, must be constantly ready to guide the rope and prevent uneven winding, or too rapid unwinding of the capstan. To lift the cloud, the capstan may be turned in the opposite direction, but to do this, as much rope must be placed about the windlass and the capstan as is necessary for the one to unwind and the other to wind.

Let AB and CD be the grooves perpendicular to the horizon, secured so that they will not move. Let FG be the beam on which the cloud E is made, its length[2] being longer by 1 foot on each side than the distance between the grooves, as AF

1. Of each rope.
2. The beam.

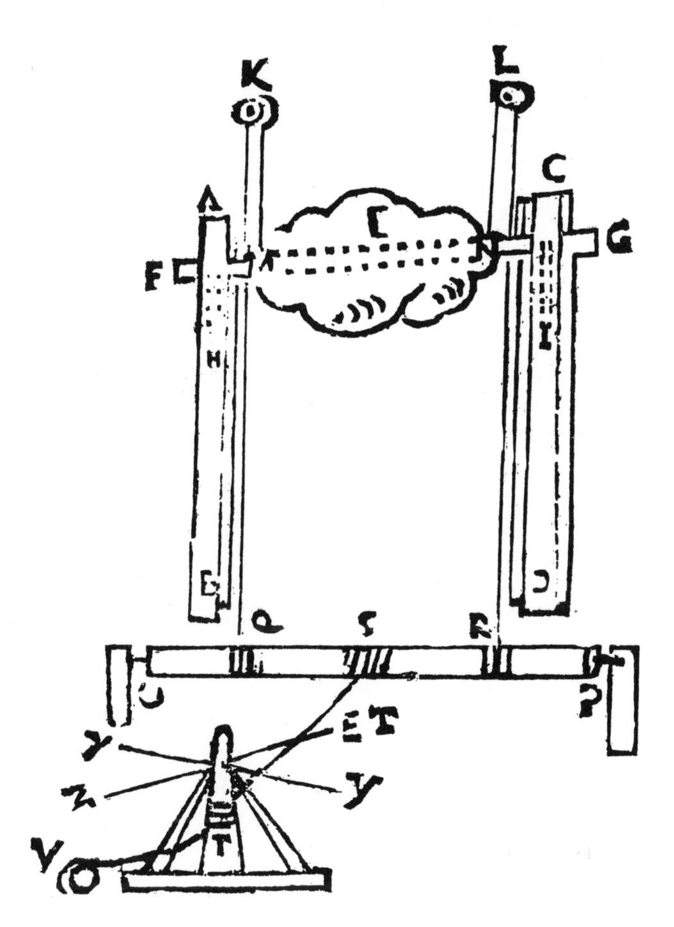


*Figure 79.*

and CG. Then on the part of that beam which is within the grooves, A and C, let us add a piece of wood of the same thickness and 2 feet long, as indicated by AH and CI. Let K and L be the pulleys placed above the heavens directly above M and N on the beam FG, where the ends of the ropes M and N are attached. Let these ropes pass through the pulleys K and L and wind around the windlass OP under the stage at Q and R. In the center of the windlass at S wind the end of a rope as many times as is necessary to lower the cloud E to the stage. Let the end of this rope pass around the capstan T, while a person standing at V guides the rope so that the capstan will unwind, and so that the other rope does not become entangled as it winds around the windlass while the first rope is being unwound. Let the men be placed at the handles X, Y, Z, ET. When we want the cloud to descend, the men will turn the capstan, the end of the rope, which was first adjusted proportionately, unwinds from the windlass and makes the ends of the ropes Q and R, which hold the beam of the cloud, unwind as well, until the cloud is lowered to its appointed place. In order to make the cloud rise, the capstan will be turned in the contrary manner.

## 45. *How To Lower A Cloud With Persons In It From The Rear Of The Heavens Forward To The Center Of The Stage*

If we wish to lower a cloud with people in it from the rear of the heavens to the center of the stage, we must follow this method: we take it for granted, however, that behind the scenes and directly behind the ends of the heavens there is adequate space of at least 20 feet. Let us take a good strong beam 25 feet long, which will serve as a lever. Let us fix its center on a very steady fulcrum held by means of supports and an iron knuckle. The fulcrum must be made out of a piece of beam bigger around than the lever. It will be placed perpendicular to the horizon and fixed on the floor of the hall directly under the last section of the heavens. Its height must be 4 feet above the level of the stage, but so far within that it cannot be seen by the spectators. Then, on it will be fixed the lever, so that its motion is easy. At 10 feet from the fulcrum and 20 feet high, let us put a metal pulley, if possible, so that it may be secure and able to sustain the weight. This pulley must be placed directly above another one of the same size and firmness at 3 feet from the floor of the hall, which will serve as a guide for the rope to the capstan. The capstan will be placed directly in line with the pulley and far enough to one side for the men to turn the handles without interference. Let us take a strong, firm rope, so that no accident may occur during the operation, and tie one end securely to the end of the lever, *i.e.*, at the back of the heavens and let us pass the other end over the pulley which was placed above the heavens. As it comes down, let the rope pass through the other pulley placed beneath it for the revolving of the capstan. At the other end of the lever, *i.e.*, that towards the spectators, a cloud must be made. Let it be made on two pieces of wood of the proper size with platforms where the people who have to go up in it may stand firmly. Once the cloud is completed, you will put it at the extremity of the lever, balanced between the two pieces of wood, so that whether the lever is moved up or down the cloud will always remain perpendicular to the horizon. Thus, as the cloud lowers, the persons will not fall out, and also the lever will not be seen. This cloud, made in this manner, will not be able to come out of a gap in the heavens as it lowers, but will move forward in an upright position in accord with its construction. It will be necessary to make an aperture in the heavens similar to the cloud but a little larger so that the cloud may descend without impediment and return with equal facility. This aperture must always be closed with a piece of heavens made on a small frame of thin pieces of wood, which resembles as much as possible the color as well as the shape of the surrounding heavens. So, the inner parts of the heavens are painted similar to the outer ones, lest any discrepancy be seen when the wicket is opened to permit the cloud to come out of the aperture. On the other end of the lever will be put a weight, which must be enough heavier than the cloud and the people to permit that end of the lever to lower by itself, regardless of the weight of the people or the cloud.

When this operation is to be done, four or eight men will be placed at the handles of the capstan, who will slowly turn the capstan while the cloud descends, until it rests above the level

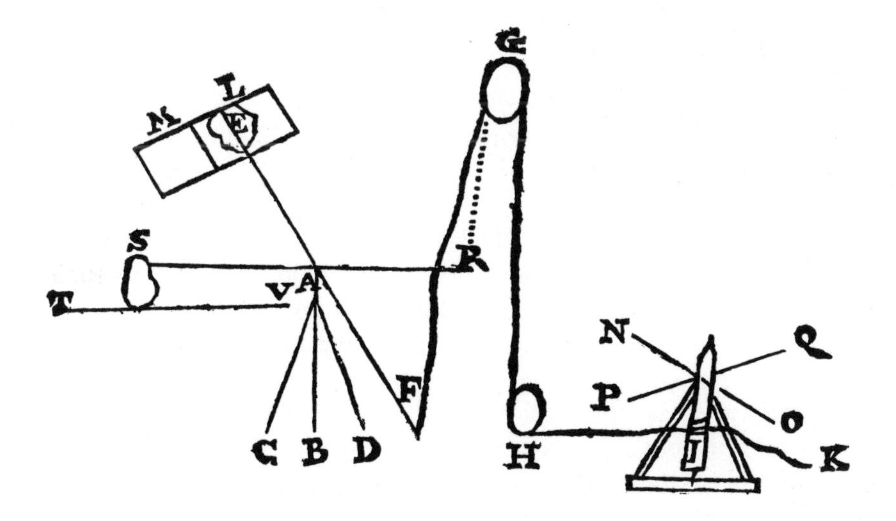


*Figure 80.*

of the stage. To make it ascend, they should reverse the capstan until the cloud has returned to its original place. Care must be taken for a man to be behind the capstan, as said before. We must take into consideration that the men turning the capstan to make the cloud ascend must be very attentive, for the cloud will ascend of itself on account of the greater contrary weight.

Let AB be the fulcrum made firm with supports AC and AD or more if necessary. Let EF be the lever placed in the center at A, made firm with an iron knuckle so that it may be easily lowered and raised. Let G be the pulley placed above and H the one below. Let I be the capstan, and F the end of the rope tied to the extremity of the lever, which passes through the pulley G and the other pulley H, turning around the capstan I. Let the other end be held by a person placed at K. Let L be the frame closing the aperture of the heavens from which the cloud E is to descend. When we wish to lower the cloud first the frame L is moved to M by the men who were placed above the heavens for that purpose. At that instant the space is open from which the cloud is to come out, and at the same time the men will slowly turn the handles NOPQ of the capstan I, until the extremity of the lever F is raised to R. Consequently, the cloud E will be lowered to S above the floor of the stage TV. To make it return to its place, the capstan will be reversed, so that R returns to F and the cloud S returns to E, its original place. Then, the frame M will be run to L and thus all things will have been accomplished.

But when, behind the scenery, there is no adequate space, as we have said above, we shall have to fix into the wall behind the back shutter, at 4 feet from the stage floor, a very secure iron knuckle in which the end of a strong beam will be placed. Its length should be according to the distance required for the cloud to come forward and it must be strong enough to support both the cloud and the weight of the people. It should be placed in such a way that the beam may be easily moved up and down as necessary. In the same wall directly above the knuckle, and a little higher than the half of the first beam, we shall put a tackle with two pulleys firmly held in the wall. In the center of the beam we shall put another tackle with two pulleys. Having done this, we shall place under the stage 2 feet above the floor of the hall a single pulley directly under the one above which was firmly fastened in the wall. This pulley will serve as a guide for the capstan, which will be placed under the stage towards the spectators on the side which is most convenient. A cloud will be made on the end of the beam, as described in the other method. Then we shall take a strong rope and tie one end of it to an iron ring which will be placed under the tackle. The rope will then go through the first pulley on the beam and come back to the first pulley placed in above it; it will come to the second pulley on the beam, and, returning to the second pulley in above, it will go below and pass through the pulley placed as a guide for the capstan, and be wound around the capstan. To operate this, let us follow the process which was used in the first method described above. We must take into consideration that, if there are so many people in the cloud that there is not enough strength to raise the cloud, more men will have to be added to the capstan, or the number of pulleys multiplied in both the top and lower parts. But it will be a little difficult to lower because of the changed proportion between the strength and the weight, as set forth in the *Mecaniche* of the most illustrious Sig. Guido Ubaldo dal Monte. At this time, however, the process may be helped by means of a person who, standing behind the cloud, pushes the beam forward. Given such a slight start, it will lower the rest of the way very easily. In order to raise the cloud, we shall reverse the capstan.

Let AB be the floor of the hall, and CD the wall behind the scenery, and E the iron knuckle fixed into it 4 feet from the

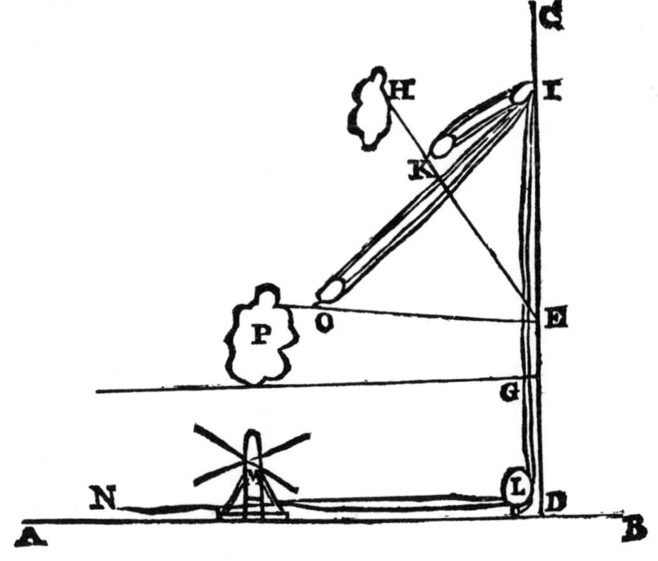


*Figure 81.*

stage floor FG.[1] Let HE be the beam, H the cloud, and I the tackle with two pulleys firmly fixed in the wall CD at I. The other tackle in the beam with two more pulleys is at K. Let the other single pulley L be secured into the wall CD under the stage 2 feet above the floor of the hall. Let M be the capstan with the person N serving to guide the rope. After one end of the rope is tied below the tackle I, it passes through the first pulley at K, goes to the first one at I, passes to the second one at K, and returns to the second one at I. The rope comes down through the pulley L, which was placed as a guide for the capstan, and is wound around the capstan M, with as many turns as necessary.

Let the cloud be made at H. In order to lower or raise the cloud, the same order which was specified in the other method will be followed: as the tackle which was placed on the beam K comes to O and as the beam EH comes to EP, the cloud H will come above the stage floor FG to P. Likewise, O will rise to K, and P to H.

## 46. *How To Represent A Cloud That Increases In Size As It Descends*

In order to make a small cloud increase constantly in size as it descends, we must follow this order: a groove, a sliding beam, pulleys, a windlass and rope will be made and assembled, as described in Chapter 43. Then 6 or 8 ribs, of the very best wood so as not to break in bending, are selected. These must be at least 1 inch in diameter and from 6 to 7 feet long. They are placed equidistant around the main beam, so that all their ends may be adjusted at its extremity. The other ends must be held with small iron hinges. One foot from the iron hinges, the same number of individual iron springs are nailed from the main beam to each rib, to hold the ribs open, like an umbrella inside out. A smooth, even hole, ⅓ inch in diameter, is bored in the end of each rib, through which a small but strong, well soaped cord will pass. The cord, fastened at the end of one rib and passing through all the other holes, runs through a small pulley which is placed on the arm of the beam at some distance from the holes of the ribs and continues along the arm through another pulley at the end of the arm. The cord has the same length as the height of the

1. The letter F is missing in the figure.

main beam. When the cloud is above the heavens, the cord must extend under the stage to be held by a person of sound judgment. Care must be taken that the cord is very strong, lest because of its length, it break, causing a very great disorder. A cloud built over the opened ribs should be of thin cloth only, painted as a cloud and attached to the ends of the ribs without any piece of wood to support it. Once the arm is in its place, the ribs will come together as the cord is pulled proportionately. If we wish the cloud to descend and increase in size, the windlass may be turned, as was said in Chapter 43. While the cloud is descending, the person holding the end of the cord must pull it. However, he must not pull it according to the speed with which he sees the cloud come down, but a little slower, so that the ribs may widen proportionately, and so that once the cloud has descended, the ribs may be completely spread. Thus the cloud will have reached its greatest size. To make the cloud ascend and decrease in size, the windlass is reversed and the person holding the small cord should let it out by degrees so that the cloud will fold up proportionately. Care should be taken to consider the opposite nature of the movements for to lower the cloud it is necessary to pull on the small cord. The tendency is to do the opposite. To do this properly, a person of judgment is needed.[1]

Let AB be the groove, and CD be the sliding beam, and E the upper pulley, and C the rope tied to the upper part of the sliding beam at C, passing through the pulley E and twisted about the windlass HI at F. Let the other end of the rope be tied to the lower part of the sliding beam at D and twisted about the windlass HI at G in the opposite direction. Let KL, ML, NL, and OL, and more if necessary, be the ribs, adjusted with their ends at the end of the supporting beam Q. Let the other ends be nailed on to the same beam at L. Let iron springs be nailed from the main beam to each rib 1 foot from L, *i.e.*, at P. Tie the cord at one of the ends of the ribs at K, passing through the holes of the other ribs M, N, and O and coming to the first pulley Q and continuing along the arm passing through another pulley at R, and coming down to be held by a person placed at S. When the time comes, this person must hold the small cord tightly so that the ends of the ribs about the cloud may remain as close to the beam as possible. In this manner the cloth of the cloud will

1. The translation here is a condensation of the Italian.

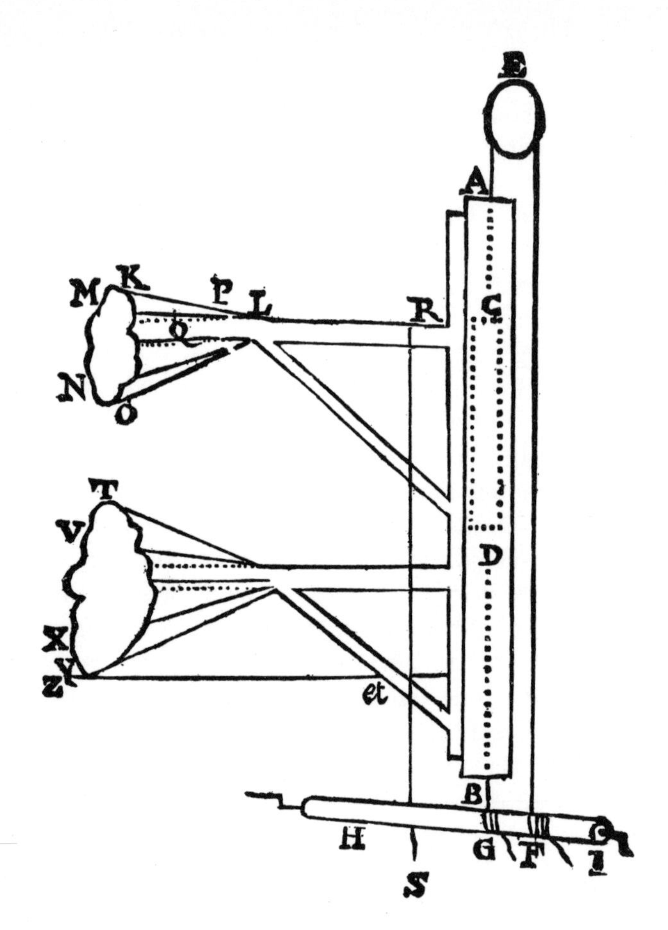


*Figure 82.*

be decreased in size. Then while the windlass is being turned to lower the sliding beam, the person placed at S must pull the small cord, but not at the identical time, because the ends of the ribs K, M, N, and O would not widen properly. We must see that the ribs are always pulled before the windlass is turned, and so that, as the ends of the ribs T, V, X, and Y widen, the end of the cloud Y comes above the level of the stage Z, &. In order to make the cloud return to its former state, the windlass must be reversed, and the person at S will pull the cord just as he did to increase the size of the cloud, but with movement proportionate to that of the windlass, and thus the cloud will be made smaller as at the beginning.

## 47. *How To Make A Cloud Move Across The Stage*

If it is necessary to make a cloud move across the stage during the *intermezzi*, we shall proceed in this manner: two grooves are built similar to those described in Chapter 42, 4 feet longer on each end than the distance traveled by the cloud. These will be placed behind the heavens, at least 2 feet apart, as high as you wish the cloud. They must be parallel and set in the same plane. An arm, as long as desired, will pass through these grooves transversely and extend equally on either side. On the side towards the audience, it must be as long as we wish the cloud to extend over the stage. However, the distance behind the groove should be the same as the distance in front of the groove, if space permits, otherwise a weight should be used to balance the arm. Within each groove a piece of wood[1] 1 foot long and as thick as the arm holding the cloud, and with another piece of equal size at the opposite side, are fastened carefully so as not to impede the smooth running in the groove, as described in Chapter 44. To wind the cords that will move the cloud, two windlasses are stationed in the same plane as the grooves, one at each side, longer than the distance between the grooves by a foot and a half on each side. These cords, two for each side, of length equal to the entire length of the grooves, are fastened to the arm in the area between the grooves and wound around the windlasses. Then the cloud will be built at the end of the arm in the center so that you cannot see where it is attached and so that it will move easily without impediment. At the opposite end of the arm a weight is placed to counterbalance the weight of the cloud while in motion. If the cloud is to be moved towards the right, the windlass on the right is turned letting out the cords on the windlass on the left. By turning the windlass on the left, the cloud is moved in the opposite direction.

Let AB and CD be the two grooves, and EF the arm placed within them equidistant from E to G on the side of the cloud, and F to H on the other side. Let there be a distance of more than 2 feet between G and H. Let two little pieces of wood be placed within the groove IK on one side and LM on the other. Let NO and PQ be the windlasses and the ends of the cords tied to RS on one side and TV on the other. The ends of these cords

1. Strictly speaking, two pieces of wood.

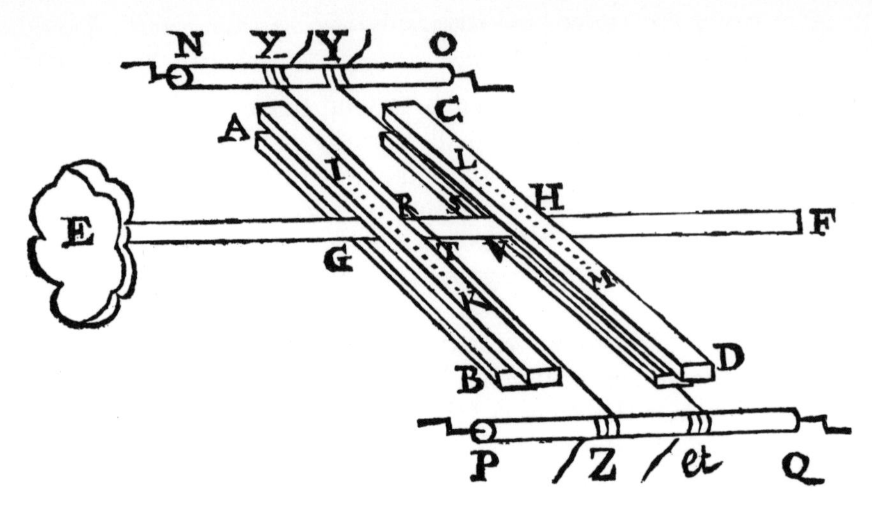


*Figure 83.*

are tied individually to the windlasses. Let RS be attached to the windlass NO at XY, and TV attached to the windlass PQ at Z, &. In order to make the cloud move, if we wish it to go to NO, the windlass NO will be turned, releasing the other windlass PQ. The contrary may be done if we wish the cloud in its former position.

## 48. *A Second Method To Move A Cloud Across The Stage*

There is another way to make a cloud go across the stage. A lever, with its fulcrum placed directly in the middle of the scene, as high as the desired altitude of the cloud, may be used to move a cloud across the stage. I thought it well to mention this method, although it would be difficult to prevent some part of the sustaining lever from being seen.

## 49. *How To Make A Cloud Divide Into Three Parts As It Is Lowered And Become One As It Is Raised*

In order to make a cloud divide into three parts as it is lowered and return to one as it is raised, we shall proceed in this manner: an arm is built similar to that described in Chapter 43, with the exception that to the supporting arm sustaining the main cloud are added on either side two shorter arms. These arms are supported by separate braces and are attached to the main arm by hinges so that they can swing open and shut. The lower ends of these braces supporting the shorter arms rest on a pin hinge.[1] Three clouds will be built, the center one being a half larger so as to conceal the other two. On the main arm a short distance from the groove are nailed two pieces of wood 1 foot long. At each end of the arms supporting the smaller clouds a pulley is placed, so as not to interfere with the movement of the hinges as the braces swing open and shut.[2]

Two pieces of rope are required: the end of one rope is nailed or very securely tied to the outer end of the arm holding a small cloud close to its back, and passes through the pulley going down below the stage floor. The same is done for the other side so as to unite with the first rope, thus serving to divide the clouds.

Then, two other ropes are taken, with the end of one rope tied or nailed on the inner side of one short arm. The other rope is tied or nailed on the inner side of the other short arm. These ropes pass through one of the two pulleys which are fastened to the supporting arm holding the large cloud, and come down like the other ropes. The ropes all join under the stage, thus serving to bring the clouds together.[3]

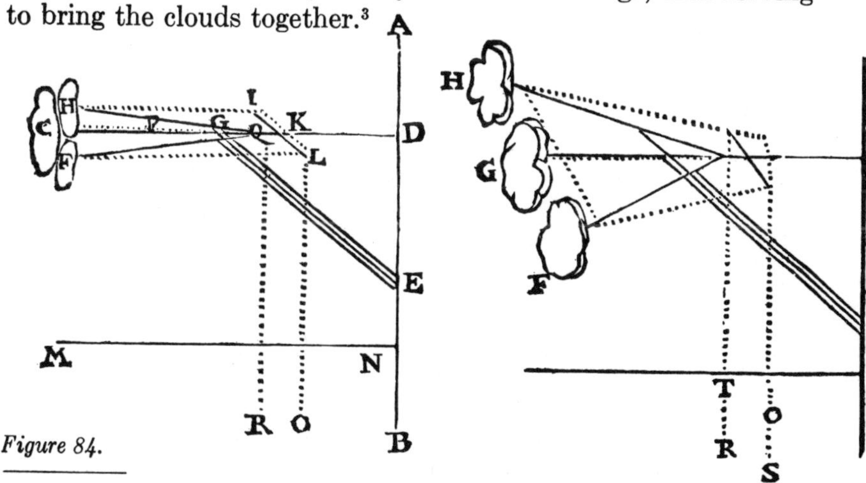


*Figure 84.*

1. A pin hinge, also used as a door hinge, consists of two hinge units. One unit has a pin which projects upwards, while the other unit has an eye which fits over the pin. This pin and eye combination will permit free movement either horizontally or vertically.

2. Sabbattini's wording is obscure. For clarity, freedom has been taken in translation.

3. This translation greatly simplifies the Italian text.

Let ABDE be the main beam, CD the supporting arm for the main cloud C, and FG and HG the arms to sustain the other clouds F and H. Let these arms be attached to the main arm CD with hinges at G nailed on to the arm CD. At a short distance from D two pieces of wood at K must extend out at least 3 feet each side, as at I and L. At each end I and L a pulley is placed. Let H and I be the rope on one side, and F and L that on the other. Let one end of these ropes be attached to the arm FG at F, and pass through the pulley L coming down under the stage floor MN at O. Let the other rope be attached to the other arm HG at H, passing through the pulley I, so as to unite with the first rope LO. Let there be another two ropes, one of whose ends is tied to F at the top of the beam on the side towards CD, and the other is attached at H. These ropes pass through two pulleys placed on the beam CD at P, and, running along this beam, pass through two other pulleys near the small piece of wood IL joining at R, as in the first figure.

To operate this machine, two men are placed under the stage floor MN, one holding the end of the rope O, the other R. To divide the cloud as it lowers, the man at O will pull the rope from O to S, while the other man will release the rope from R to T, as in the second figure. Thus, the arms FG and HG will spread and the three clouds C, F and G will be seen. To unite them again, the man at T will pull the rope at R, and the man at S will release the rope at O. Thus the three clouds will be united, as in the first figure.

## 50. *How To Lower A Person On To The Stage Without Using A Cloud, So That He May Immediately Walk About And Dance*

If it is necessary during the *intermezzi* to make a person descend from the heavens without a cloud, this order must be followed: a supporting arm is made, similar to that described in the preceding chapters, except that the sustaining arm and the braces are of a rod of iron strong enough to bear the weight of a person. At the end of this arm is securely placed the very smallest saddle possible, wider at the front, so that one can easily sit astride it. It has a stirrup as long as the person's leg, which will be placed so as to hold the heel instead of the toe, thus concealing the stirrup.[1]

1. This sentence has been condensed.

After the person is placed on the saddle with his heel in the stirrup, the machine lowers slowly. As soon as the stirrup touches the stage, the person quickly alights by stretching his legs and the machine will then disappear through an opening made especially for this purpose in the stage floor, leaving the person instantly free to begin to dance on the stage.

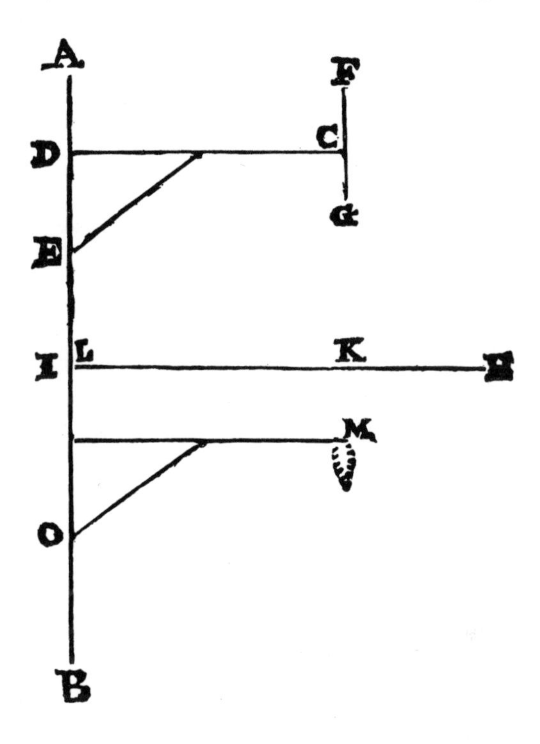


*Figure 85.*

Let AB be the beam, and CDE the supporting arm with CD and CE made of iron rods strong enough to support the weight they must uphold. Let FG be the person placed in the small saddle at C, with one foot in the stirrup at G. In order to make the figure descend onto the stage, the supporting arm may be lowered, and once it has arrived, the person will rapidly lift his foot from the stirrup G and the arm is lowered under the stage floor HI through the aperture KL until it arrives at MNO.[1] The opening is closed immediately. Thus the person will be able to dance immediately upon the stage.

1. The letter N is missing in the figure.

## 51. *How To Imitate The Wind*

To imitate the wind we follow this procedure: thin pieces of walnut or other hard wood, 1½ feet long and 1 inch or a little more wide, are required, which must be pliable like a ruler used in drawing. At one end of each of these a hole will be made through which is tied a cord, or small piece of rope of the same length. The ends of the cords are given to the men who will rapidly spin the small pieces of wood to imitate the wind, and they will continue to spin them as long as the wind is required.

*Figure 86.*

Let the ruler AB be 1½ feet long, 1 inch wide and as thin as we have said above. Let B be the hole and BC the small cord attached into it, and the end C held in the hands.

## 52. *How To Imitate Lightning*

We considered, in the preceding chapter, how to represent wind. Now we must tell how to imitate flashes of lightning. To do this, let us take an ordinary board as long as we wish the size of the flash to be. It must be 1 foot wide and cut in two in a wavy line, similar to the effect of lightning. These two pieces of wood are placed on the cloth of the heavens. The upper piece is made stationary by nailing the cloth of the heavens at points along the cut. The lower piece, which is movable, is held in position, to keep the cut closed, by two or three pieces of rope with their upper ends attached to a beam in the roof, or some other firm point, and with the lower ends fastened to the bottom of the board.[1] These ropes must not hang perpendicular but rather should incline at least a foot towards the stationary piece. Then the cloth of the heavens is carefully cut to correspond with the opening between the boards. Another board, 1½ feet wide and a little longer than the opening for the bolt of lightning, is fixed

1. Translation is simplified for clarity.

behind the opening and a foot above it so as not to interfere with the ropes. This board is covered with shining golden tinsel. Ten or twelve small candles are placed on the stationary board ½ a foot inward from the opening about three or four fingers apart. They must be lighted.

To make one or more flashes of lightning, a man commissioned to each rope gives it two or three quick jerks so that it separates from the stationary board about three fingers, thus revealing the tinsel. After giving these jerks, he suddenly lets go of the movable piece and the fissure closes concealing the tinsel. Other large or small flashes can be made in the same way.

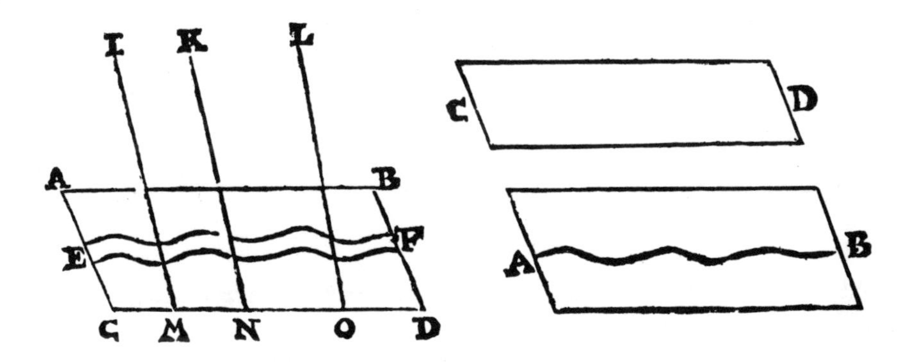


*Figure 87.*

Let ABCD be the board, cut along the line EF, attached here and there on the cloth of the heavens. The part ABEF must remain stationary, while the lower piece EFCD must be held with the ropes IM, KN, and LO or, rather, attached at I, K, L above and at M, N, O on the board in such a manner that it remains movable. Once the aperture is closed the ropes are not perpendicular. When we wish to represent lightning, we shall take the movable board CD and draw it toward us. Then the fissure EFGH will immediately be opened, as in the first figure. When released, the board must close by itself. The other board CD, which was covered with shining tinsel, must be placed 1 foot above the fissure AB, as shown in the second figure, so that it may not hinder the ropes.

## 53. *How To Imitate Thunder*

After describing flashes of lightning, it is now necessary to show how to represent thunder. This effect is very easy to produce for it requires only a channel made of ordinary boards long enough to give duration to the thunder desired. Once having made the channel, it must be firmly placed above the heavens, and within it some steps ½ a foot high must be made according to the directions below: when we want to imitate thunder, a man, placed for that purpose, must take two or three iron or stone balls, about thirty pounds in weight, and must release them into the channel, one after the other, according to the judgment of the director. Care must be taken that the channel must not be placed horizontally, but slightly inclined. The larger the channel may be the more natural the thunder may seem.

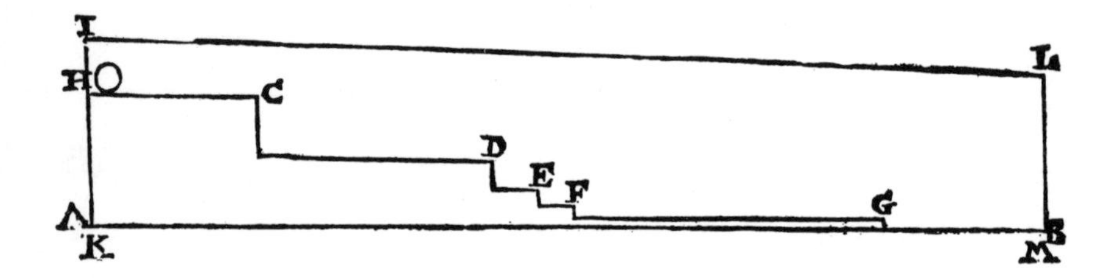


*Figure 88.*

Let AB be the bottom of the channel placed on an inclined position to KM. Let C be the first step 1 foot high, which must be a short distance from the beginning A. Then, a little farther let us make three other steps at D, E, and F, ½ a foot high. A little farther, and separated by an equal amount of space, let us make another step G, the same height as the preceding ones, but a little further from F than F is from C. Then, from G to B, which must be the end, the distance must be much further.[1] The faces of the channel IK and LM must be 2 or 3 feet high, completely closed. Above will be left the opening through which the ball H may be put, so that it may run at the allotted time from A to C. Consequently, it will be left to run down the other steps as required.

1. In the figure the distance is less.

## 54. *How To Make A Paradise*

Sometimes there is an occasion in the *intermezzi* to show a paradise. Then we must act in this manner: a circular opening is made in the heavens as large as the paradise to be shown. Then eight or ten concentric circles are made of strips of board 1 foot wide and of unequal size: the first larger than the second, and the second larger than third, and so on. Each circle is covered with clouds the color being graded towards white as the circles decrease. They are fastened firmly with nails and cross pieces of wood, one behind the other at least 1½ feet apart in the form of an apse with the largest at the opening and the smallest at the other end. A sufficient number of lights is distributed between the circles out of sight of the audience. The opening in the heavens is always concealed by means of a shutter, as described in Chapter 45 concerning the lowering and bringing forward of a cloud. A little before showing the paradise, these lights will be lighted. The shutter may be run to the side, and thus a very beautiful flight of clouds may be seen. Truly it will seem a paradise.

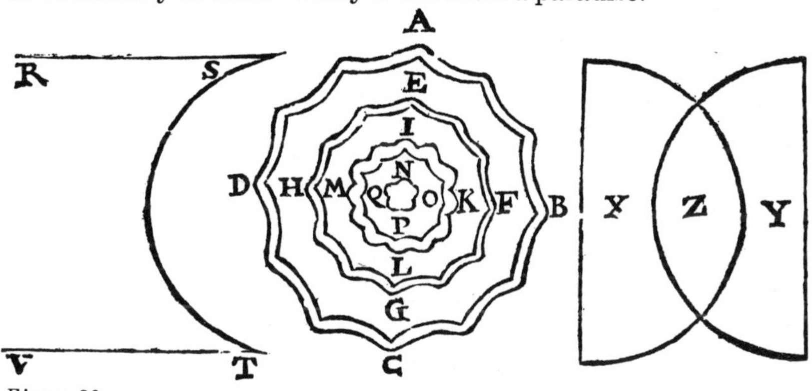

*Figure 89.*

Let ABCD be the aperture of the heavens made in the shape of a circle. Let EFGH be the first circle, IKLM the second, and NOPQ the third, which are covered with clouds. Behind each one of these a large number of lights must be placed, as was said above. Let RSTV be the shutter which must close the aperture. When we wish to show the paradise, we must run the shutter to the side and thus the paradise will be seen immediately. The aperture might also be opened and shut by means of two shutters made in the shape of half circles as shown by X and Y, and which superimpose each other at Z. To open them each runs to its own side and to close them the contrary motion is followed.

## 55. *How To Make The Dawn Rise*

The dawn can be made to rise either at the center or at one side of the stage. First is made a piece of heavens, of a suitable width and depth and a little higher than the person who is to represent Dawn. This section of heavens is painted at the top with skyblue and white, next with orange, then with red, and finally with blue fading off. It is to be placed on the machine which is to bring Dawn forth, as explained below. As the head of Dawn rises, the blue and white part is already visible and the orange begins to appear. Then as Dawn rises farther, the red portion is seen and when she has risen to full height, the pale blue part appears. When she is as far up as verisimilitude demands, the section of heavens is raised into and becomes part of the main heavens.

If it is desired to have Dawn come up in the middle of the stage, the machine described in Chapter 43 of Book II, from beneath the stage, will bring up both Dawn and the piece of the heavens. But if Dawn is to rise at the side of the stage, then the machine described in Chapter 47 of Book II is to be used, and the piece of heavens with it as in the other case, or in this case a lever might well be used. But the effect is not so good when brought in from the side, because, of necessity, a portion of heavens will be made to move contrary to the main heavens.

Hence, for greater illusion and verisimilitude, the entire stage should be darkened in the manner described in Chapter 39 of Book II. Then a large number of lamps are placed beneath the stage at the edge of the sea where the Dawn is, that is, parallel with the last wave. Over these lights is placed a board cover to hide the glistening light. When Dawn begins to rise, this board is raised a little at a time and a resplendent light gradually comes from beneath the stage. When Dawn is almost completely raised, the lights of the stage are again covered, so that when she has disappeared, the stage will be lighted as it was in the beginning.

## 56. *How To Make A Ghost Or Apparition Appear And Disappear Rapidly In Various Places On The Stage*

The outline of the ghost is designed upon a piece of cloth the size and shape desired and colored to show relief. At the back of this cloth are sewed two or more small pieces of wood ½ by 1 inch, according to the length of the arm or other members of the ghost, multiplying them in conformity with your need. These small pieces are nailed to a center pole 2 inches square and 3 feet longer than the height of the ghost. To the top of the pole is fastened that part of the cloth representing the head of the ghost. The bottom of the pole is held below the stage by the person operating the ghost. Two or three or more of these ghosts may be made, according to the places where they must appear on the stage. We must warn you that the ghosts must not only be made just alike but also be the same in height and color. If we want to make this figure appear in the center of the stage, an opening must be made there, long and wide enough to let the ghost appear and disappear with ease. This aperture should be left closed until the time of the apparition scene, when the person already prepared under the stage quickly raises the pole described above and the ghost will suddenly come into view.

To make the ghost disappear, we must lower the piece of wood rapidly and close the aperture of the stage immediately. To make the ghost continually appear and disappear from place to place upon the stage, other openings must be made in the stage floor similar to the first one. Several persons are stationed beneath the various openings, and as one pulls his ghost down the other immediately thrusts his up.

The ghost may be represented as increasing and diminishing in stature, as twisting, as bending down, and immediately becoming erect, and as moving and folding its arms or any other members: all these movements being accomplished by the same person who holds the pole under the stage. By raising and lowering the pole its height is increased or diminished. To move and bend the arms two cords, with their ends going below the stage, are first fastened to the end of the small rod to stiffen the arm, so that by pulling on one cord and releasing the other the arm is raised and lowered. A similar set of cords is prepared for the other arm. To make the ghost bow and bend, the center pole is tipped at an angle.

Should you wish to have the ghost come from the side wings and walk about the stage, from time to time increasing and diminishing in size, an actor instead is used. He wears a long full dress, similar to that worn by women and gathered at the waist, to make him look larger. To make the ghost look taller, in his belt a 3 foot center pole is held under the dress so that it cannot be seen. The lappet of the garment, or a mask is firmly attached to the end so that it does not wobble. This pole is held away from the face of the operator a little more than its thickness. The neck is covered with cloth or pleated paper, like certain lanterns used by coachmen, so that it can lengthen as the pole is raised.

The pole is raised to make the ghost look taller. To make it diminish in height not only is the pole lowered but the actor himself bends down as much as possible.

To make the ghost increase or diminish in size, five or six wooden ribs 1 foot long, similar to those of an umbrella, are attached to a wooden hoop around the waist of the actor so that they will move easily. The ribs are sewed underneath to the dress. To the lower end of each rib a small cord is attached. All these cords are tied together and fastened to the wooden hoop. To increase the size of the ghost, you pull up at the ends of the cord attached to the hoop; immediately all the ribs are raised, increasing the size of the ghost from the waist downward. To increase the size upward, a similar set of ribs is used with this difference, that the ribs attached to the same wooden hoop are ½ foot long and extend in the opposite direction. By pulling down on the attached cord, as in the previous instance, the desired effect is obtained.

Greater verisimilitude can be attained by making a ghost say a few words. A speaking tube is run from the face of the mask down to the mouth of the operator who will speak into it the required words at the proper time, making them seem to come from the face of the mask.

If the reader should wonder that I tarried too long in describing such a fantastic action, I did so to avoid being ambiguous, which might have been the case if I had followed out my original plan of being brief.

## 57. *The Simplicity Of Practical Experience*

Theory is not difficult to follow but practical experience is easier. To give a pertinent example: the machines described in both these books have been to a great extent used in the very noble spectacles which recently were presented in the Teatro del Sole at Pesaro, and they worked so satisfactorily that they received particular admiration and gave pleasure to the spectators.

The theatre was erected last year on the occasion of presenting, with elaborate *intermezzi*, *Asmondo*, a tragedy by Sig. Giovanni Hondedei, a nobleman of that city. The conception and execution of this work, which is worthy of its author and very highly regarded by experts, brings praise to the poet who, keeping to the rules of artistic composition, has known how to give flight to his genius.

Therefore, experience has proved that what has been said regarding the construction of scenery and machinery can be easily put into practice.

## JOSEPH FURTTENBACH THE ELDER
## 1591–1667

# *Introduction*

Like Inigo Jones, Furttenbach is important as one who came from a distant country to spend some time in Italy and carry back to his native country the principles and methods of the Italian theatre. Both he and Jones came under the influence of Parigi in Florence, and both were influenced by a production of 1608. Both were primarily general architects and were only incidentally interested in the stage. Both were deeply influenced by Italian practice, but each introduced important adaptations and original developments. Both have left us valuable materials for the study of the Renaissance theatre. While of Jones' work we have hundreds of sketches and designs for scenes and costumes, Furttenbach left us in three of his books treatises on scenery and lighting. These treatises, except for the treatise of Sabbattini, form the most extensive general account we have of back-stage practice, and the only detailed account of instruments of lighting in the Renaissance.

Furttenbach[1] was born on December 30, 1591, in Leutkirch in southern Germany, the son of Hieronymus Furttenbach, city comptroller and banker. About 1610 he went to Italy and spent some ten years there. In his account of the journey to Italy we can see in the young man the interests that he followed in his later work and writing. In Italy, as later in Germany, he was most interested in the building arts, both on land and on the sea, and in the spectacular trappings of festivals, processions, and dramatic performances of the court and church.

---

1. This account is based on the biography in Thieme-Becker, *Lexikon der bildenden Künstler*, and on Furttenbach's own account in *Newes Itinerarium Italiae* (1627) and later books. Cf. A. M. Nagler, "The Furttenbach Theatre in Ulm," *Theatre Annual*, XI (1953), 45–69.

He comments on the many little towns he passes, and his precise mind notes the exact distance from each one to the next. He comments on the customs fees and on the necessity for tipping. He is interested in fishing, in horses, in athletic contests. There are many detailed accounts of buildings. Hospitals, churches, chapels, and palaces are described; both the old Roman amphitheatre of Verona and the water system of Genoa are commented upon. He inspects the construction of harbors. Ships fascinate him, and he tells many things about their construction and operation and about his experiences on the water.

Most interesting for us, he describes many spectacles and shows. At Milan he joined the procession of a splendid church festival where fireworks were set off, fountains burst forth, and little scenes of religious plays were presented along the way.[1] He describes a large ball in the palace and notes a court where actors came yearly to put on plays in the loggia. In front of the palace, platforms were set up at the sides for spectators, and a rich tournament with interspersed dances was performed.[2] At Rome he measured the Colosseum, and speaks of it as a "Theater" where "Schawspielen" are seen. He examined the hospital and the Marcellus theatre. At Rome and elsewhere he was interested in the grottoes that were scenic ornaments in many formal gardens.

It was in Florence that he came under the spell of the Renaissance stage. He must have spent some time with Giulio Parigi, engineer and architect of the Duke of Tuscany and designer of some of the finest musical spectacles in Italy, whom he speaks of as his "patron, master, and teacher." He was especially interested in the designs for *Il Giudizio di Paride* which Parigi made for an elaborate production at the Medici wedding festivities of 1608. One of the settings he describes is that "Jardino di Calypso" which was the third *intermezzo* at the Florence production; another corresponds exactly with the description and the engraving of the fourth *intermezzo* — a scene with the ship of Amerigo Vespucci.[3]

In his account of the marvels in the Medici palace, he writes of a religious spectacle:

"In this palace was prepared on a Good Friday, through the arrangement of the very able and famous Herr Giulio Parigi

---

1. *Newes Itinerarium Italiae*, pp. 25 f.
2. *Ibid.*, pp. 16 f.
3. For the indebtedness of Inigo Jones to this production, see Nicoll, *Stuart Masques*, pp. 69 and 91 and Figs. 43, 44, and 64.

(whom I honor as my worthy patron, master, and teacher) the engineer to the Grand Duke of Tuscany, a lovely heroic and beautiful perspective scene or *sepolcura santa,* in a great hall completely closed and made dark. Its front was completely surrounded with clouds on which sat angels that sang to the accompaniment of lovely music. The impression of great distance and width was created by a good use of the art of perspective. In one direction, through a forest, was seen the city of Jerusalem. At the right side was the *castrum doloris,* or *sepulchrum Dominicum.* It was eight spans long and about six spans high, decorated like a well-formed coffin completely covered with black velvet on which was a large quantity of expensive diamonds that can not be described . . . A great spectacle of riches was created by the glow from standing lights put in hidden places within the heavens. The diamonds sparkled as though the stars in heaven were shining.

"Further were seen many other shows, as especially, real persons lying in hell fire made to look so natural that one could believe he saw the streams of fire flame out. Several hundred oil lamps were so carefully placed that the actual lamps could not be seen, but their glow sent out such a light that it seemed to be day . . . A sight no less than the earthly paradise."

Furttenbach continues with an account of other marvels of the palace, such as the clocks, statues, and paintings, especially those in a long gallery:

"From windows there, one can see into the *Theatro* where princely plays are presented in lovely well-contrived scenes appropriate to the action. With great dexterity the whole scene may be changed. Such varied spectacles as these have never been equaled in our times. I present here in plate 14 just such a scene, a street open to a great distance, shown by means of perspective art. Here the actors present their play. At the end of the act the whole scene changes into a pleasure garden, a sea, a wood, or some other place, with such dexterity that those who are watching can not see the change and think that they have lost their senses. What other delight this splendid work may bring I leave to the imagination. Such changes of scene often are made six or seven times in the same play. How the clouds appear to the accompaniment of lovely music, and the *Dii* or Gods are let down to earth in the many forms traditional to poetry, would take too long to tell."[1]

1. ***Newes Itinerarium Italiae,*** **pp. 81 ff.**

Furttenbach was interested in the Eastern actors he calls "Japanese" and shows in a plate the costume of one — a conventional Renaissance costume to denote a character from the Orient. He was also interested enough in an artificial perspective niche in a church to present an engraving of it.

1. Street Scene from *Newes Itinerarium Italianae*

Back in Germany, he settled in Ulm and started a long, successful career as architect and universal engineer. Besides publishing a number of books and building many important structures, he was named city architect, served on the city council, and received many honors. Among his building accomplishments were a large, well planned hospital, a waterworks system, a schoolhouse designed for the comfort of the students, a small theatre for the children in an orphan asylum, and a number of dwellings. He built a church in Scharndorf and a Gymnasium in Munderkingen. A number of fortifications on the banks of the Rhine were his work, and a tower on the Danube that still stands. In his later days he was honored by hundreds of foreigners and many neighboring princes. He died in 1667, leaving a son by the same name almost as well known.

The list of books by Furttenbach indicates the wide variety of his interests. His first publication was the account of his journeys in Italy, in the form of a running notebook of what he had learned. His next work was a treatise on gunpowder and fireworks, with formulas and methods of manufacture. Then followed the six treatises on architecture: books on civil, naval, and military architecture, a miscellaneous collection of projects, a book on recreational architecture mostly about parks and gardens, and a book on private dwellings.

After the passing comments on performances in Italy, in the *Newes Itinerarium Italiae,* Furttenbach included formal treatises on theatrical practice in three books, appearing in 1628, 1640, and 1663. Although the later treatises cover the same material as the first, each contains information not included in the others, and all must be consulted for a full picture of Italian stage practice in Germany.

The first of these accounts appeared in *Architectura Civilis* (1628). The title page of this work shows an arch and a street scene diminishing into the distance with the same principles of perspective design used in stage scenes. Plate 12 is definitely a stage scene, and two pages are devoted to an account of the structure of the stage and scenery. Later in the book Furttenbach includes a small theatre in his plans for a mansion, and in the ground plans for the two floors shows us what relation the theatre should have to a princely residence. Here, however, the stage is little more than a decoration to the building; it is only slightly larger than the little stalls under the balcony, where small working models of machines, ships, and buildings symbolize branches of study.

The next treatise, in *Architectura Recreationis* (1640), covers the same ground as the two-page account in *Architectura Civilis,* but adds much information and includes several drawings and designs he had made for actual productions.

After a lapse of many years, Furttenbach brought out late in his life the curious compendium he called *Mannhaffter Kunstspiegel,* or "noble mirror of art" — a collection of sixteen treatises: Arithmetic, Geometry, Planimetria, Geography, Astronomy, Navigation, Perspective Scenery, Mechanics, Grottoes, Water Fountains, Fireworks, Gunpowder, Military Architecture,

Naval Architecture, and Island Architecture. In many of his books are descriptions and plates not only of actual works he had finished but also of projects of what might be built. Thus a very interesting part of the section of *Mannhaffter Kunstspiegel* on Civil Architecture is devoted to an imaginative project of a theatre hall with four stages surrounding a revolving banquet table.

The treatise on Perspective Scenery in *Mannhaffter Kunstspiegel* is much the longest and most interesting of Furttenbach's accounts of stage practices. His plan for an auditorium in a long narrow hall shows interesting differences from the arrangement in Italian halls, where tiers of seats partly encircled the dancing area of the floor. He gives extensive descriptions of cloud and wave machines that differ in many ways from those described by Sabbattini. This is the only Renaissance account with a detailed description of various lighting instruments planned for different positions about the stage.

As an architect in Württemberg, Furttenbach may have been able to satisfy his interest in public and private building; but in his provincial world there were very few opportunities for producing the scenic spectacles that had so caught his eye and warmed his heart in Italy. In his descriptions of stage effects he repeatedly comments on how splendid such effects would be in Italy, where tons of gold might be spent on a single production.

For all his tremendous love for plays and spectacles, he probably was actually engaged in the designing and construction of only a small number, and those few were produced in quarters and with means far more restricted than he considered suitable. When he came to write about them, he described them as they should have been. After an account of a full scene on a scale that would still have seemed fairly small in Italy, he admits that he had built the actual stage exactly half as large as the dimensions he gives.

The account in *Mannhaffter Kunstspiegel* is based on plans for two productions. When Furttenbach was gathering material for this comprehensive book late in life, he doubtless included the plans for the most ambitious spectacles he had worked on. One of these may be the same play about Jonah which he had mentioned in 1640. The other took place in 1650. It may be that these were the only interesting productions, besides his small stages for children, with which he had ever been directly concerned.

However magnificent they may have seemed to the burghers of the little German city, these scenes he describes are small and simple judged by Italian standards. For us there is a note of pathos in the comment of the designer, "They would in no wise have been unworthy of the presence of far greater persons — of Princes, Dukes, and Electors, who are fond of having such plays presented." For Furttenbach found no such great prince or rich churchman, "enemies to ugly stinginess," as the Italian architects found. His only patron was his admired Herr Merchius, who, along with his other duties as rector, historian, professor, librarian, and director of music, put on a play about Moses.

These plans and descriptions are important to us for three principal reasons. They tell us much about Italian practice that we can learn from no other source, and show how that practice was adapted in a country far from Italy. Second, they give us the most extensive information we have about the form and use of the inner stage. The use of the inner stage as a regular part of the continental theatre has not always been recognized, and its importance as a parallel to the English stage has not been fully explored. Third, they show Furttenbach as an advanced thinker in lighting practice. While he was far behind current Italian scenic practice in his dependence on the *periaktoi*, yet in the development and specialization of lighting instruments he was far ahead of what we know of Italian practice. As we have no evidence of such interest in instruments elsewhere in the whole century, we may conclude that Furttenbach made important contributions to the development of lighting. He certainly records for us creative thinking far ahead of much of the practice for centuries afterward.

## *From "Civil Architecture," 1628*

[Figure 2.] Here is the scene and stage for the presentation of plays (similar to that described in my *Newes Itinerarium Italiae*, p. 87). Such a stage should be 36 feet[1] wide at the front, 18 feet wide at the back, and 30 feet deep. In front of the stage is a parapet together with side [proscenium] frames painted with

1. "24 braccie." The *braccia* varied in length in Italy. It is taken here to be 18 inches.

drapery, each 4½ feet wide, to keep the audience from seeing within. Behind the proscenium frame and the parapet are placed numerous candles or oil lamps which throw such a splendor on the scene and up into the heavens that they make the scene bright as day. Behind the parapet is the front pit, 2½ feet wide, an excellent position for the musicians, out of sight of the audience. Since the parapet is 4½ feet high, almost at the level of the eye, the stage must begin at that height, and the perspective lines, set thus high, will give the scene an excellent effect. As the lines of perspective require that the vanishing lines should run not only from both sides in towards the center vanishing point but also from the foreground upwards, the stage should be raised at the back 6¾ feet above the front level.

2. Stage and Scene for a Play

At the back of the stage is another pit 3 feet wide. In this also many oil lamps are concealed, to throw their splendid beams on the scene above. Spectacular effects — lightning and flames, for instance — can be simulated by setting the lamps on pivots so that they may be turned by pulleys. This rear pit is so situated that it may be used not only for carriages, horses, processions, and marching armies, but also for ships, galleys, or other machines that pull or roll, according to the needs of the play.

Immediately behind the rear pit is the shutter, 13½ feet high in all. In order to draw and build the entire scene correctly according to the art of perspective, the vanishing point of the scene should be placed on the back wall 4½ feet above the stage level.

For the heavens, five *cerchie*, or curved frames covered and painted with clouds, are built and placed one behind the other, each at a lower level than the one in front of it. The foremost frame is set 36 feet above the stage level at the front pit; the rearmost rests on the back shutter. Between the *cerchie* are spaces 4½ feet wide to allow *deastros*, or gods, and triumphal cars to be let down from above or moved over the stage.

Three side wings (*telari*) of frames covered with cloth are placed at each side of the stage on lines which converge at the vanishing point. Between them are streets, or entrances, for the use of the actors. These side wings are triangular frames covered with cloth and so arranged that two corresponding ones are set together, to match at the corners. By turning them, various scenes are presented; as first, a scene of palaces and houses, changing to a second of a garden, and to a third of wild rocks in the sea. They are built on strong wooden shafts or pivots which extend under the stage. There, by means of two bars, men can turn them around as quick as the bat of an eye, and the scene is changed to another place. When these *periaktoi* are painted according to the art of perspective to represent palaces and houses and the back wall is painted in the likeness of the heavens covered with clouds, and all is inclosed by a curtain, then the whole scene for the first act or the prologue cannot fail to present a fine appearance. Later the scene can be changed in a moment by the turning already mentioned, because on another face of the *periaktoi* the scene is painted for the act that follows.

On things of this kind the Italians generously spend large sums. For what can produce greater entertainment for great lords and ladies than to have such a beautiful, marvelous, ever-changing show before their eyes? Thereby heavy thoughts are quickly lightened and joyous ones take their place; for, first of all, the eye loves to look on something beautiful; second, the ear is charmed by the accompanying music, and third, the mind takes vivid delight when the soul-stirring players, coming forward, make graceful discourse. Among such actors there are many so excellent that they cause great wonder by their performance . . .

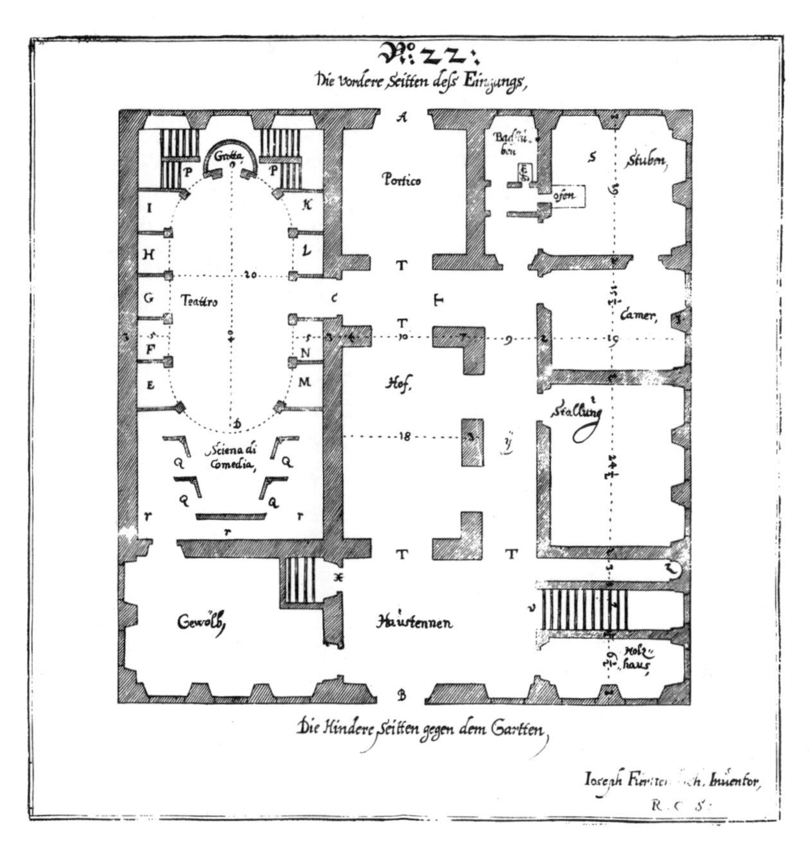


3. Ground Plan of an Exhibit Hall with Stage

[Figure 3.] . . . C is the entrance to the *Theatro*. This theatre is a large hall wherein an architect or some other amateur may put on display things which please.

O is a small grotto with sea-plants and little fountains. Here may be placed the grotto I present on page 221 and plate 16 of my book of travel.

D is the *Sciena di Comedia*, or the stage where the plays are presented. The scene I present on page 87 of my travel book may be used here. At Q Q Q Q are the streets through which the players pass. These players have a space at *r r r* to dress and to wait until they get their signal to enter.

At P P are two stairways leading to the gallery. Between the grotto and the stage at the two sides, nine little rooms or cabinets are built of strong wood and finished with columns and cornices in the best architectural style. Above them the gallery or passageway is finished with *pallaustrelli* of little columns and pedestals.

In these compartments are prepared the following designs and instruments: in I, mechanical displays of mills, wind machines, etc., set in motion by pulleys; in H, an exhibition of naval architecture with galleys and ships and instruments of navigation; in G, military architecture; . . . in E, civil architecture with plans of palaces and houses and models of wood built to scale; . . . in F, astronomy; . . . in G, geography . . . .

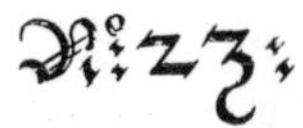

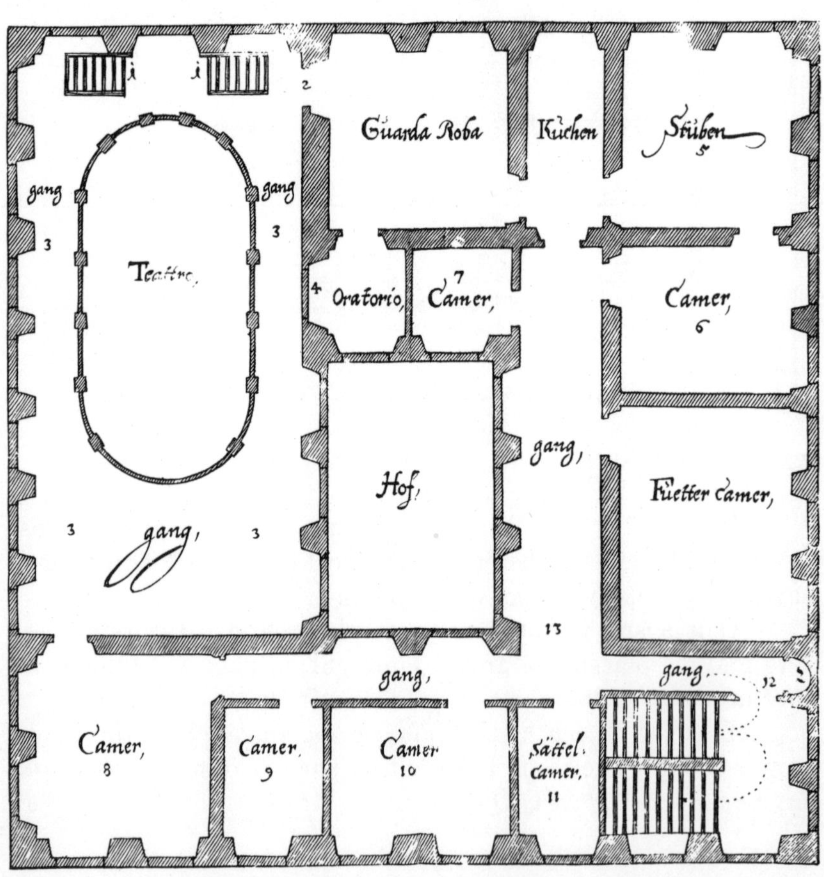


4. Second Floor Plan of Exhibit Hall

[Figure 4.] This is the second floor plan of the house. It shows the *mezari*, or the middle rooms used for children and servants, with the landing at the stairway and the passageway to all the rooms. Here is seen again the *Theatro*. Its height is about 15 feet (30 palms). Its ceiling is decorated with designs wrought in plaster, and over the gallery are hung paintings. One comes to the gallery above the cabinets by the stairs *i i* and passes by the passages 3 3 3 3 to the seats placed around a circle like a Roman theatre, to see the play or whatever is presented. At 2 is a door leading to a wardrobe where there are many boxes and chests to store the table cloths and other household effects. At 4 is a quiet, secluded place, called an *oratorio*, for prayer. It is convenient for the women, for from it they can look into the theatre unseen.[1]

## *From "Recreational Architecture," 1640*

[Figure 5] shows four designs for *fuora;* that is, painted cloths or curtains which are called the first, second, third, fourth, etc., which may be used before the acts begin. Since the spectators, on entering the theatre, should not be able to see the complete scene on the stage, a curtain appropriate to the following action is hung in front of the scene. This curtain must be made in such a way that it can either be drawn to the two sides or let down into a special pit in front of the stage. When the spectator takes his seat he must be content for a short time with anticipation, which will only whet his appetite. To increase this expectation, it is good to arouse attention by the introduction of cries and dialogue while Mezetino and Scapino move about behind the curtain, or else choruses and instrumental music of lutes and theorbos may

1. Apparently, at the court spectacles in Italy the ladies usually were seated in the open, though separated from the men. The princely box was highly ornamented and perhaps balustraded, but its occupants must have been visible. A secret box, however, is not unknown in Italy. Boxes with blinds for cardinals and high prelates to watch the performance unseen were built in an academic theatre in Rome in 1549. Eduard Flechsig, *Die Dekoration der modernen Bühne in Italien* (Dresden, 1894), pp. 73 f. Cf. the "palco segreto ben turato" from which the grand duchess, the princesses, and their ladies viewed the theatrical spectacle in Florence in 1613. A. Solerti, *Musica, Ballo e Drammatica alla Corte Medicea dal 1600 al 1637* (Florence, 1905), p. 73. The nobility fairly early had a covered "Lords' Box" in the public theatres in England. Lawrence, "The Royal Box" in *Old Theatre Days and Ways*, pp. 143–151.

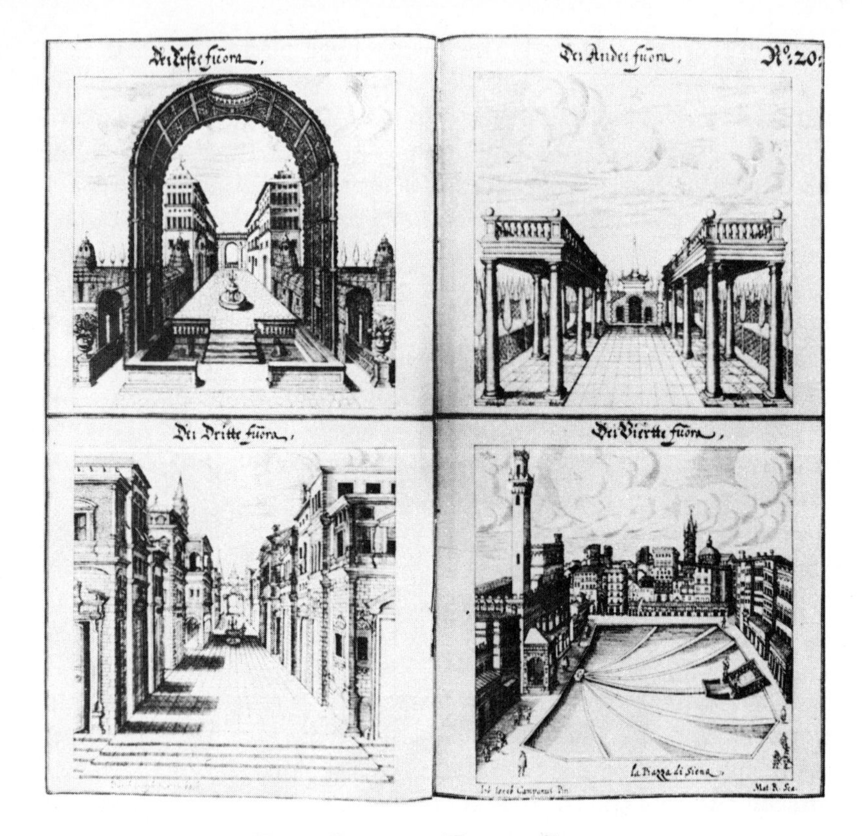


5. Four Painted Front Curtains

be introduced. These should eventually rise to a violent din and crashing as if everything were coming to destruction, until finally, with the sounding of drums and trumpets, the curtain suddenly falls down. Then is disclosed the stage setting, magnificent in its perspective lines. At the same moment the speaker of the prologue — the first player — steps out on the stage and by his gracious discourse charmingly makes known the story of the play. The spectator is so overcome with wonders that he scarely knows whether he is in the world or out of it. In this manner the play is continued and the other acts revealed in their turn.

It is to be noted that these four *fuora*, or curtains, may be used on many other occasions, not only in the great hall but on the portico or on the stairs and in vestibules. Above all, they may be used with the greatest delight on a wall of a pleasure garden. The understanding painter will know without further explanation how to use them correctly.

## THE SCIENA DI COMEDIA

I have presented two designs for scenes and described the acts that go with them in Plate 14 of my *Itinerario Italiae* and in Plate 12 of my *Architectura Civilis*. Since many people wishing to build according to right proportions and well-founded architectural methods have asked me for designs for settings, I have sent some of them the ground plan and cross section of a stage in my own hand. To make complete designs, however, I did not have time or leisure; and accordingly all I can do is to set down here in the form of plates some indications which may be of service.

I acknowledge that far more famous and far more expert architects are to be found today, especially in Italy, men who understand far more of what concerns stage decoration than insignificant I. At the same time, it is to be noted that some of these masters are not willing to communicate the details of their methods, that others will not go to the cost of having copper plates made, and that still others, and these the most prominent masters, are not willing to take the necessary pains to prepare such things for print. I hope that the understanding reader, remembering that if we do not catch the fleeting moment many good things will remain unrecorded and will be carried with their creators to the grave, will appreciate the good intentions and sincere love I bear for my fellow men, and that above all he will forgive the difficult terms and rest content with my good intentions . . .

When the curtain has fallen down, then the first scene, as shown here, representing a street built of stately houses, stands before the eyes of the spectators. On this *sciena*, or stage, the *prologus*, or first actor, begins the performance by making his entrance at A to tell the story of the play. His graceful gestures and charming delivery (*alloquium*) bring special delight to the spectators. At the two sides of the design at B and C we see Mezetino and Scapino, who, though very unattractive in appearance, have personalities apt to render them entertaining figures in the *intermezzi*.[1]

1. Furttenbach shows in both plates the settings designed for the main acts. The characters shown entering from the wings, however, are the Commedia dell' Arte characters of the entr'acte entertainments. Separate scenery for the *intermezzi*, while frequent in Italian productions, was not to be thought of with the restricted means available in southern Germany. Furttenbach evidently considers these three or more scenes an impressive spectacle.

6. The First Scene of Houses for Comedy

On the stage there should be a large number of oil lamps, as will be explained in the commentary on the cross section, placed within the scene, above between the clouds, at both sides, and in the front and rear pits, all of course completely concealed. These will give out such a splendid glow that it will seem as if daylight were breaking through the clouds. An exact representation of the sun, too, can be secured by a special device; this consists of two pieces of glass, the space between which is filled with water, and behind them a brilliant lamp of the kind described fully in my *Halonitro-Pyrabolia*, folio 27.[1] Stars are simulated by

1. There Furttenbach describes a mixture of oils, volatile spirits, gums, and perfumes to give a bright flame with a pleasant odor and no smoke.

7. The Second Scene for Comedy: The Pleasure Garden

devices of tinsel, placed in the heavens with an oil lamp in the center to make them shine. No less marvelous is the manner of having the *deastros*, or Gods, swing down from the heavens to the stage in triumphal cars, according to the poetic tradition. Likewise at the rear pit, wagons, carriages, and processions of horsemen may pass across. Indeed many other similar *apparati*, as occasion demands, can be prepared. Further information is provided in connection with the ground plan and cross section.

When the first act of the play is brought to an end, the corners of the houses swing from each other, the back wall is divided, and the scene suddenly changes to a beautiful garden —

all this so rapidly that none of the spectators, no matter how keenly he looks on the stage, can see how it is done.

The second scene is *il jardino di Calypso*, a beautiful pleasure garden. Here also are seen three actors entering to present their pleasing *intermezzi*, Mezetino [down right], Madonna Nespola [center], and Scapino [stage left].

At A, [at the left] in the clouds above, Jove is seen in his glory. At B Mercury is seen in a similar position sitting on a cloud. He orders Calypso to free Ulysses, whom she has been holding captive, — or whatever else the play demands. The clouds at the center open up to disclose a group of seated musicians, who give great delight to the spectators by their singing and playing. A *Dea* or *Dama* sitting on an eagle causes great wonder and delight when, to the accompaniment of music, she is let down from between the heavens and returns back into the clouds.

After the ending of the second act this *sciena di comedia* may in an instant be changed to a wild sea for which there is no need of a design. This third setting[1] of great ranges of hills, with monstrous animals, represents the fourth part of the world; that is, America or the West Indies. The stage floor is covered with tempestuous waves. In this great tempest moves the ship of *Americo Vespucci the Florentine*. When he and his mariners see the shore, they express their joy with songs of delight. They proceed to the land and find there the chariot of Tranquillity decorated with sea shells and similar sea effects, drawn by two *Ballenen*, or whales. In the center is seen Immortality, represented, according to the poetic tradition, in a cloud sitting on a sphere. At both sides are numbers of musicians who play and sing as they pass over the heavens. Whatever other settings or actions are demanded by the play may be prepared in a similar way. Thus the scene may change for a fourth, a fifth, and even more times.

Here are shown the proportions and dimensions of the *Sciena di Comedia* with the "houses," and the "streets," or entrances, and the front pit and rear pit. From ♎ to ♒ the entire width of the scene is 50 feet. From ♎ to ♀ and from ☿ to ♒ are two vertical board [proscenium] frames 7 feet wide to

1. This description corresponds exactly with one of the scenes (which Inigo Jones also used) from Parigi's *Il Giudizio di Paride* (Florence, 1608). Cf. Nicoll, *Stuart Masques*, p. 69 and Figs. 43 and 44.

keep the actors or anything else behind the wings from being seen. The front pit for the musicians is 36 feet long and 3 feet wide. At both its ends must be concealed a number of oil lamps to throw such a splendor above that the heavens are pleasingly lighted. The front parapet, made of boards, is ¼ foot thick.

If the hall is sufficiently large, the stage should be fully 50 feet deep so that behind the rear pit the actors may have ample

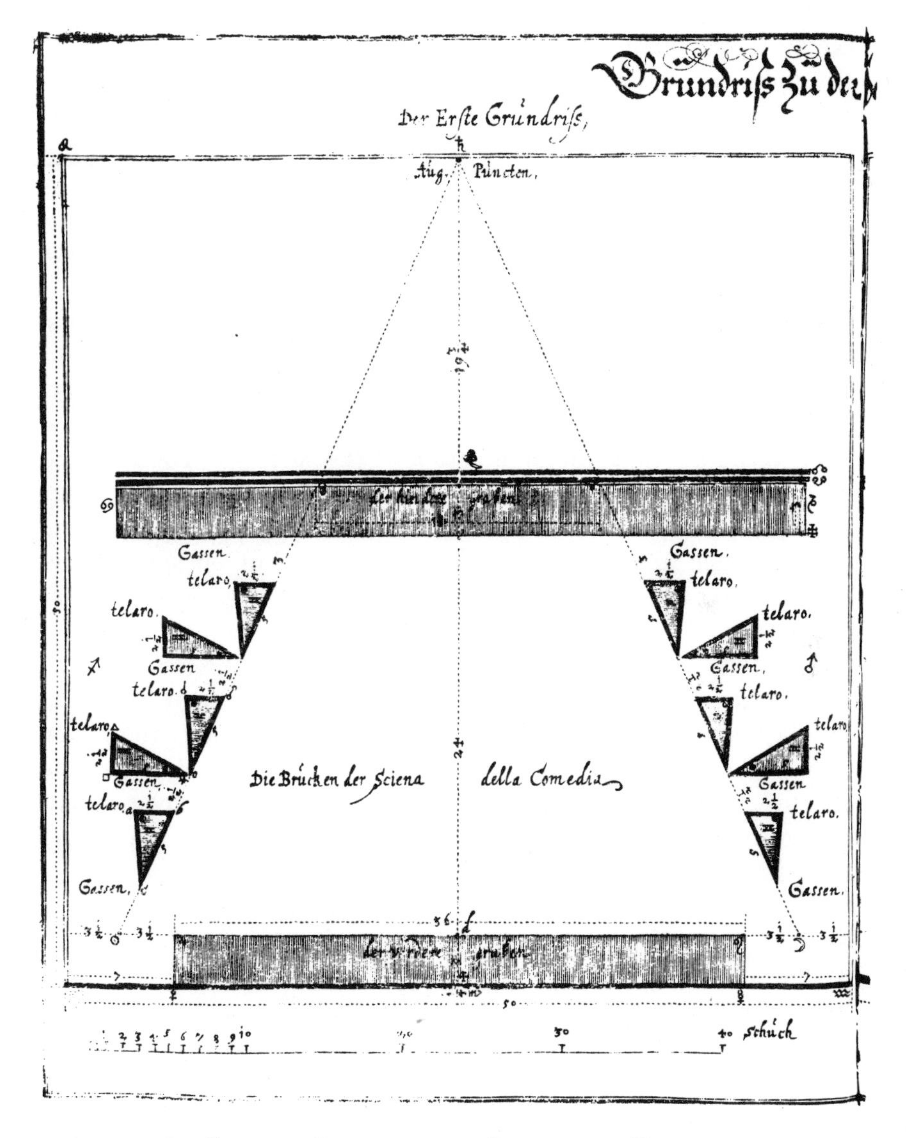


8. Ground Plan of the Scene for Comedy

accommodation in the shape of a covered place or passage for changing their costumes as the play proceeds.

When a sea is to be represented, then the loose boards of the level rear floor covering the rearmost pit are to be taken up altogether or in parts and the waves placed there. Between the waves, in the stormy sea, whales may draw across a ship. This arouses a feeling of pleasure and wonder. Recently, at a place not far away, we had proof of this in the production of a play of the story of Jonah; there were in this two changes of scene with charming effects in the sea as also in the heavens. On that occasion, for lack of space and to keep down costs, I built the stage only half as large as the ground plan here indicates, but the proportions were the same.

At ♄ the vanishing point is placed; from this all the proportions of the scene must be drawn and also the lines on the floor laid out. At this vanishing point three cords must be firmly nailed; the first is drawn to the point ☉ , the second to ☽ , and the third to ♂ . These must be stretched tight and made fast. Twenty-four feet from the front pit, at *d* on the line of the middle cord, is established a point to mark the depth of the main area used for acting and for the erection of the setting. The rear pit is 3 feet wide and the painted shutter behind it is 18 feet long. This pit usually serves for the passage of wagons, coaches and horses, ships, galleys, etc., and is left open, but on some occasions the rearmost pit, from ♃ to ♄ , may be used for this purpose.

At ♉ behind the pit there is the first groove for the foremost frame which is painted with houses and divided in the middle. One part of it can be drawn quickly to the left, the other part to the right, to effect the change of the shutter. On the rear shutter, which is made in the same way and which moves in the groove indicated at ♌ , is painted a beautiful garden. Like the first shutter, it also divides in the middle.

At the end of an act this shutter must be drawn apart by hand or be so fastened to a counterweight that it comes apart by the force of a blow. Thus when this first shutter is pulled back, we see the second shutter, representing a garden. So much for the changing at the rear pit. In front of that pit, along each of the stretched cords, are erected five *periaktoi* (*telari*). One of these *periaktoi* is indicated on the ground plan at *a*, *b*, and *c*. The *periaktoi* are triangular units constructed of strong frames joined together, covered with cloth, and painted to represent buildings. Each stands on a very strong iron rod or on an oak pole, so that the entire unit can be neatly changed, quickly and suddenly, just as a door is turned, by a movement to the right or left. Each pair of *periaktoi* must be so placed that their pointed edges form a corner together, as is shown at ✱ ○ on the ground plan.

At *o*, δ , 8 is the first of the *periaktoi* and at ✱ , □ , △ the second. Each has one side 5 feet long and another 2½ feet long. Each perspective face, as from 8 to *o*, is painted to represent buildings, and likewise each front face, as from ✱ to □ .

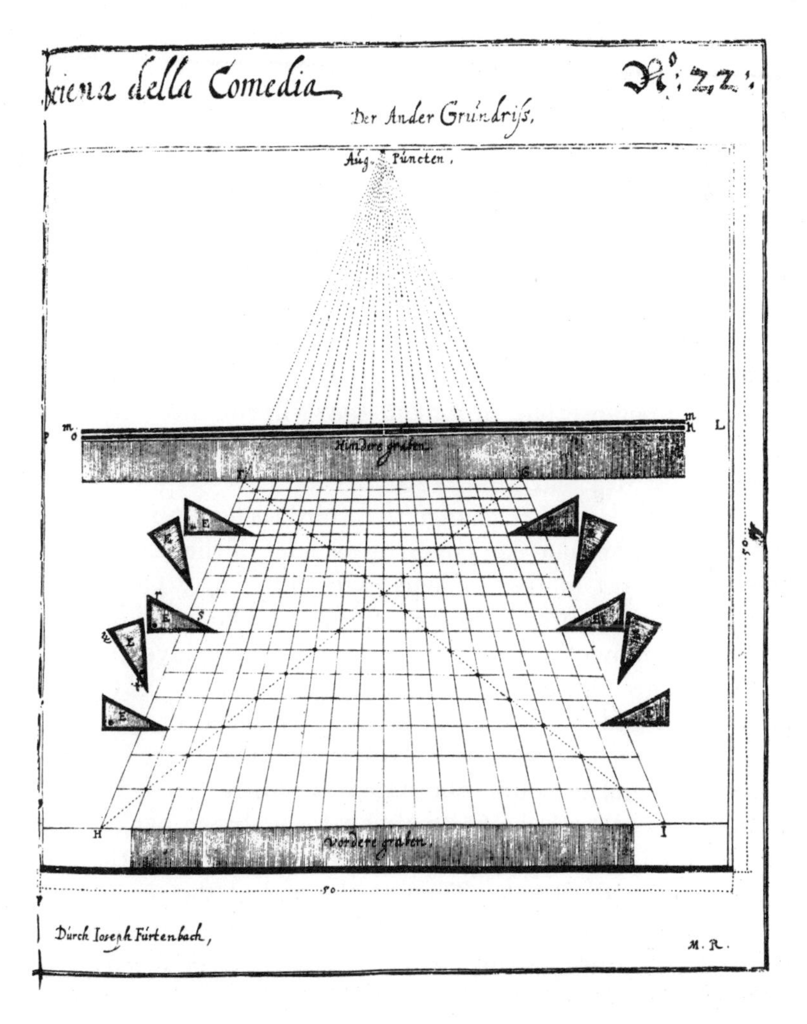


9. Second Ground Plan of the Scene for Comedy

Further, on the two rear sides of the *periaktoi* is painted a garden, so that when they are turned the houses disappear and quickly this garden is shown. Passages are left between the *periaktoi*. In this manner the *periaktoi* are put on both sides of the stage, so that the *Sciena di Comedia* stands before the eyes complete, with its painted houses and clouds.

For the second act, these *periaktoi* (as will be considered later) are changed from under the stage in an instant by means of handles on rods. The corners separate and suddenly (*impito*) and furiously (*furia*) the buildings disappear and the garden presents itself. In this manner the *periaktoi* are all turned, the first rear shutter is changed, and the scene is suddenly transformed into a garden. The plan provides convenient space for the actors behind the scene, and also entrances onto the scene by the "streets" between the houses.

We have considered how the *Sciena di Comedia* instantaneously is changed to a garden by the turning of the *periaktoi* here shown at E already changed. When the two parts of the first rear shutter are drawn back from K to L and from O to P, then the second shutter, MM, which is still closed, presents the form of a garden. Such a quick change will arouse in the spectator both delight and wonder. In order that the entire floor may be laid out in perspective, so that it, too, will run into the distance, we lay out and draw the lines of the pavement on two diagonal lines from F to I and from G to H.

If it is desired to change to a third scene, during the course of the second act one can cover those sides of the *periaktoi* which are out of sight of the audience with differently painted cloths representing mountains or the sea or the like — taking care of course to remove the pieces of cloth already displayed in the first act, which are painted in the semblance of houses. These are put on at *r* to *s* and at W to X, or secured by means of specially contrived grooves. Naturally the other *periaktoi* must be similarly re-covered, and of course the first rear shutter must be changed as well. As soon as the first act shutter is drawn back, while the second act is in progress, new shutters are put into the grooves ready for the third act. Then at the end of the second act the *periaktoi* and this first rear shutter instantaneously change, and we have the third setting, which is the scene of America which we have described above, or some other place. So we see from this discourse how settings may be changed to whatever scene is desired and as often as is desired.

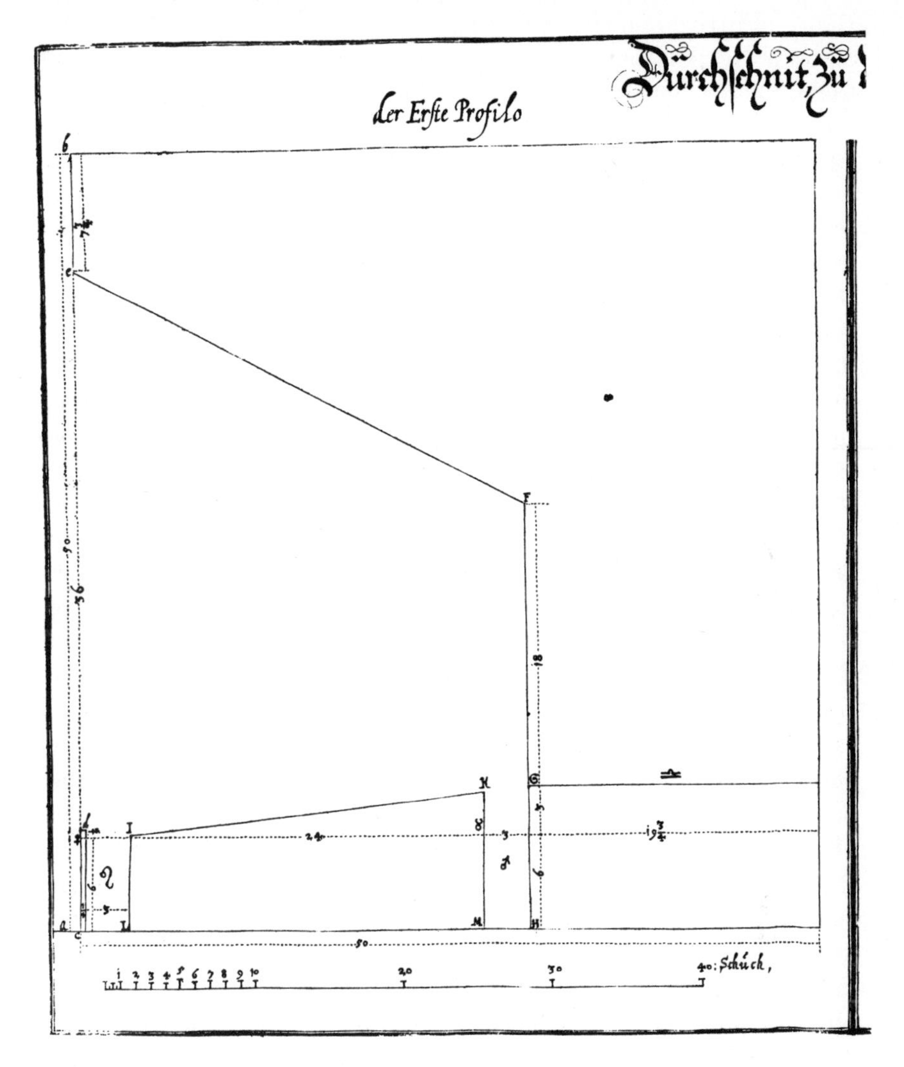


10. Cross Section of the Scene for Comedy: First Profile

Here is presented the first profile or cross section of the *Sciena di Comedia.* If there is space enough, it would be well to establish the distance from *a* to *b* as 50 feet; then, in proportion, from *c* to ♀ is 6 feet and from ♀ to *d* is $\frac{1}{4}$ foot, which together make $6\frac{1}{4}$ feet as the actual height of the stage at the front pit. There should be a wooden parapet to mask the front of the stage platform from the spectators as they enter the theatre. The front pit where the musicians sit is 3 feet wide and 6 feet high. The stage proper extends 24 feet from the front to the back, where its height is from M to K. Next is the rear pit ♂, which is also 3 feet wide. Then the height H to G is fixed at 9 feet.

Along a line drawn from I to G, that part from I to K represents the sloping part of the platform, and the rest from K to G remains as the width of the rear pit. We set up G to F as 18 feet for the height of the first shutter or rear wall. From F to *e* an imaginary line is drawn, below which the clouds must not hang. The clear space behind the shutters, at ≏, can be used in two ways: either as a room for the actors to change their costumes, or as a rearmost pit wherein ships are made to pass. Of course, the understanding architect who proposes to follow these instructions will recognize that they apply only to a very large, imposing *sciena di comedia.* If there is too little space or the hall is found too low or too narrow, then the height of the stage may be altered. The height of the scene at both the front and the rear may even be halved, so that the front will be only 18 feet and the shutters only 9 feet high. In such a case, the dimensions throughout must be reduced so that, for example, the depth of the entire stage will be only 25 feet, or even smaller, but always in the same proportions.

The second profile or cross section shows the *periaktoi,* painted as houses, along with the beams from which the heavens hang. On the first rear shutters, which are indicated at O, is placed the vanishing point[1] from which all the lines on the faces of the *periaktoi* are drawn. On the painted houses lines are drawn from this vanishing point to mark the cornices as well as the windows and doors. Each of the *periaktoi* rests on its own special rod or pole, which is cut through the boards of the stage and turns in a socket on the floor. A man placed by each pole, at the sound of a bell takes three steps forward and turns the *periaktoi* by means of a bar or handle, so that the side painted as a garden appears with a suddenness that astounds and delights the spec-

---

1. Here Furttenbach specifically places the vanishing point on the shutters. That this is a mistake in the text and the plate is clearly shown, not only in the theory of the time, but by Furttenbach's ground plan, Plate 22, and his two designs for scenes. There the vanishing point is clearly far behind the shutters. If the point were on the shutters, then the perspective lines of the houses, as Serlio points out, would vanish far too quickly. Of course the lines of the front faces could be laid out from a point on the shutters, as Serlio recommends. Perhaps Furttenbach has confused the faces in writing about the lines. His designs show that he did not make the mistake in practice.

tators.[1] At the same time the first pair of shutters are pulled back to disclose the second pair painted to complete the garden scene. S is the back stage, used by actors to cross over and to

11. CROSS SECTION OF THE SCENE FOR COMEDY: SECOND PROFILE

1. It is not clear how the *periaktoi* could turn if the bottom edge conformed with the slope of the stage as drawn here. Probably Furttenbach in practice followed the method recommended by Sabbattini of building the bottom straight and painting the sloping line. The tops of the *periaktoi* which Furttenbach shows in the *Prima Scena* in his *Mannhaffter Kunstspiegel* are clearly built with a straight line and painted with the sloping perspective line of the building. The corner above the top of the building was painted to blend with the heavens above and behind it. Such painted tops continued into the eighteenth century. Cf. Richard Southern, "The Staging of Eighteenth-Century Designs for Scenery," *Journal of Royal Institute of British Architects*, xlii (1933), 1021–1037.

change their costumes; or, when the floor boards are temporarily taken up, it forms a large rear pit in which the sea can easily be presented, showing, for example, the ship of Jonah together with a whale passing across — indeed here can be presented whatever is wished for the occasion.

Above we see where the heavens are made fast and how the floating clouds are strung between them. Pairs of strong beams are set at *t t*, V V, W W, X X. On each pair of beams, a frame on rollers, as at X X, can be pulled across, suspending an angular brace ♐ , △ , ⊙ on which clouds are fastened at ⊙ . As the cloud machine passes over, it opens up to show the Gods as well as lovely musicians sitting in it. This gives the spectator great delight. In like manner triumphal cars, and whatever else is desired, can be hung and swung down according to the action of the play. Lower supporting beams are set at *hhhhh*, to nail the heavens to. Another supporting beam is set above the shutters for the rearmost section of the heavens. The heavens are formed of five *cerchie*, or curved frames, at II II II II II, cut out skillfully in the shape of clouds. Behind these frames at the positions marked Z are placed a number of glass oil lamps, which cast such an exquisite glow on the scene that although it is night in the theatre it seems as if purple-colored dawn were drawing after her the longed-for day through the rich clouds. Also above at the front of the scene at U, and again in the pit at *z z z z z* are put a great many other oil lamps, which are of the highest importance for the lighting.

At P is the front pit where the Fellows of Orpheus [the musicians] have their seats. The parapet of this front pit should be 6¼ feet high. Still much more might be said of these lovely things so pleasing to all people; but I believe that a resourceful man will have enough from these instructions. And so I bring the construction of the *Sciena di Comedia* to a close.

# *From "The Noble Mirror Of Art," 1663*

## CONCERNING PERSPECTIVE SCENERY

[Furttenbach begins his discourse with a poem expressing the delight in seeing actors represent humanity, in delightful costumes, in old customs and manners, Gods, combats, sun, moon, and clouds, thunder and lightning, and the raging sea. He ends with a couplet praising the power of perspective art, "And thereto the stage must be formed lovely and beautiful by perspective art, for without that there is nothing."]

What a splendid moving thing is a perspective scene in a theatre. The perspective lines carry the eye so well into the distance that not only the ordinary spectator but the master himself will be carried away against his will and be astonished and entranced. Perspective presents such a lovely new world that even a melancholy spirit would be refreshed, strengthened, and persuaded to a longer life.

Sometimes as many as seven changes of scene are built at no little expense. Especially in Italy no expense is spared. It is well known that there as much as a half ton of gold has been spent for a play that would have only one performance at a princely celebration of marriage and would be seen only by the great lords present.

The putting on of plays is a most delightful and useful training for growing youth, who are to be brought up to a life of devotion to God and worth and nobility in the world. Acting in a well-equipped theatre will give boys a pleasing appearance, a confident speech, and a heroic spirit that will prepare them well for later discourses on both spiritual and secular occasions. Therefore there is a special need for the private citizens of cities to build such beneficial theatres to save the growing youth from sins, shames, and vices.

It is not necessary for every occasion to build a large expensive structure. For very little, one can build on a small scale in the same form as the princely theatres. In my *Architectura Recreationis* I have described how princely theatres as well as small stages are easily built. I refer those interested to that book.

Here it is the best course to give an account of large construction from my actual experience in planning and building two large stages, and in the plates that follow to present details in an architectural form. Further I would emphasize that the site should be of suitable size, and comfortable accommodations be provided for the actors. It is especially advisable that in the summer, when a crowded audience can get very hot, boards in the upper floor be raised to let out the stale air and to let in fresh air to quicken the people.

On the first of those occasions the noble and most learned Herr Ioan. Chunradus Merchius, Rector, Hist. Prof. Bibliothec. & Direct. Mus., with his students presented the very moving and memorable tragi-comedy of the life and history of Moses, especially the delivery of the Israelite people from the bondage of Egypt. The production used 120 people, lasted for six hours, and presented three principal changes of scene.

On the second occasion, in the year 1650, there was presented at the conclusion of the peace celebrations a play concerning the fortunes of the old Christian church during the rule of the Roman emperors Caius, Diocletian, Galerian, Constantine, Maxentius, and Constantine the Great. The lovely settings with five changes of scene won the praise of all who saw them. They would in no wise have been unworthy of the presence of far greater persons — of Princes, Dukes, and Electors, who are fond of having such plays presented. Some of the scenes with dimensions and the machines for this performance are shown in [Figures 12, 13, 14].

Here the building of the theatre hall is shown with an overall width of 50 feet and an overall length of 175 feet. Allowing for a wall 2½ feet thick, the inner dimensions will be 45 feet wide and 170 feet long. The distance from the floor to the roof structure should be 30 feet. If the hall has had[1] partitions and floors to make smaller rooms, they can be removed. Any flooring or ceiling suspended in the roof beams should be left so that there need be no supporting column to obstruct the view of the spectators. In this open hall the whole structure for the stage and for the audience can be built for less than a hundred *Reichstaler*.

1. Here Furttenbach uses a past tense. He shifts from present to past tense without consistency because, although his main purpose is to give general principles, most of his particular details come from the two productions which he mentions in the beginning. We have kept the present where a general principle seems involved and used the past only when the reference applies to his particular experience. Here he speaks of the stalls and sheds he had to remove. This tells us something of the kind of building he had to use.

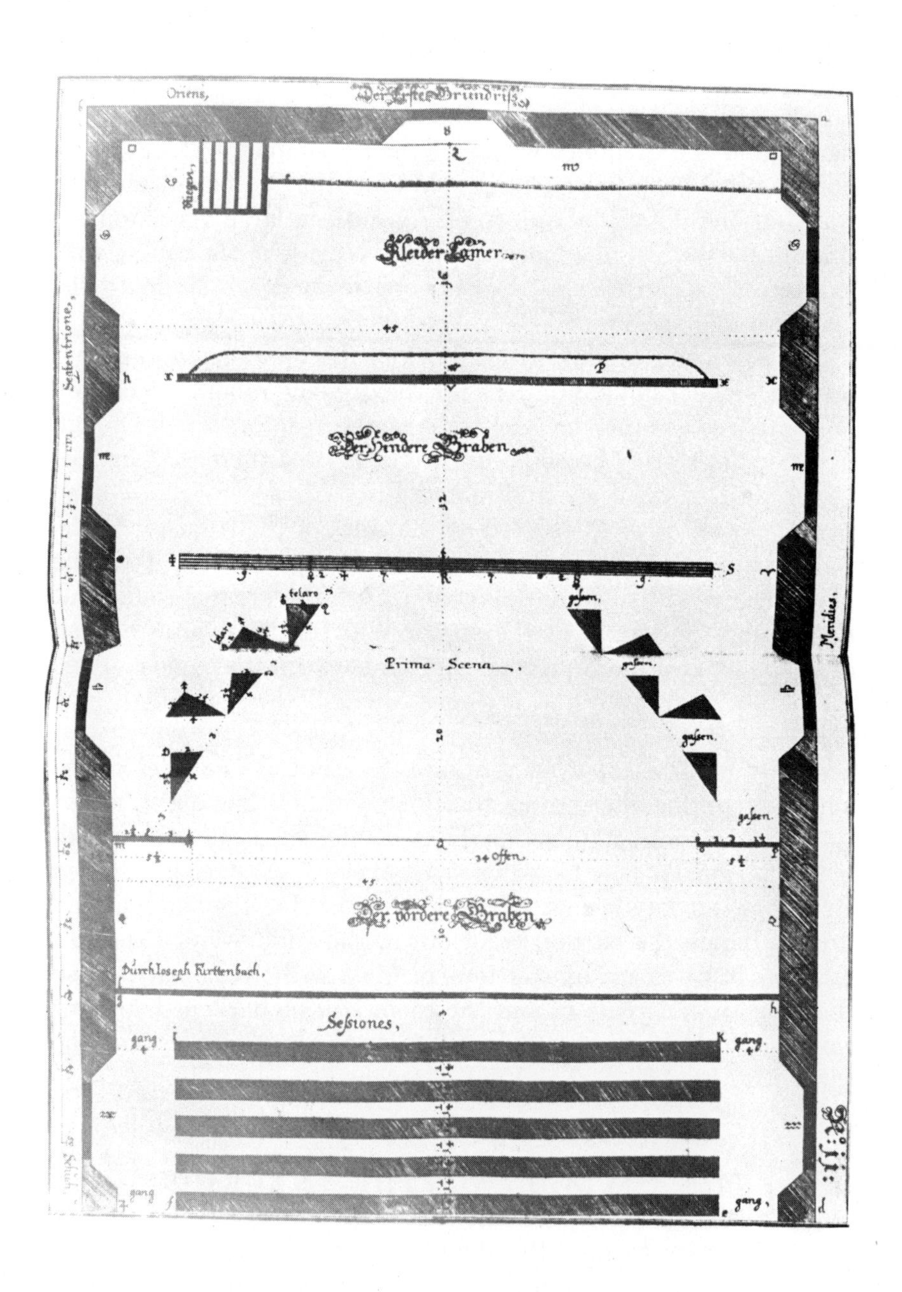


12. Stage and Auditorium: First Ground Plan

For these directions the four sides of the hall are named for the four parts of the world, *Oriens, Occidens* [back of the seats, outside the picture], *Meridies,* and *Septentrione.*

It is very important that the windows be planned at the right places for the proper lighting and for plenty of air. So many people so close together cause the air to become very warm and damp, and the architect would be held a simpleton if, after the building had been finished, more windows had to be cut into the walls, or the upper flooring spoilt by cutting large vents for air. At suitable places small openings may be made in the ceiling with shutters that can be closed or opened to let fresh air in to the audience and the actors.

A winged window at the back of the building and another on each side let in light and air for the dressing room. Two more opposite one another on each side of the rear pit let in enough light so that by day no oil lamps will be needed there. Again two at the sides of the scene add more light.

No windows are placed at the sides of the front pit. The walls there are left unbroken so that the spectator will not be blinded, but will sit in darkness and have the greater wonder at the daylight falling in at the streets between the houses as well as at the light of morning coming from between the clouds. Then the actors appear for the prologue and tell the contents of the play.

It were better if no windows were put at the sides of the audience, so that the spectators, left in darkness like night, would turn their attention to the daylight on the stage. But it is still better to have a pair of windows at every tenth bench to let in air before the play begins. Then at the sound of the trumpet and drums, before the curtain is let down, the windows of the auditorium can be closed by shutters, or filled with green leafwork so that the air can come in and the room still be darkened. Every care should be taken for the welfare of the audience — that the spirit may be refreshed and not dampened.

## THE DIVISION OF THE INTERIOR

In order to give the dimensions of the place where the audience is seated, beginning at the corner *g*, over the point 4 a straight line is drawn 110¼ feet long. (In the small space of the plate the entire dimension could not be shown.) Forty benches each 37 feet long and 1¼ feet wide are placed with a 1¼-foot space between. Each bench will accommodate 20 people, even though some large persons will need 2 feet. At the sides the aisles run 101¼ feet, and a 3-foot passage is left at the front and an 8½-foot passage at the back where the audience comes up by double stairways from the 12-foot portal.

Within the entire dimensions of the room, 45 feet in width, 30 feet in height, and 170 feet in length, the architect must calculate how wide he will make the dressing room, the rear pit, and most important, the stage itself, to provide for the needs of the play, of the actors, and of the machines. The following dimensions will take care of those needs:

16 feet for the width of the dressing room
½ foot for the partition wall
12 feet for the rear pit
1 foot for the grooves of the shutters at S
20 feet for the stage from R to Q
10 feet for the front pit
¼ foot for the board parapet

(making 59¾ feet to be allowed exclusively for the stage and actors)

Then from *g* towards I —

3 feet for the front passageway
98¾ feet for the benches and spaces between
8½ feet for the passage at the entrance

(making 170 feet in all for the interior of the building).

## DETAILS OF THE INNER BUILDING

For the most important part — the stage itself — a 45-foot straight line on the floor of the hall from *m* to P is marked out, by carpenter's method. Then a ¼-foot base is laid for posts to support the sills, to form a wall 5 feet at the front of the stage as shown in the cross section in [Figure 14].

Then ¾-foot bases are laid for 5-foot posts for 20 feet along the straight line ‡ to S [Figure 12] to support firmly the one-foot-square beam for the grooves and the back shutters (as shown in the cross section of [Figure 14]). These four grooves are 1¼ inches deep and 1¼ inches wide and are made slick for the four painted shutters to slide in.

From the front of the stage the floor slopes upwards to a height of 7 feet at the shutters,[1] but from there to the end of the hall it is horizontal.

The whole floor of the stage is supported by strong cross-beams. But those must be placed to allow four stage traps, each 2 feet wide, at the four entrances between the wings. These are covered with boards and fastened by hinges and open downward when the sliding catches are removed from below. Through them, according to the play, may issue on occasion plants, buildings, fire, smoke, and lightning, and buildings and persons may sink and disappear, and various kinds of machines may be drawn, to the great wonder of the audience.

The whole stage is covered with good boards or slit deals and nailed, and the trap doors are fastened firmly by their sliding catches, so that the actor can move freely and the stage be entirely smooth.

The 12-foot back pit is laid with strong but light planks left unnailed so that they can easily be taken up and replaced. There should be braces at the center to support the planks lest they should bend with an actor on them.

The upper floor of the dressing room is of slit deals nailed. At the back is a stairway for the actors to enter by a separate entrance at the north end of the building and get to the dressing room and behind the wings unseen by the audience.

The front pit, 10 feet wide. as shown in the cross section of [Figure 14], serves not only as a barrier to prevent the curious from getting too near and speaking ill of the scene painting, but much more for the curtains that are let fall into it to disappear in turn. According to the action, there are used one, two, three, four, five, or on such occasions as the play of the Creation of the World which God finished from day to day, as many as six different curtains.

A parapet separates the pit from the audience. For the seats a structure of strong boards is made as shown in the cross section of [Figure 14]. Here only five benches are shown, but in the actual construction 40 may be built to seat in all 800 persons. After the important people are seated, about 200 common people may find a place to stand in the 4-foot aisles, or seats of narrow boards may be placed in the aisles. Experience has shown that they can be accommodated quite comfortably there.

1. Here Furttenbach seems to say the shutters back of the rear pit, but the cross section shows a level floor at the rear pit.

So much for the stage and the pits. We must turn now to consider the changing of the scenes.

## HOW TO DESIGN THE WINGS AS SHOWN IN THE FIRST SCENE

In the space between the front pit and the shutters, wings that revolve [*periaktoi*] are to be erected to form the scene. These must have their pivots carefully placed so that they not only present one scene, such as this one of houses, but also revolve to show another, such as the garden of the *secunda scena*, and on occasion still other scenes. They must permit entrances or "streets" for actors and for various machines. Hence their construction is most important.

The whole scene must be planned in good proportions for the best perspective effect, and so planned that the lamps that stand at the sides will have good position for lighting the successive scenes. This scene I made 34 feet wide at the front and 14 feet wide at the back, and 20 feet high at the front, decreasing to 10 feet at the back.

[THE PROSCENIUM.[1]] To mask and cover what is not part of the setting, thin boards well joined and planed are built at the sides (at *m* to *n* and *o* to *p* on [Figure 12]) 5½ feet wide and 30 feet high to the ceiling. The proscenium is finished by a section (*Schirm*) between the side walls 4¼ feet wide, made of smoothly planed boards and fastened to the ceiling. On this planking is painted a beautiful curtain tied in rosettes. This gives a beautiful finish to the front — then the scene opens and you cannot see behind at all but only a well proportioned perspective setting 34 feet wide and 20 feet high.

To place the setting according to perspective art, four principal points must be established on the stage floor. The front points are established at the back of the proscenium walls 3 feet to the right and the left of the scene opening (at ☽ and ☍ on [Figure 12]). The two back points are at the shutters, 7 feet on each side of the center. Then two red lines are laid out by carpenter's chalk-line from the front points to the back points. On

1. Furttenbach nowhere uses the word *proscenium*. As was usual in the Renaissance in dealing with temporary stages constructed in buildings not designed as theatres, he regarded the proscenium as part of the scene that was to be erected. We have used the word *proscenium* to distinguish these frames used as parts of the proscenium from those used for the scenery.

these red lines, beginning at the back, first a 3-foot street is left, then the 4-foot face of the *periaktoi.* Then from the two front corners of the *periaktoi,* the point for the other corner is found by drawing with a compass two arcs with radii of 2 feet and of $3\frac{1}{2}$ feet. These three points mark the sides for a triangular wing or *periaktoi* with a 4-foot front, a $3\frac{1}{2}$-foot back, and a 2-foot end.

The main difficulty is to find a point for the iron pivot, so that when the *periaktoi* turn they may have the proper positions with respect to each other and to the entrances. The point is found in this manner: From the middle point of the 2-foot end a line is run to the opposite corner. Then the point for the pivot is on that line, $1\frac{3}{4}$ feet from the end.

The two secondary *periaktoi* (marked ↥ ), which join two of the main ones to form complete houses, have sides of the same dimensions as the three main ones on the red line, but the sides are in different order. The 4-foot sides are visible to the audience at the same time as the 4-foot sides of the three main *periaktoi.* To find the point for the pivot of the two secondary *periaktoi,* a line is run from the center of the 2-foot end to the opposite corner just as in the case of the other three prisms. But here the point is marked 1 foot from the 2-foot end instead of $1\frac{3}{4}$ feet.

These *periaktoi,* with the frames that are fastened on them and the top and bottom into which the iron pivots are fixed, can easily be made by an ordinary carpenter or cabinet maker with the instructions here given. The two farthest back on each side are made 9 feet high. After another 3-foot street is left, the next pair are made 12 feet high. After another 3-foot street there is a single *periaktoi* at each side, 14 feet high. In all there are five similar *periaktoi* on each side of the stage with four 3-foot streets or entrances.

For the back shutters (*Schnurramen*) four grooves from ǂ to S are cut into a supporting beam at the level of the stage. Each shutter is a frame of wood 9 feet long and 10 feet high covered with cloth. The two shutters for the first scene, painted as part of the scene of houses, run in the first groove. They fit together at the center so that no space can be seen between. They can be drawn apart to the ends of the groove, where they are out of sight, to disclose the second shutters painted as part of the garden scene. When the scene is to be changed again, the second pair of shutters are drawn to the side in the groove to show the third pair of shutters painted as a camp, and finally the fourth pair painted as a grove or a desert or mountain. At the center at R an iron stop 1/4 inch thick and 1 inch high is set in each of the grooves so that when the shutters are pushed to the center they will not go too far to one side.

When all the shutters are drawn aside there is a large opening to the inner stage,[1] where a tapestried room like a hall may be shown. At V at the back of the inner stage a royal throne may be placed for a prince, king, or emperor with his councillors at each side, with excellent effect.[2] Such a room can be used for many other occasions. If the boards are removed it becomes a rear pit where the sea is shown with waves, where ships, whales, and similar maritime objects can be seen.

The wall back of the inner stage may be made only 1/2 foot thick or only of boards. When there is need, openings for machines may be made in it. Here the fiery bush was shown (as told in the third chapter of the second book of Moses) in a beautiful wood of natural trees and shrubbery. By means of an opening in the wall the *parisol* was operated to simulate fire. This is described in detail later.

Further back is the dressing room, with a long table and a bench of the same length. It is easy for the actors to pass unseen through the two doors to the stage,[3] so that the spectators will wonder how the large number of people came to fill the stage.

The Placement of the Oil Lamps. At the front of the stage oil lamps are set 3 feet apart[4] on the floor behind the 3/4-foot board shown in the cross section. From this hidden position they send light only over the scene. Behind the side walls of the proscenium next to the scene opening oil lamps are placed in iron rings one above the other 2 feet apart up to the heavens.

---

1. Furttenbach uses the term "rear pit" (*hindere graben*) for the portion of the stage back of the rear shutters, whether it is used as a rear pit or is covered with boards and used as an inner stage. He nowhere uses the term "inner stage."

2. The inner stage would naturally be a favorite place for the throne. Compare the interior scenes on the inner stage in the hell scene reproduced by Lee Simonson, *The Stage Is Set*, p. 469, and the throne room described by Laurent for *Le Divorce* in Paris, 1683: "Théâtre est des maisons sur le devant et une salle sur le derrière. Il y faut un trosne . . ." (*Le Mémoire de Mahelot, Laurent et d'autres Décorateurs* (ed. Lancaster), p. 132). Furttenbach describes the throne and its use later, in the section on machines.

3. Compare the location of the dressing room or *vestuario* of the Spanish stage. It was immediately back of the playing area and separated from it by a curtain. A man killed on the stage generally managed to fall in the dressing room (Rennert, *The Spanish Stage in the Time of Lope de Vega*, pp. 92 f.).

4. Two pages later, he says 2 1/2 feet apart.

Behind these lamps[1] are placed glittering pieces of gold tinsel.[2] Other lamps are placed behind the clouds, so that one cloud lights the next, sending down a glow like day. Also in the rear pit 50 oil lamps should be placed, each filled with ¼ pound of olive oil.

In order to change the scene, one man is assigned to each pair of *periaktoi;* in each hand he grasps one of the handles fastened to the ends of the *periaktoi.* When the signal for the change is given by a little bell, he pulls the handles towards each other simultaneously, turning the *periaktoi* so that the backs are turned to the audience and new corners come together to show the second scene. At the same time men turn each of the single *periaktoi,* and pull the first pair of shutters back by means of strong leather straps. These men, eight in all, change the scene with a quickness that excites the admiration of the audience, who can scarce divine how the change is brought about. The *periaktoi* are shown in their new positions in [Figure 13]. The new sides of the wings and the second back shutters are painted to represent a garden.

The turn of the *periaktoi* to the new positions makes the scene larger by the spaces marked *Spatium.* These provide good places for the actors to go out of sight in the course of the action, as behind mountains or rocks. Above all, the perspective lines are kept intact; there are still sides of houses on the main perspective line, though that line is further to the side than in the first scene.

For the change to the third scene, the military camp, preparations are made during the second act. Out of sight of the audience, new painted frames with new scenes to cover the first scene are put on the backs of the *periaktoi.* To hold these frames, guards are glued on or set into the top and the bottom of the *periaktoi* and the frames are inserted or fastened on with an iron turnbuckle so that they can be taken off at will. When the signal is given by the bell, the same eight men turn the *periaktoi* in an instant to the first positions and pull to the sides another pair of back shutters. Thus the whole scene is changed to a military camp as quickly as a man can open and shut his eyes.

For a change to a fourth scene, painted frames are fastened by turnbuckle to the *periaktoi* on the other side. At the

---

1. See the section on machines later for these reflectors.

2. *geschlagen Flendergold.* This seems to consist of beaten pieces of gold alloy or tinsel.

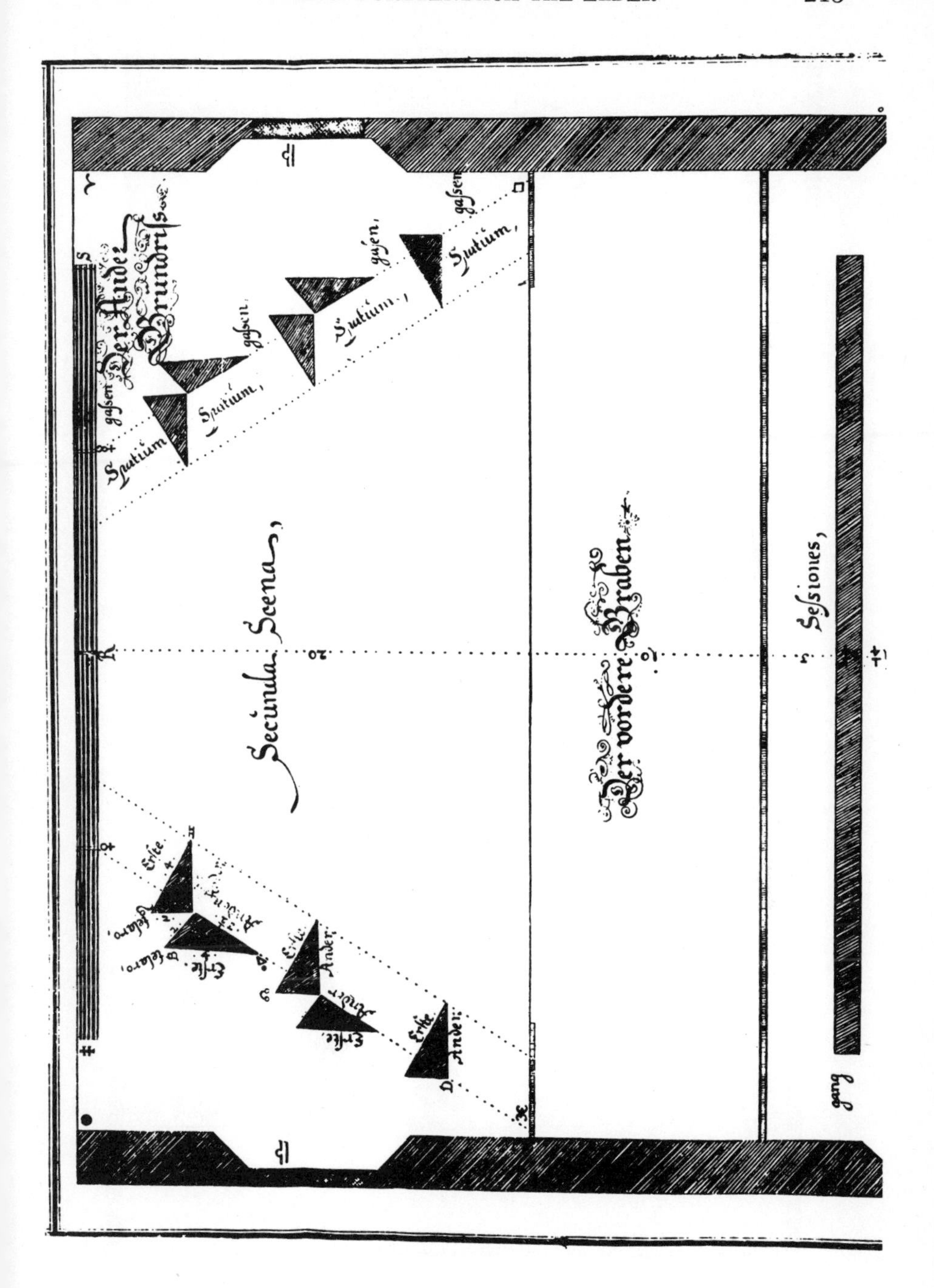


13. Stage and Auditorium: Second Ground Plan

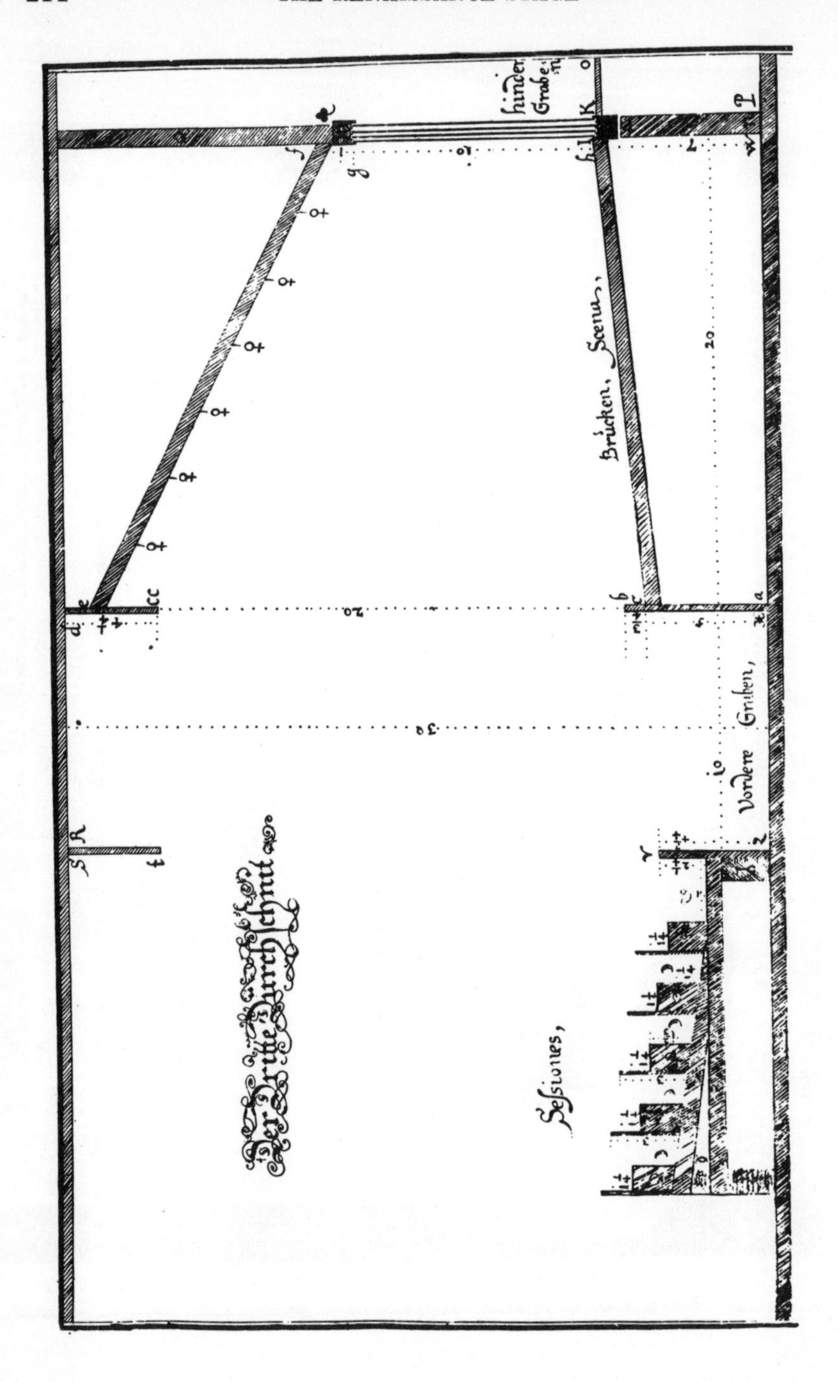


14. Stage and Auditorium: Cross Section

sound of the bell the *periaktoi* are turned and the shutters are pulled aside to show the fourth pair, painted for the fourth scene, which may be of mountains, hills, and rocks. In this manner the scene may be changed as many times as desired.

Here is shown a section through the length of the theatre. The stage platform is 5 feet high at the front from *a* to *c*. For the proper effect of perspective it rises to 7 feet at the back shutters at W to I. The stage is 20 feet deep from A to W. At the front of the stage at *c* to *b* is a board or screen rising ¾ foot above the level of the floor to conceal the oil lamps placed behind it every 2½ feet.[1] Round holes are cut into the floor to hold the pointed under part of the lamps. By these lamps the scene may be lighted from below, evenly like day. Behind the lamps a piece of beaten brass or golden tinsel covered with a piece of mica will reflect glimmering rays that will cause the spectator to wonder how the effect is achieved. At the back of the stage is the row of posts to support the lower grooved beam I, K. In this beam are cut four grooves for the shutters. The shutters are 10 feet high from I to *g*, and their tops are held in a similar beam with four grooves.

Only the beginning of the rear pit is shown in this cross section. Further detail has been shown in the first ground plan. When this space is floored it serves as a room. When the board floor is removed, it is a pit 7 feet deep where the sea is represented and where ships, galleys, and whales are made to pass on the lower floor P. When a land scene is shown, carriages, wagons, horsemen, or such other machines as may be desired, are made to pass over.

In order that this rear pit may be well lighted, at least ten oil lamps with shiny reflectors behind them are set in iron rings 2 feet apart along the upper grooved beam.

The scene opening at the front is 20 feet from *b* to *cc*. Above the opening, from *cc* to *d*, is the 4½-foot board section of the proscenium on which drapery (*Umbhang*) is painted.

Above the scene at *e* to *f* are two sloping beams to give the heavens the proper perspective form. These beams, called *Anhafftungs* or *Seitenträger*, are ⅓ by 1½ feet and are placed one on each side of the stage above the red lines laid out on the ground plan. In them are set the upper ends of the iron pivots of the

1. Two pages before, Furttenbach gives 3 feet as the distance between these lamps.

*periaktoi*. To the bottom of them are nailed at ♀ , ♀ , ♀ , etc., one behind the other, the six sections of the heavens cut in the form of clouds (*Wolcken*), about 2 feet wide, and a seventh section is nailed at *g* to the grooved beam above the back shutters. Behind each section of the heavens, as explained and shown at *z z z* on plate 23 of my *Architectura Recreationis*, a large number of oil lamps are fastened by iron rings. Behind each lamp is nailed a 6-inch-square reflector of gold tinsel.[1] In the fluctuation of the air, the glimmering of these lamps will light up the heavens and send down beautiful beams to the great delight of the audience. Lights with reflectors should be placed in rings behind the upper part of the proscenium frame at *cc* to light the first cloud.

The front pit at X to *z* is 10 feet wide. At the ceiling above it, at *d* to R, is a similar space between two frames. Here at the top are hung two, or sometimes as many as six, curtains. They are let fall into the front pit to lie out of sight of the audience. If a curtain covers the scene when the audience first comes into the hall, it will whet the interest and cause the greater wonder when the curtain falls. If anyone desires to paint on the curtain a perspective scene of buildings, he will find four different designs in plate 20 of my *Architectura Recreationis*.

The seats for the spectators must be planned with care. A floor is erected on strong pillars, and over this a sloping floor. The seats of the benches are 1⅔ feet from the sloping floor and 1¼ feet wide, with backs 1⅓ feet high. A space 1¼ feet is left between the benches for entering and for comfort when sitting. The fact that the benches are set on a sloping floor enables all the spectators to see the stage clearly — a very important provision in a place intended for graciousness and delight.

In the space between the first benches and the front pit are placed sixteen well-appointed chairs for the most distinguished spectators (*Principales*) with their wives, and for their youths.

This space is separated from the front pit by a parapet (*Galleriae*) 2¼ feet high. The board frame immediately above at *t* to S is painted with ornaments of leaves and fruit.

THE DESIGN OF THE FIRST SCENE. Here we consider the scene as a whole as it is painted ready for the audience. The overall width from *e* to *f* is 45 feet; the overall height from *e* to *g*

1. The reflector was not shown or mentioned in the *Architectura Recreationis* of 1640.

is 30 feet. The width of the scene itself from M to M is only 34 feet. The height of the opening from C at the stage floor to *a* is 20¾ feet. All around the scene, from *a* to *g*, *b* to *h*, *c* to *e*, and *d* to *f*, is a proscenium frame painted with draperies caught up in rosettes. On the 5-foot front parapet are painted in perspective two flights of steps as though one could mount to the stage. The front parapet is shown only to the height of the stage. The ¾-foot additional screen or shield in front of the oil lamps has been omitted in the engraving because it would hide part of the scene, though of course in actual practice this would not be true.

PAINTING THE SCENE. On the back shutters a street with houses is painted with a fountain in the center, such a fountain as I show in plate 28 of my *Architectura Recreationis*. The shutters should be so carefully fitted together at the center of the scene that they will appear to be one frame. The vanishing point must not be placed too high or too low but in the proper place. I usually start from the level of the stage floor at the center and locate the vanishing point 4 feet above. Then all the lines of the perspective, both on the floor and in the entire scene, are to be laid out from that vanishing point.

The *periaktoi* that come together to form one house, as shown on the ground plan, must be fitted together so well that they look like the corner of a real house, and so that nothing can be seen between them. These *periaktoi* and the single *periaktoi* at the front are to be drawn and painted as houses of Florentine design with big red stone blocks (*Quatterstucken*) and white lines. But the windows and door frames are to be painted in shades of gray (*graw in graw*), so that they will stand out in the light of the lamps. When the heavens are painted to simulate clouds, in shades of gray with a reddish tinge in natural proportions, the first scene is finished.

When the *periaktoi* are turned and the first back shutters drawn aside as explained in connection with the ground plans, the scene is transformed into a graceful pleasure garden.

THE DESIGN OF THE SECOND SCENE. On the second pair of back shutters is painted a garden in the middle of which is shown a beautiful open grotto, such as I show in my *Architectura Recreationis* in plate 28. At either side of the grotto are painted lovely trellised arbors. These back shutters, like the first pair, should be well fitted together as a continuous wall. Here also the vanishing point for the entire scene is placed 4 feet from the floor.

15. The First Scene

16. The Second Scene

Each pair of the *periaktoi*, as at L and K, must fit together at the narrow corners so that nothing may be seen between. On the *periaktoi* are painted splendid trellises or arbored walks with topiary cupolas. The foremost one is painted with a sizable trellis of shrubs trained in a formal pattern, painted green with the clear blue sky shining between.

At I, I, I, etc., on the two sides are the streets or entrances between the pairs of *periaktoi*, as marked out on the ground plan of [Figure 13]. Then the second scene is complete.

After the lovely pleasure garden, if it is desireu to have other changes, such scenes may be designed as a wood or a wilderness, or a scene of the shore with rocks and other rugged objects (*Rilppen*) painted directly on the faces of the *periaktoi*. Again after the sound of the drums and trumpet the performers will come on in costumes appropriate to the scene and once more please the audience.

## MACHINES FOR THE PLAY

### *Clouds That Are Lowered To The Stage And Raised Again*

Here we give directions for preparing in an inexpensive way the machines for special effects on the stage. For this work an expert in mechanics who knows the means of drawing machines across and of raising objects can be of great assistance. Without a good craftsman it will be difficult to carry out these things satisfactorily.

When it was desired to present the play of the birth of Our Lord and Saviour Jesus Christ in the theatre at night by means of the lighting of oil lamps, it was necessary to show the Celestial Hosts and the lovely angels coming to earth in a cloud. For this a frame of clouds 5 feet square was made of boards in the shape shown in [Figure 17]. This frame has an opening 3¾ feet wide, and to its back is nailed a box 4½ feet wide at the front, with sides that run back on perspective lines to a back 1½ feet wide and 2 feet high from the bench. Its depth is 2 feet.

Inside the box there are a rear bench *aa* and two side benches *bb* and *cc*, on each of which was seated a young boy dressed as a beautiful angel, with white frocks with red silk bands about the body and with curly hair put on the head. The entire interior of the cloud is lined with pieces of beaten brass or gold tinsel so cross marked and mottled that they scatter shimmering light from the candles. Concealed on the flooring at the front just behind the frame of clouds at *ee* is placed a large wax light which brightly illuminates the faces of the angels so that they appear to have a high color. To make the whole interior radiant and to send a light out on the stage, large wax lights are placed at each side, from *dd* around to *dd* at the other side, ¾ foot apart behind the frame of clouds. Above each light is a copper funnel-like chimney to take the smoke up and out behind the cloud, so that there will be no danger to the boys sitting in the cloud. The front frame is painted in the form of clouds and ornamented with the heads of angels.

When the time comes in the play that the shepherds in the field fall to their knees in wonder at the beautiful light from heaven, then, after the shutters are opened, this cloud is let down through the other clouds into the inner stage (rear pit), which is now made to look like a field. This descent is accomplished from the floor above by means of a reel of a kind commonly used for

17. The First Cloud

opening and closing weirs. By means of two ropes wound on the roller of the windlass, the cloud is hung in a horizontal position and counterweighted. When this cloud descends to the accompaniment of charming music, the likeness of the Celestial Host seems to be shining with the glow from the cloud. When the three angels sing, with many unseen persons joining in, and turn their heads, hands, and voices toward Heaven, then, though at little expense, the spectators are made to believe they have a foretaste of heavenly joy.

After that, by the same windlass, the cloud is drawn up and disappears from sight. The windlass will serve for lowering many other things. The understanding architect will find many other uses for such a machine to delight the audience.

In presenting the tragi-comedy of the life and history of Moses, we had need to make the destroying angel appear in a cloud, not at the rear pit, but in the middle of the stage between the buildings. For this is used an inexpensive machine out of sight of the audience, with a supporting frame of two 10-foot boards which are nailed with their lower ends at the upper floor. It looks like a village well-pole, with the foot fastened down at PP and the upper part made fast in the roof structure so that it can carry a great load. The boom is an oak beam 16 feet long, with the cloud hung on at one end and a counterweight of oak wood blocks heavy enough to lift the cloud at the other end. Where the bucket is on the village well-pole, there the cloud is hung. The cloud, which is 9 feet long and 3½ feet wide and is cut from boards and painted, hangs from the pin at the end of the boom by a wrought iron hook 2 feet long and 2 inches thick. Behind it at Q Q is a hidden bench for the destroying angel to sit on. To make the cloud hang straight, a strip of lead a half hundredweight heavy is screwed on behind the cloud in the middle, in a vertical line from the top.

When the time comes for the destroying angel to appear, the cloud is let down between the heavens to the floor of the stage by two men out of sight of the audience who grasp and raise up the counterweights. The destroying angel with his naked sword steps out on the stage and the cloud is drawn up to disappear in the sky. When he has done his part he is taken up to heaven again in the cloud. A similar use was made of this device in the tragi-comedy about Diocletian. An angel was let down to present to Theophilo the fruit from the garden of the martyr

Dorothea. It can also be used in many other effective ways.

At another time, for the presentation of the history of the Patriarch Abraham, another inexpensive machine for letting a cloud down was used. Two beams 16 feet long, $\frac{1}{2}$ foot wide, and $\frac{1}{6}$ foot thick are fastened together by means of four cross-rails to make a frame 2 feet wide. A round bar is set through the center of the frame so that its projecting ends can fit into

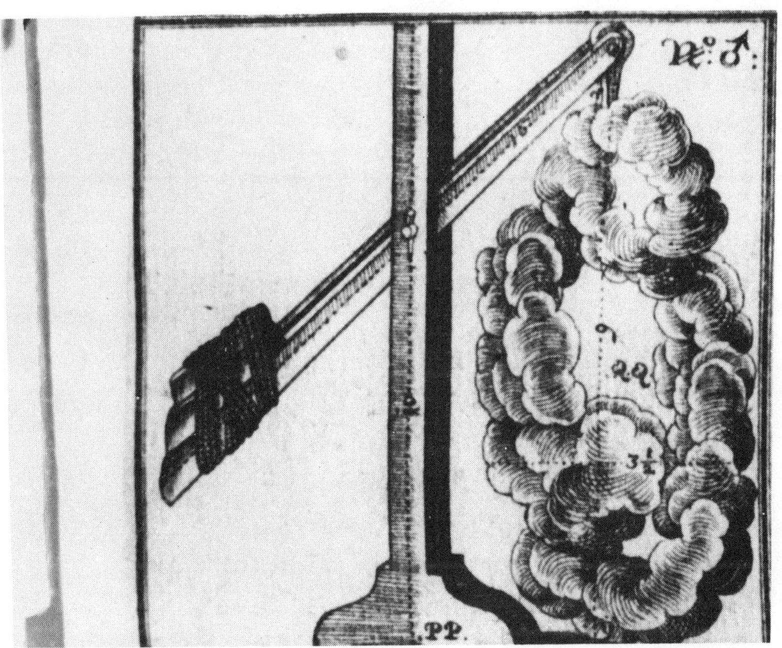


18. The Second Cloud

holes in two beams of the upper floor, and thus, just as a cannon pivots, the frame pivots between the beams, raising or lowering the end of the frame that holds the cloud. At one end a heavy counterweight is fastened by means of some strong oaken bars. At the other end the angel sits on one cross-rail with his feet on another cross-rail, surrounded on both sides by clouds so that only the upper part of the body is seen. For this action the inner stage is made into the scene of the land Moriah, the mountain of the Lord. When the time comes for the angel to appear, then two men grasp the iron handles at the sides and lift the frame at the counterweight end to let the cloud with the angel down some three or more feet below the opening between the sections of the heavens, so that he is at the right height to seize the sword of

Abraham. Afterwards the men let the counterweight pull the cloud back into the sky as though it had disappeared. It was especially pleasing to the audience to see in the inner stage this distant scene of a wilderness with wild mountains.

This cloud can also be used in the play of the birth of Christ when the angel announces to the shepherds in the field the happy birth of our Savior Jesus Christ — and also for many other occasions.

When the tragi-comedy of the life and history of Moses was presented, there was need for a beautiful heroic "splendor" of a radiating circle of sunbeams from which the Almighty God spoke to Moses. With very little expense a powerful light can be placed behind a round double glass filled with water and put at the very center of the *glory*, as will be explained in the following paragraphs.

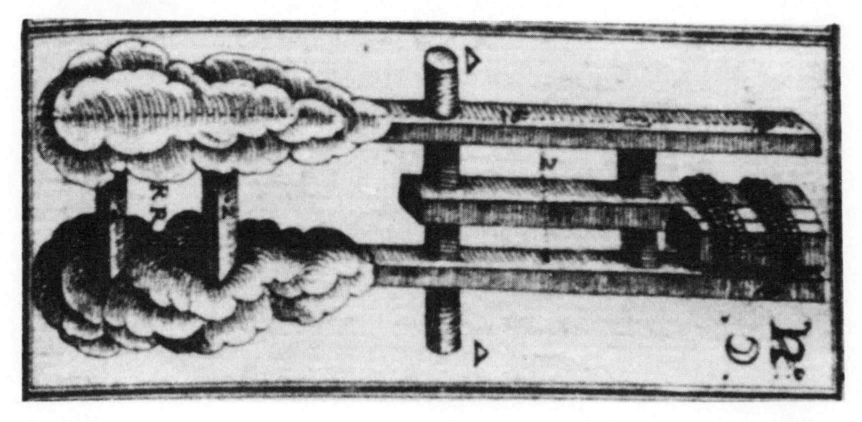

19. THE THIRD CLOUD

At the bottom is shown one of the four identical polished side walls that are to be fastened together. Each is 3 feet wide at the front, 2 feet wide at the back, and $1\frac{3}{4}$ feet deep.

On the opposite page is shown a perspective box which is 3 feet square around the front opening, and 2 feet square at the back wall, and about 2 feet deep. In its rear wall is cut a hole $\frac{5}{6}$ foot square, by means of which a strong light can be put at the outside. The light from it, especially when a water-filled glass is set before it, will seem like an eye that sends out sunbeams toward the spectators to cause great wonder by its shimmering.

Onto the back of the front wall, at PP, and on both sides,

at *oo* and *oo,* are fastened three strong lights which will illuminate not only the inside of the box but the sun which is to be put in. A copper hood must be set over each light to carry away the smoke. Then the entire box is to be lined with gold tinsel marked out in cross lines so that a golden glow will come out.

[Figure 21] shows the front wall or cover, II to II and *hh* to *hh*. This cover is nailed on the inner box so that only the 2-foot opening is left, and it can be so completely closed by the sliding door *kk* that not a ray comes out. Finally the front wall, together with the door, is painted so that it looks exactly like a cloud floating in the air.

Figure 22 shows us the completed *glory* above Mount Sinai. When the door is drawn up, it stands open 2 feet wide, from *ff* to *ff* and across from *ff* to *ff*. At ⊙ the sun is placed in such a way that by a thin iron rod it can be moved from right to left, so that the beams of the sun will catch up the lights from the bottom and the sides. When the light is placed behind the glass with water at the center, it will look like an eye which sends out beams, and the four lights will not be seen. That light behind the half-rounded water glass and the reflection of the gold tinsel give out such a shimmering and shining splendor that the man who looks at it too closely would lose his sight.

As for the sun itself, it is 1½ feet in diameter and has 16

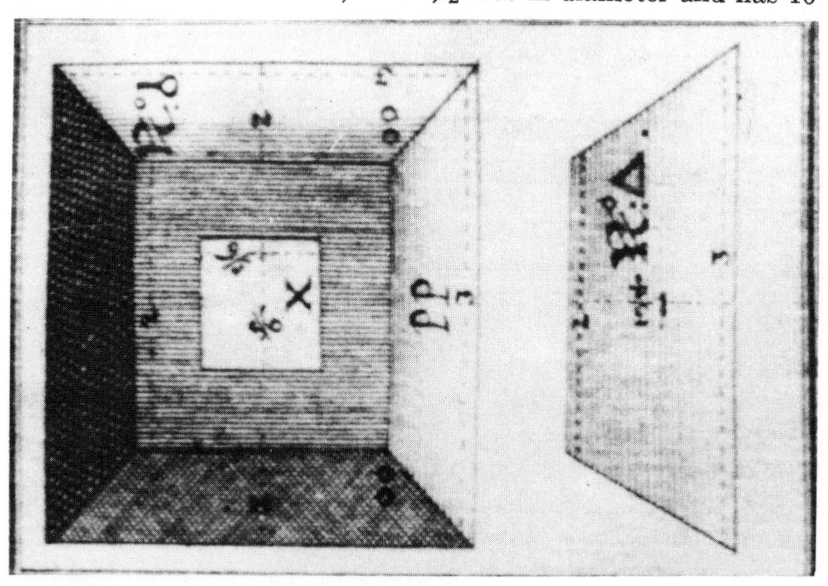

20. THE "*Glory* BOX"

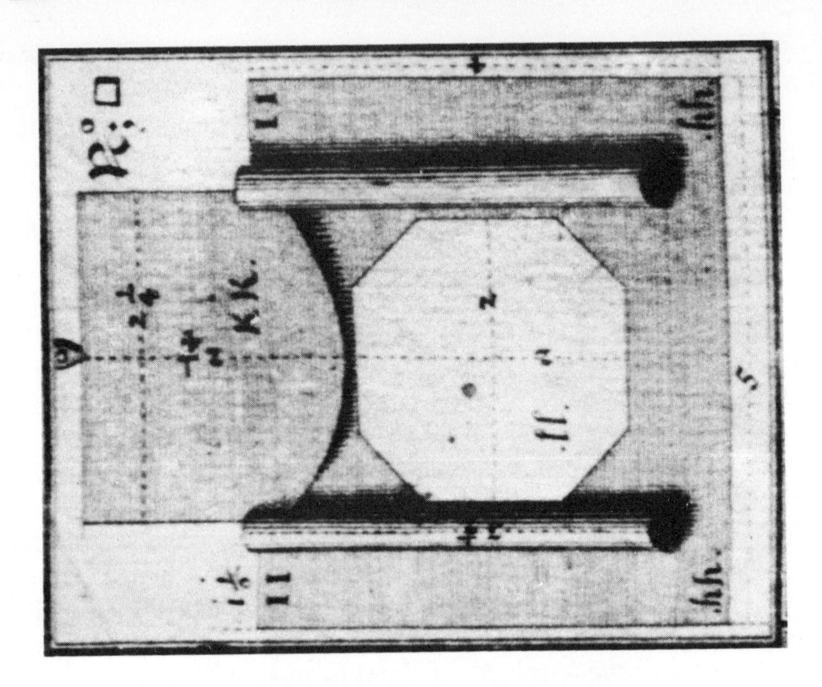

21. The Cover for the *Glory* Box

points or flames, no thicker than a knife blade, of well-colored brass cut from a barber's basin shining like beautiful gold and highly polished with brickdust.

In the middle at ⊙ is a crystalline globe 5 inches in diameter rounded at the front. This globe must be carefully made by the glassmaker from two pieces of crystalline glass set two fingers' distance apart. It is filled with water to which a little bit of red coloring is added. It must be made with a neck or hole the width of a finger to put the water in by, and also with a peg (*Zapfen*). By the peg and the neck it is made fast to the box. Or if no better can be had, a glass flask with a curved side can be used. The globe is placed in special grooves soldered to the back of the sun and fastened with hooks so that it is held upright and fast. By this method the sun is made with little expense and trouble.

A thin iron rod from 5 to *ff* and another from the upper *ff* to 3½ serve to turn the sunbeams, fastened in such a way that no rods pass across the sun lest they darken it.

At *gg* this box has a special piece by which it is hung from a beam of the upper floor at the inner stage near Mount Sinai (which will be described shortly) and kept closed until the proper time to open it.

Now when the time comes in the play when the Lord God speaks from the heavens to Moses to the accompaniment of thunder and lightning and the sound of the trumpet, then the door is drawn up and the sun is turned a little to the right and

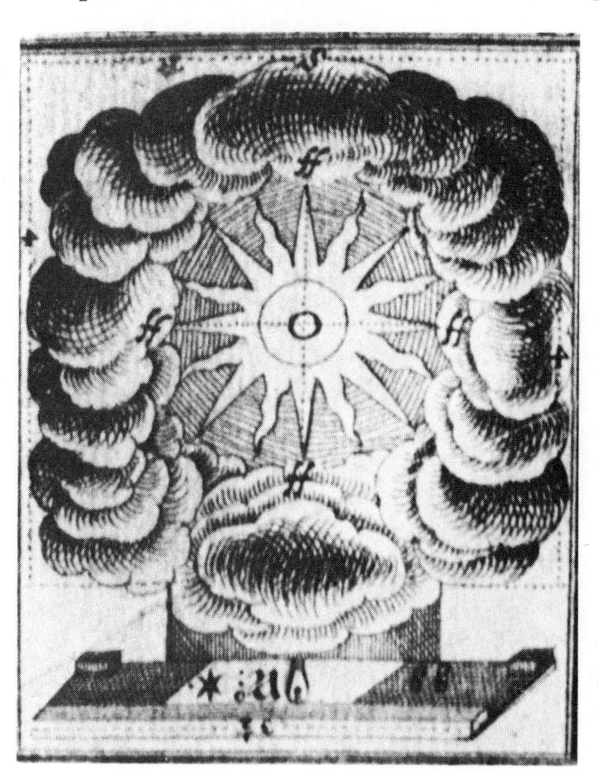

22. THE COMPLETED *Glory*

then a little to the left to send a beautiful splendor with shimmering beams toward the spectators, causing them great wonder. This *glory* will serve for many other actions besides Mount Sinai, and the lover of such things will produce great delight with it.[1]

*Machines For Bringing Objects Up From The Ground As Well As For Letting Objects Down From The Sky*

In the presentation of the play of the prophet Jonah when he prophesies the fall of the city of Nineveh, there was need to show a gourd vine that suddenly grew from the ground and later suddenly withered and then disappeared. For this a vine is cut out 7 feet high and 4 feet wide. Behind it at SS is a bench as a seat for Jonah. When the time comes for the vine to grow from the ground, a 2-foot-wide trap door (*Fallen*) in the floor is let down on two iron hinges, just like the lid of a trunk, and the vine is suddenly shoved up. It is painted with live green vines on one side, but the other side is painted as withered and dead. When the time comes for the vine to wither, the whole vine is quickly turned around by means of a 4-foot handle set into the middle of the base. Then just as suddenly it is pulled down under the stage and disappears. The trap is closed again. Such a trap may serve for many other uses.

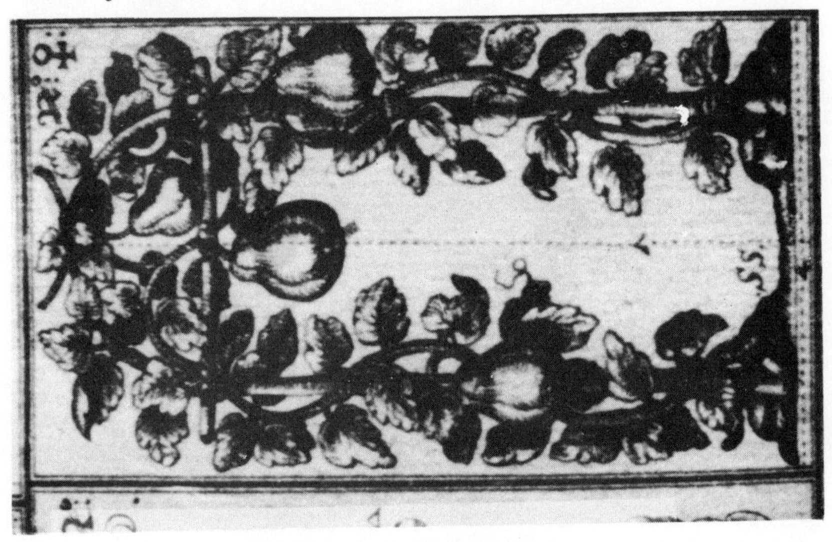


23. JONAH'S GOURD VINE

*A Floor That Lets Godless People Be Swallowed Up*

In another scene in the play when Core, Datan, and Ibirim were to murmur against Moses, the earth was tc open and swallow them up with all their houses and people. For this action a section of boards in the floor of the stage is left free, but suspended as a platform by four ropes at the corners where it is cut across.

1. Two such suns in *glories* used in Paris are shown in Mahelot's sketch for *Les Travaux d'Ulisse* by Durval, printed 1631. "Au dessus de l'enfer, le ciel d'Appolon, et, au dessus d'Appolon, le ciel de Jupiter." The printed text Act V, 5, calls for "le Soleil en son char de lumière" and "Jupiter en son trone de gloire." (*Le Mémoire de Mahelot*, pp. 82 f.)

These ropes go through small round holes above the stage and back through holes in the platform itself, and from there are wound on two windlasses under the stage. When the time nears that Core, Datan, and Ibirim are to be swallowed in the earth, they stand close together on this trap. Of course the audience are not aware that the floor is cut. Then when Moses calls down curses on them, the windlasses are turned loose and the platform with the men sinks slowly under the stage. They disappear with a great cry before the eyes of the audience. When at the same time the moans and wailings from the hell are heard and smoke and flames come from the hole, the spectator's heart will throb and his eyes fill with tears.[1] The audience, glad to be rid of such arrant sinners, will take this inexpensive spectacle to its heart.

How such fires are prepared will be explained in the next chapter. By the first kind of platform, fastened by hinges, Lucifer would be brought on quickly from hell and let down again amidst flames and smoke. Especially when the lights are dimmed for night, this gives quite a terrifying effect. Such a platform next to the rear shutters would serve as the river Jordan when the godless Pharaoh has the innocent child thrown between the small waves.

### *How Flames And Lightning Are Made*

In the palm of the right hand, in a well shaped piece of tin to keep the hand from being burned, is put a quantity about the size of a hazelnut of *colofonio* or Greek pitch. This is a fine meal-like powder of a beautiful yellow color like resin, sifted through a hair sieve. A lighted wax candle is held between the four fingers of the same hand, so that the flame is scarcely a half inch from the *colofonio*. Then the whole arm is extended and the meal is thrown through the light. It makes a long bright flame in the air like lightning. This flame can be used from under the stage to show hell, or above between the clouds to represent lightning. It will not set anything on fire or cause any damage; moreover it leaves a pleasant odor behind.

---

1. Trap doors for the smoke and flames of hell were well known in England. Fire issued from a trap door for the performance of *Progne* in 1566. (L. B. Campbell, *Scenes and Machines*, p. 91.) See also the description of *The Masque of Queens* in 1609: ". . . the part of the scene which first presented itself was an ugly Hell: which flaming beneath, smoked into the top of the roof. . . . these witches, with a kind of hollow and infernal music, came forth from thence." (A. Nicoll, *Stuart Masques*, p. 67.)

*How Thunder Is Made*

On the upper floor a runway is made of dry boards, 4 feet wide and the length of the entire building. The boards are not nailed down fast, and side walls 1½ feet high are built so that the stone balls do not roll out of the runway. Two men are stationed at each end of the runway and twelve stone balls about eight-pound size are placed ready for the thunder. When the signal is given by the bell for the sound of the thunderstorm to begin, a man gently rolls one ball upwards the entire length to give the low sound of the beginning. Then a ball is rolled gently downwards. When the storm is to grow stronger, one man throws a ball violently onto the boards, and a man from the other end starts one violently so that there are two heavy strokes like powerful claps of thunder just over the heads of the audience. Then more are added until all twelve balls are in action. At the same time two other men at opposite sides of the scene throw or swing the lightning between the clouds. When to this is added the sound of a strong wind roaring and moaning, the storm seems to be tremendous.

*How Rushing Wind Is Made*

Several thin rulers or pieces of veneer 2 feet long, 3 inches wide, and no thicker than a knife blade have a small hole the size of a quill at one end where a cord 1¾ feet long is tied. Someone takes the cord in his hand and swings the ruler with all his might. When many rulers are whirling, they roar like a hurricane. At the same time great bellows may send a wind out through hidden bored holes so that a strong wind actually blows on the audience. This whistling wind with the thunder and lightning, especially if the lights are darkened, will seem like a natural storm.

*How To Change Day Into Night*

During such a storm the daylight should get dimmer and gradually become dark like night. It could be arranged that the oil lamps and lights behind the scene be put out and later relighted. But that would require time, and extinguished oil lamps produce a bad smell. Hence we have little boxes or covers specially made of black metal that by cords are drawn over and then away from the oil lamps on the floor behind the masking screen, as well as over and away from the oil lamps behind the proscenium. They can be drawn over all of the oil lamps at a time, or only part. They cover the lamps but still permit them to burn, so that it seems night on the stage. The cord from each lamp is led up above the stage and thence to a single handle for all the cords. When this handle is forward, the lamps shine as for a bright day, but when the handle is drawn back then each cap covers its oil lamp so that not a ray is seen. Thus it was made to grow dark with the thunder and lightning in the scene where Pharaoh grew obdurate, and through the act of Moses it became night for a time in Egypt. This effect for such occasions gives great delight to those who see it.[1]

*How To Produce Rain And Hail*

Towards the end of it, fresh interest and wonder is created in the audience, especially on a warm day, by producing a splendid rain of water perfumed with rose and other odors, dripping through many holes bored through the upper floor but only over the heads of the most prominent ladies and their sons.[2] Such effects are held in the highest esteem by the Italians, and of course are not accomplished without cost.

Or, instead of rain, a sugared hail can be produced of sugared confections of coriander, almond, cinnamon, etc., to bring the play to a happy close. If some important lords are present, such *intermezzi* are means of showing them great honor and bringing them great delight.

In this play there was need for an impressive throne for Pharaoh. Its height is 9 feet, its width 3 feet. The back of the throne is covered with gold tinsel which reflects the light from the oil lamps of the rear pit and throws out shimmering rays like pure gold. The throne is given a majestic appearance by means

1. Cf. the similar method of Sabbattini, Book II, ch. 12. The use of darkness for dramatic effect was known at the time in both Paris and London, though different means may have been used. There are a number of references in the *Mémoire* of Mahelot to the creation of night, as for *Le Trompeur Puny* by Scudéry, 1631: "Il faut aussy une nuicht au premier acte." The text has, I, scene 7, "il fait nuit." (*Le Mémoire de Mahelot*, pp. 68 f.) That darkness was attempted by the closing of windows in the private playhouses of London is indicated by a line from Dekker's *Seven Deadly Sins of London*, 1606: "All the city looked like a private playhouse, when the windows are clapped down, as if some nocturnal or dismal tragedy were presently to be acted." (Lawrence, *Elizabethan Playhouse* (Sec. Series), pp. 8 f.)

2. Cf. the perfumed mist used in *The Barriers* of Ben Jonson. "There appeared at the lower end of the hall, a mist made of delicate perfumes; out of which (a battle being sounded under the stage) did seem to break forth two ladies, the one representing Truth, the other Opinion." (Lawrence, *Elizabethan Playhouse* (Sec. Series), pp. 5 f.)

of figured flower work in lacquer, a canopy of red damask and gilded circles, a crown with green velvet set with precious stones, and a seat and steps covered with Turkish tapestry. The throne scene is prepared on the inner stage for discovery; the rear pit is covered with boards, a well-tapestried room is prepared, and the throne is placed at the rear wall facing the audience. At the sounding of the trumpet, the rear shutters all open, and there stands the royal hall with Pharaoh sitting on his throne and next to him, attending at both sides, his council — a scene which affords special pleasure to the spectators [Figure 24].[1]

*A Fiery Bush*

When there was need for a fiery bush in the play of Moses, it occurred to me that a homely device, namely an Italian *parisol*, could be used. This, generally covered with black fine leather, is customarily used in Italy on a journey as a little roof over the head, to protect one from either the heat of the sun or a shower of rain. It can be opened 3 feet in diameter like a peacock fan, and afterwards closed together for handy carrying. If you take the 3-foot handle in the left hand, and the knob further up in the right hand, and shove the knob up, then the twelve ribs will open up. When the knob is drawn down, it closes compactly so that it can be put into a sack. For the present purpose the twelve leather sections are gilded and painted in figured streams like flames of fire issuing from a central point like the rays of the sun. When the knob is pushed up the flames spread out like a flaring fire that leaps around. When the *parisol* is closed the fire seems to be dying down and about to go out. This device must be handled with great care and skill if the effect is to be convincing [Figure 25].

For this inner stage scene, the rear pit is covered with its boards. At the left side is placed Mount Sinai, to be described later. At the right side, where there is more room, is set this rather large bush among trees, made the more like nature by natural leaves. Behind it a hole 1 foot square closed with a little door is cut in the wall at the rear of the inner stage about 4 feet from the floor. Through this hole is thrust the closed *parisol*. A man concealed behind the wall works it continuously by pushing and pulling the knob and sometimes turning it round from

1. Cf. the description of the inner stage, above.

24. A THRONE FOR PHARAOH

side to side. In the meantime two perspective lanterns, as described below, are placed in the inner stage in order to make the opening golden flames seem like a strong fire, as if the bush were burning without being consumed. This brings great wonder to the spectators. This *parisol* is also very useful in many other kinds of scenes, as for instance when hell is to be presented.

## FOUR DIFFERENT METHODS OF LIGHTING

*First By Oil Lamps*

For lighting the stage a glass oil lamp of medium size is used, 5 inches high and 4 inches wide above at the mouth, but tapering to 1 inch at the bottom — just the sort that is ordinarily used in church. This lamp is filled with fresh spring water up to the widest neck, leaving 1½ inches at the top of the container for the oil. A quarter of a pound of heavy olive oil will float on the water and fill the vessel almost to the top. A floating wick is prepared as follows. For a base a brass wire ring is made 2½ inches across; to this ring are fastened, at equal distances, six little cork blocks about the size of a small hazelnut. A little ring or collar, the size of a feather quill, which will hold the wick rather loosely, is fastened above the brass ring by twisted wires. A cotton wick, about 3 inches long and no thicker than a little quill, is inserted. When the entire float is set down in the lamp on the olive oil, the top of the wick will stand ⅓ inch above the little ring for burning and the rest will remain below to draw up the oil by the heat. Then the lamp is ready to light [Figure 25].

The whole lamp is placed in a wrought iron ring with a 4-inch screw to fasten it where it is needed. There should be a number of these rings ready for the lamps at the back of the parapet, back of the side walls of the proscenium, between the sections of the heavens, at the rear pit, and at other places. The screw of the ring is set in 1½ inches, leaving 2½ inches out to keep the light from coming close enough to burn the board.

For greater effect and safety, we use behind each lamp a piece of gold tinsel 5 by 8 inches marked out in lozenge shapes with cross lines. Or better, behind each lamp a flat thin piece of mica (of a shape we shall soon describe) is set up or fastened on so that it throws out a glowing reflection of the lamp. If the mica gets smoky, it can easily be cleaned by a wool cloth. It also provides an excellent fire shield.

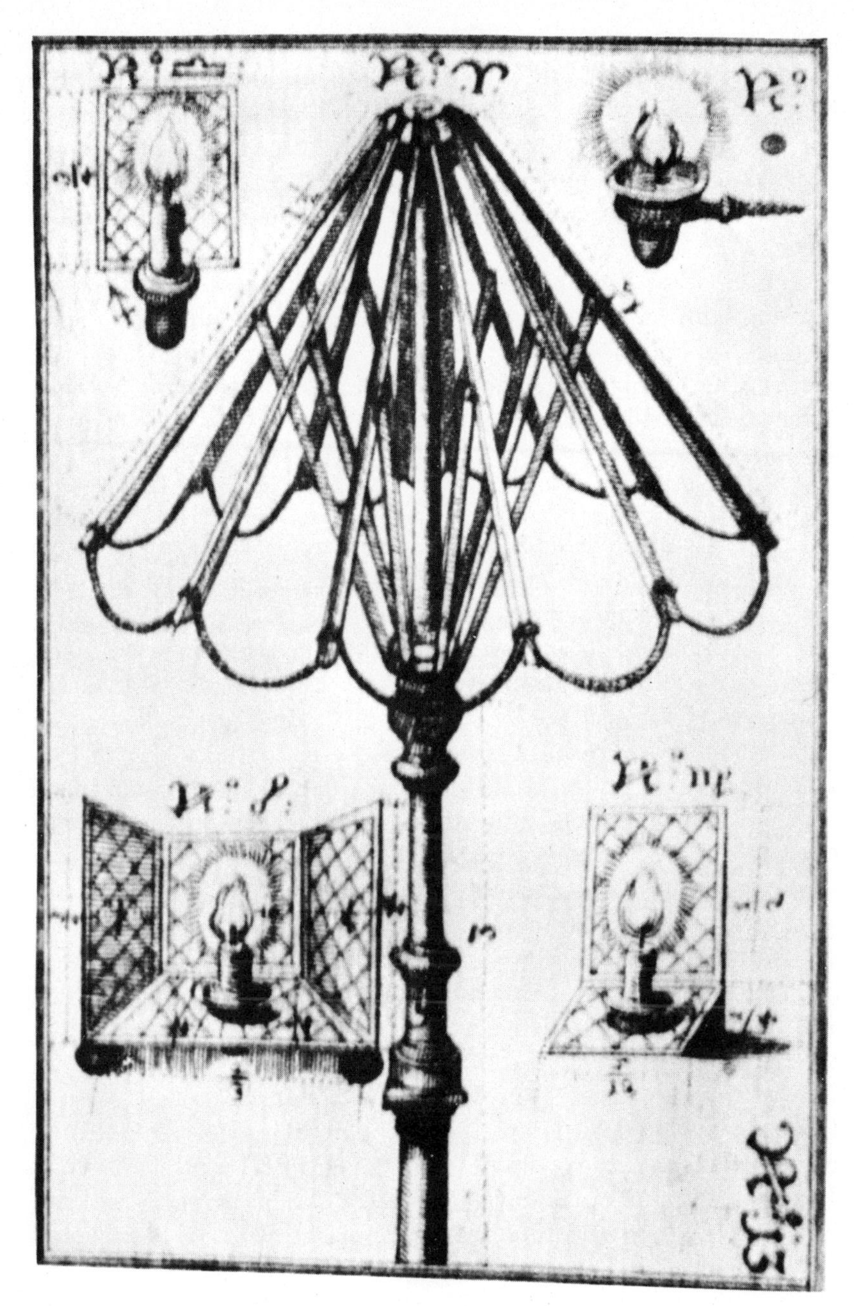

25. *Parisol* FOR THE FIERY BUSH AND FOUR LAMPS

In practice such an oil lamp has often given a good light as long as twelve hours with ¼ pound of olive oil, for water is continually poured in to raise the oil and the floating wick until the last drop of oil is burned and only water is left. This saves considerable trouble and expense. As many as 50 lamps can well be distributed around the stage and up in the heavens to light a scene.

At other times, especially for churches, to secure a long-burning lamp, a different wick is used. You search in the fields among the marshes for little rushes, peel them, and use their tender fiber. This fiber, white and rich as silk, makes a wick that gives a soft and long-burning light.

*The Mica Reflector*

The lantern should have a fairly strong white tin reflector[1] some ¾ foot high and 5 inches wide. For it a piece of gold tinsel the same size is marked out in crossed lines (lozenge shapes) with a wooden model or with a bone knife until its flat surface is broken up to give a diffused shimmering glow. Over the tinsel is laid a thin piece of mica of the same size.[2] All three pieces are bound together at the edge by a piece of lantern tin the width of two knife blades, with the mica outside and the marked-up tinsel between it and the white tin at the back. Then on the back of the white tin at the center is soldered an oblong tin sleeve, which is slipped onto a wide hook screwed into the board of the wall, so that the reflector is hung securely, just as we hang antlers on the wall. By this method a piece of mica is fastened or screwed behind each oil lamp. Experience shows how strong a splendor will be cast by lamps fitted with such reflectors and screwed in the heavens and about the entire scene.

At other times, especially for quite small scenes, to save the cost, I use no oil lamps but only good clean slowly burning candles (those candles poured from wax are the best), with which I experimented in a small theatre with a miniature stage which I have erected in my own humble shop. I had practice plays acted

1. A specialized reflector does not seem to have been known at the time of Serlio. He mentions only a barber's basin behind a torch. Ingegneri in 1598 mentions tinsel reflectors for the lights behind the proscenium valance. (Nicoll, *Stuart Masques* p. 134.)

2. Furttenbach uses the term *Frawen Eiss* as a parenthetical explanation of *Steinhorn.*

by children who could scarcely be more than ten, eleven, or twelve years old at the most — a modest and virtuous recreation, well pleasing before God and the honest world. By these and other useful arrangements, at very little expense, everything can be well lighted with as few as ten candles. Besides, a "perspective lantern"[1] was hung just in front of the scene and added its part.

Besides the lighting from lamps and from simple candles, there are three types of lights with candles and mica reflectors. The first is shown here. To the bottom of a flat mica reflector of the kind just described, a small iron ring is screwed as at ≏. In this ring is placed a little mushroom-shaped socket (*Pfifferling*) to hold a candle 5 inches long. The candle will give as rich a glow as a large lamp, though it will not burn so long. This candle and reflector is the best light for the back of the side walls of the proscenium and will serve well in other places.

### *The Third Method Of Lighting. The Leaning Light*

This is like the mica lantern described before except that for the present purpose it has a wedge-shaped (triangular) base where it is attached to the wall. Like the other light, it will have its vertical side and also the sloping top of the wedge base covered with gold tinsel marked in diamonds and then with mica. Then, as at *q*, a little socket, or, as it is called, a *Pfifferling*, which holds a candle light is set into the inclined top of the wedge base. When these lights are placed about 2 feet apart behind the board shield on the floor at the front of the stage, they will cast a strong splendor downward to the floor of the scene as well as upward into the clouds of the heavens. Indeed these leaning lights can be very useful and safe in many other places besides the stage, as in rooms and on staircases.

### *The Fourth Method Of Lighting. The Standing Light Box*

Except that this has no roof or door, it is exactly like the perspective lantern. It too is made of white lantern tin. It has a vertical back, a perspective base and two sides, all covered with marked-out gold tinsel. It is ⅔ foot wide at the front and ¾ foot

---

1. A lantern shaped like a perspective box or a perspective stage, with top, two sides, and bottom all set at an angle to send more light to the front. Cf. the "standing light box" described below as the Fourth Method of Lighting.

high. A candle in a *Pfifferling* placed at the center will send out a splendid glow. It can be placed equally well on the floor or on a table. But its principal use is at the rear pit [the inner stage], where it is hung by a sleeve at the back as an antler is hung, and will serve to light the royal throne or the sea. It can also be used away from the stage, as for reading, writing, or drawing at night.

In the same tragi-comedy there was also needed the form of Mount Sinai,[1] as shown here, 8 feet high, 5 feet wide, and 3 feet thick. It is so put together of cut-out boards that it can easily be set in place and afterwards taken away. At V V are hidden steps by which Moses can easily climb, but the rest of the mountain is painted wild and craggy so that at a distance it looks quite natural. The Mount Sinai is made ready in the inner stage for the discovery, and large shrubs set beside it. Then the *glory* already described, closed, is put in position among the clouds. When Moses is in the wilderness, the rear shutters open where Mount Sinai is seen in the distance. When he goes up the moun-

26. Mount Sinai

1. Cf. the account of the *glory* above.

tain, great streams of fire and lightning are seen; also thunder (produced as already explained), together with the sound of trombones, makes such a great uproar as to shake the earth. The *glory* of Mount Sinai is opened by drawing up its door, and the sun within is turned back and forth so that it shimmers like the rays of the sun.

## FOUR MACHINES FOR VARIOUS WAVES OF THE SEA

### *The First Machine. Still Waves*

For occasions when the sea that is shown at the rear pit is to be calm and quiet, this first machine of waves cut out of a board is placed in position, leaning against the rear wall next to the dressing room. Above the machine, the wall is painted as a sky with drifting clouds and sunbeams coming down.

### *The Second Machine. A Sliding Wave*

The first wave machine is too quiet for the usual idea of the sea. To produce an effect of movement that is yet not wild or tempestuous, the second wave, a sliding wave, is used. It is cut from a piece of board and is painted with waves more billowy and active than the first. The fourth, rearmost, pair of shutters are taken completely out of the groove, and this sliding sea wave is put in and slid back and forth. The sea will seem to be coming in to shore at the place where the shutters open. When in the rear pit, between this moving wave machine and the other still one, the ship of Jonah or other ships and galleys pass, an excellent effect is produced. When this sliding wave is moved continuously back and forth in its groove, then the ship will seem to move in a natural sea, and the audience will be delighted.

### *The Third Machine. Violent Waves*

When a *fortuna,* or stormy sea, is to be presented, this machine is made by cutting and painting four boards in the form of wild waves falling one over another and fastening them to a roller. The ends of the axles of the roller are set in supporting iron brackets high enough so that the roller will be at the level of the horizon of the sea, and the blades will rise above when the roller is turned, like a roast-spit. When the ship of Jonah, or some other ship, passes behind this machine, it seems to the spectators that the ship passes through the terrible waves. Two or three such machines, one behind the other, produce a tremendous effect which can be used in many different actions.

*The Fourth Machine. An Upstanding Wave*

In the tragi-comedy of the delivery of the children of Israel from Egypt, when they pass through the Red Sea, there were needed two waves that stood up where the sea divided. Each one is made of wood and is 3 feet wide and 14 feet long. It is cut in the form shown here and painted with a wild appearance. When the sea is prepared in the rear pit, as explained before, with a still wave at the back wall and a sliding wave in the groove, then both these upstanding waves are fastened by a pin onto the lower shutter-beam. They are set with the points *tt* and *tt* facing each other and at such places that when they are lowered they will be scarcely a hand's distance apart. The lower ends are cut as levers where counterweights are attached to raise or lower or churn the wave as needed. When they are down they can scarcely be seen, but when Moses throws his rod into the sea they rise and stand until the children of Israel have gone through. When Pharaoh pursues them with his army and gets to the middle of the Red

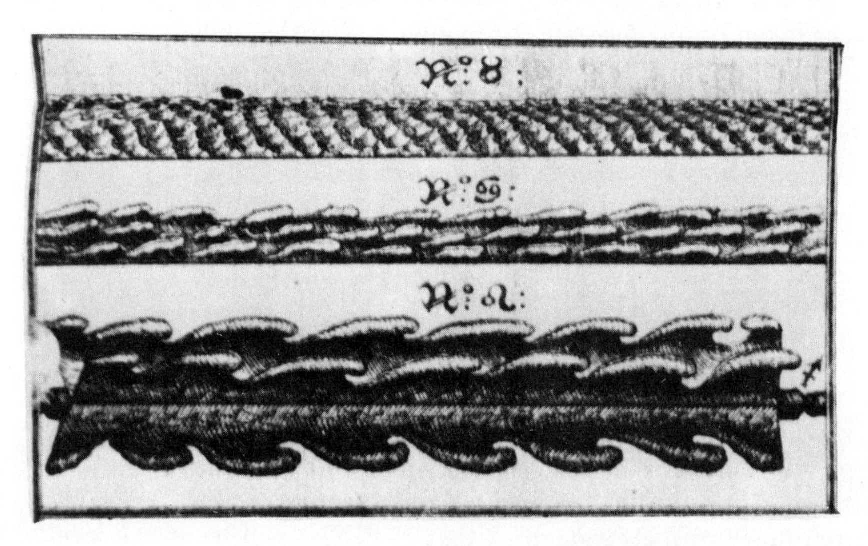


27. Waves: Still, Sliding, and Violent

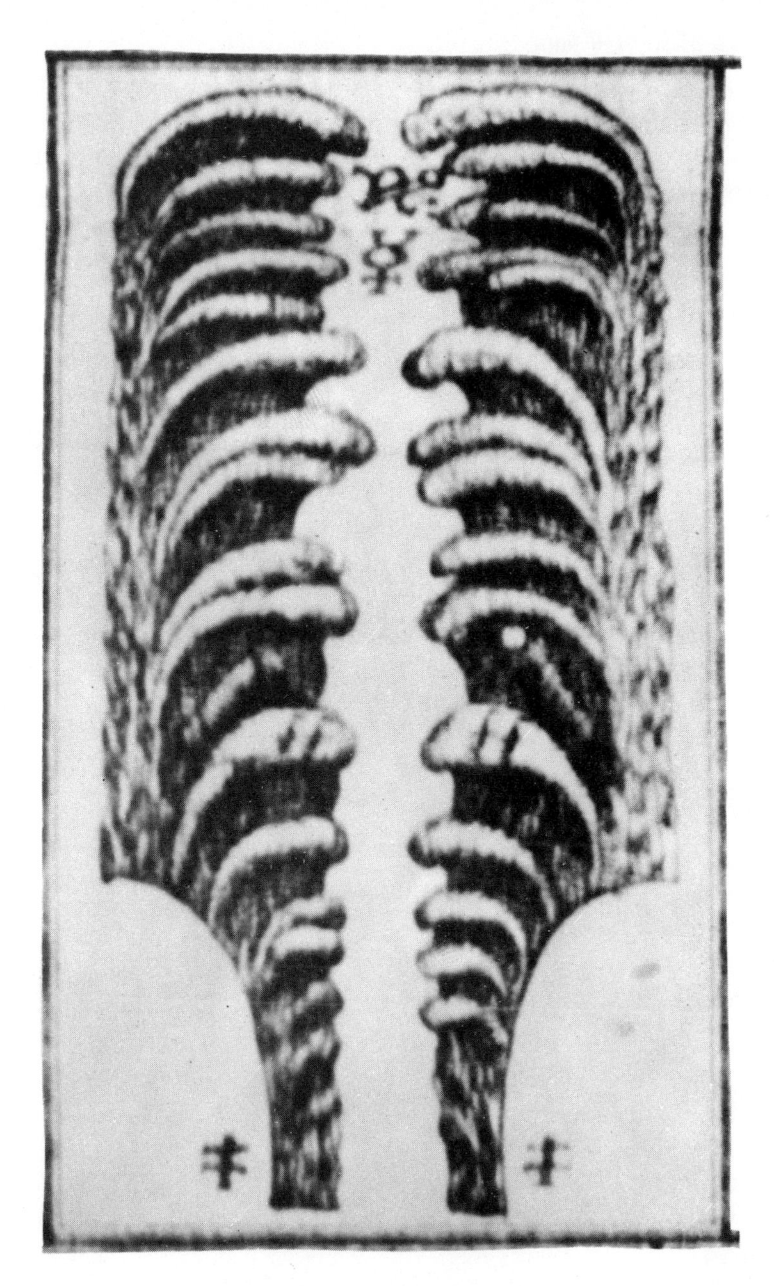

28. An Upstanding Wave

Sea, the waves come down. Amidst terrible cries and raising of hands, all are drowned.

*How To Make A Whale*

For the play about Jonah there was need to make a whale 11 feet long with jaws that stood 2½ feet across and opened up to 3¼ feet wide. The lower part of the body is cut from one piece

29. The Whale

of linden wood, hewn out like a trough, but left thick so that the whale can seem large enough to hold a man inside. The upper part is formed of small hoops of wood (*Raiffen*), and the whole thing is covered with cloth and painted as a horrible sea monster. Its eyes are made 3 inches in diameter with little mirrors in them to send out glimmering reflections of light. On the side away from the audience there is a hole over which a cloth is hung. When Jonah is swallowed he goes out this back hole into the rear pit and waits out of sight of the audience until the time comes when he is to be cast out again. Then he slips the upper part of his body into the oblong hole and the whale casts him out into the sea or onto the stage floor. This whale, as shown in the figure, is set on a three-wheeled trestle frame 10½ feet long and 5 feet high. By means of the handle WW the whale can be tipped forward on a wooden pivot or swung from side to side and raised and lowered by a screw.

The sea for this occasion is made by the first and second wave machines; the stormy waves in the middle are not yet needed. The trestle rolls between the waves with the fish carried so high that the head rises above the water. The upper jaws, like a trap, can be opened by a hidden cord. They are pulled closed by a 12-pound lead weight (*Kifer*). Two men operate the whale from behind the pit. While one pushes the trestle from behind the head of the fish, the other at the handle turns the fish from side to side and makes the head rise and fall, and with the cord raises the jaw and lets it snap shut. In practice this can be most convincing.

*How To Make A Ship*

For this same play of Jonah, we used a ship as shown here 12 feet long, 2 feet high, and 2½ feet wide, built of thin boards according to naval architecture, like a sea-going vessel. It is painted in wood color as if it had been stained with pitch. It is supported by a rocker on a chassis (*Karren*) similar to the carriage of a cannon, 10 feet long and 6 feet high with four 2-foot wheels. The ship has side pivots or axles which fit into sockets cut into the carriage. On these axles the ship is made to toss by the two 4-foot handles *yy* and *yy* at the front and the rear. The carriage for the ship is pulled across by a windlass at each end of the rear pit.

By this means the ship with Jonah and five mariners

30. The Ship in the Sea

sitting in it was shown to sail in the sea at the rear pit in a tremendous terrifying storm (*fortuna*). Here the stormy sea wave was laid in the sockets and turned like a reel so that one wave fell on top of another as though engulfing the tossing ship. Lightning and loud thunder strokes, together with the rushing wind, produced a tremendous storm. Jonah and his company cried out to God in heaven and with heads and hands upraised prayed for help and guidance. Such a sight made the hair of the spectators stand on end and brought tears to their eyes.

To produce a still greater *perturbation*, this great whale was made to pursue the ship with his jaws snapping, ready to swallow Jonah and all the company. It came up and snapped up Jonah. He was thrown into the mouth by the mariners with such dexterity that it looked as if the whale had swallowed him by itself. After Jonah was in the stomach of the fish, the sea became quiet and calm. The stormy wave was taken out and shoved under the stage, and the sea was left at its normal *tempo*. This whole action produced a great effect and almost broke the hearts of the audience.[1]

In the same manner, at very little expense, other ships may be made to cross the sea. Armed galleys may be made to sail one against the other or to pass one after the other. Without the use of powder and without any damage to the scenery, they can be made to seem to shoot at each other by the use of stage fire and thunder as already described. Thus an heroic sea battle can be presented.

For further designs for painted perspective scenes the reader is referred to the lovely summer room and the pleasure and flower gardens in *Feriae Architectonicae* by Joseph Furttenbach the Younger. In plates 18 and 19 he shows these as they are to be painted and gives a description.

With this I close the account of scenery (*Prospectiva*) and leave such things for those interested to think further on.

## THE SCHAWSPILSAAL[2]

We now come to a consideration of the Schawspilsaal, which will be delightful and pleasing to treat, because, God be praised and thanked, a noble peace has been ratified, and those people who remain in this life will rejoice and celebrate with noble praiseworthy entertainment. Hence there is need for a princely, splendid room for gatherings — for fencing, for foot-tourneys, for

1. Cf. the sea chariot in Davenant's *Temple of Love* in England, 1643–45. "The masquers appear in a Maritime chariot, made of a spungie Rockstuff mixt with shel, Sea-weeds, Corral, and Pearl, born upon an Axeltree with golden wheels with a rimme, with flat spokes like the blade of an Ore coming out of the Waves. This chariot was drawn by sea monsters, and floated with a sweet motion in the sea; Indamora Queen of Narsinga, sate enthron'd in the highest part of this chariot, in a rich seat, the back of which was a great Skallop Shell . . . This sight thus moving on the water, was accompanied with the Music and the Voyces of the Chorus . . . The Song ended, all the forepart of the Sea in an instant turn'd to dry land, and Indamora with her . . . ladies descended into the room and made their entry." (Nicoll, *Stuart Masques*, pp. 106–111.)

2. From "The Discourse on Civil Architecture."

acrobatics, for dances, banquets, and plays. To provide a suitable place for exhibitions and performances, it will be necessary to build a large wide room to permit a large number of people to see freely.

> [A poem in praise of J. Furttenbach by M. Jacob Honold, the elder pastor in the Minster at Ulm, and professor in the school. — The theatre or Schawspilsaal is needed for assemblies of all the burghers . . . delight . . . fencing and leaping, foot-tourneys, singing of lovely music . . . happy dances . . . princely persons . . . lavish banquets . . . plays . . . plays to make real what imagination conceives . . . bring before us now what has taken place long ago . . . such a Schawspilsaal to refresh men in the noble time of peace . . . for whatever concerns the artistic achievement of such a building look to Herr Joseph Furttenbach.]

*Ground Plan For The Schawspilsaal*

First let us consider the central room. It is to be 73 feet wide, a width which easily allows for the construction of a ceiling suspended in the roof. (No posts or supporting columns which might obstruct the view are to be considered.) The ceiling is to be finished with burnished plaques and beautiful panels in plaster. These will cost less than a wooden ceiling and look more finished, and be a better protection against fire.

The central room has eight similar sides.

At ******** will be eight windows, quite high like church windows. A person comes to the main entrance, the "Eingang," by wide well-built stairs, and by the "Ausgang" leaves by similar stairs.

This Schawspilsaal can easily be made ready for foot-tourneys, combats, solo dances, and rope dances. A number of benches may be brought in according to the occasion. But principally the hall will serve as a meeting place for foreign princes and such occasions as splendid marriages when banquets and dances are held.

At two sides at K and L are two similar alcove buffets (*Credenz*) somewhat like that drawn on plate 19 and described in folio 58 of my *Architectura Recreationis*. High above each buffet a heaven is made of clouds where the singers and performers on trumpets, cornets, drums, and the organ can make music out of

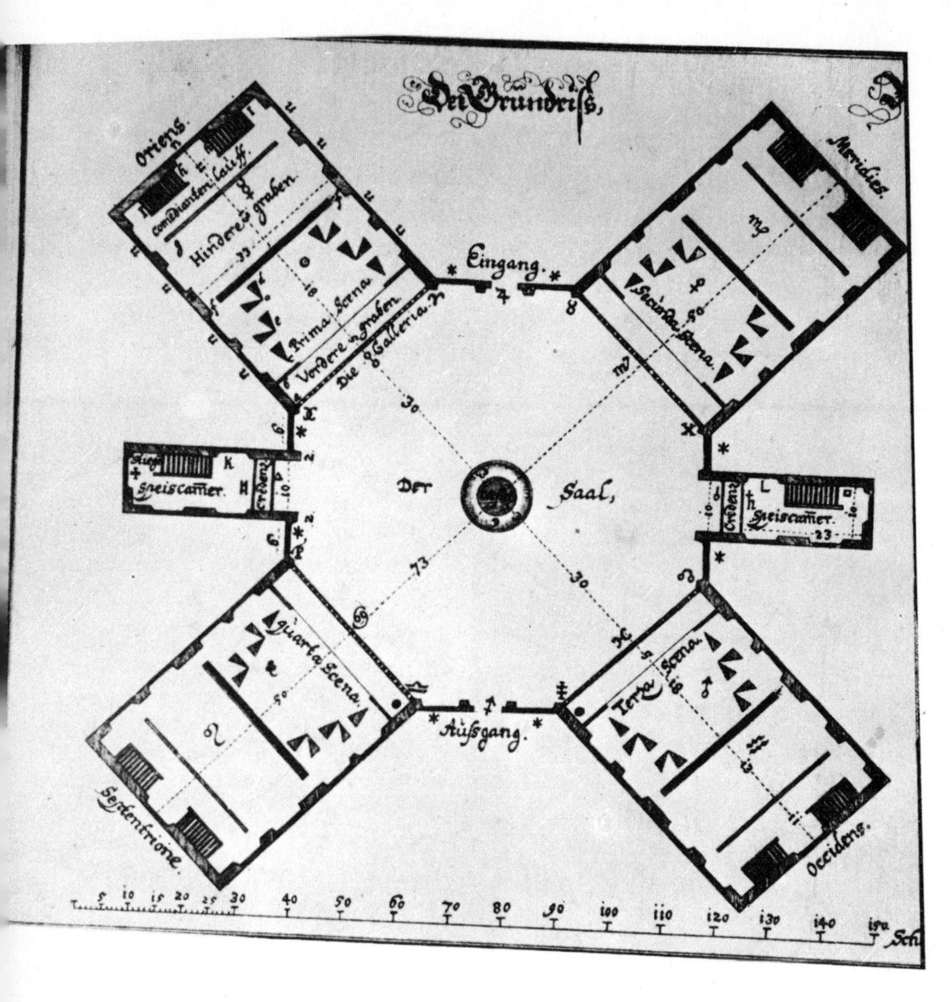


31. BANQUET TABLE SURROUNDED BY FOUR STAGES

sight of the guests. Below, these side cabinets have doors which open to allow food to be carried to the table without anyone's guessing how it could be brought so quickly or be kept so warm. At the rear of the cabinet are doors to allow the dishes to be put in from behind; and at K is a table for the warm food, and the buffet at the opposite side is for carrying away the empty dishes. The food room is conveniently located at the head of the stairs, accessible to the kitchen. A special kitchen is built next to the building so that the main hall will be kept free of smoke, steam, and the danger of fire.

. . . . . . . . . . .

When it is desired to use the hall as a playhouse, then only one corner — namely, at *Oriens* — can be opened and a supplementary structure for the stage be erected. At the front is the *Galleria*[1] [parapet]. The front pit is from *a* to *b*. The scene is from *b* to *f*, 18 feet long and 33 feet wide; *c* is the first, *e* the second, and *o* to *d* the third *periaktoi*, which can be turned for the needs of the play. From *f* to *f* is the grooved beam in which the rear shutters may be shoved on or drawn back. The rear pit is used not only when a princely room and a throne are needed, but also when its floor is taken up it is used to present a river or the sea.

A *g* is the rearmost partition wall behind which the actors have an unseen passageway.

The stairs at *hh* lead to the lower floor where the actors change costumes; the stairs at II lead to the upper floor of the theatre, to arrange there all the things necessary above. At *nn* at various places are windows, but how the scenes of the stage are lighted by lamps, how the *periaktoi* are turned, and how the scene is changed to water or land are fully explained in the section on Perspective in this book, in plates no. 11, 11½, 12, and 13, to which the reader is referred.

When the Schawspilsaal is thus made into a playhouse and the chairs and benches are put in, it will hold many hundred persons who can see freely the *Prima Scena* at *Oriens*. The hearts of the spectators will be enthralled by the action on the stage with the accompanying music from above in the alcoves.

---

1. The term *Galleria* is used earlier for a free-standing parapet before the front pit.

If one is not satisfied with one stage but wishes to make a really princely banquet and have a number of actors present plays (as between and during the courses of the meal there is time for special entertainment), then one may have four stages,[1] as at *Oriens* a stage (marked O) to represent the Air; at *Meridies*, the Fire; a third at *Occidens*, the Water; and a fourth at *Septentrione*, the Earth. All are formed like the first. These four stages are not left open, but they are hung with *fuori*, curtains or tapestries, so covered at the front that no one knows what is taking place behind.

In the middle of the room is a round table, large enough for twelve persons to be seated and served. Now the table and all the seats are placed on a round platform fully 13 feet in diameter, to turn on a pivot resting in a die on the lower floor. While the guests sit quietly, unnoticed the platform is turned by the capstan. However, when the princely persons are having a banquet of peace and rejoicing, it were enough to have only a half table shaped like a half moon with six lords seated at one side, and the other side left empty that their view might be uninterrupted.[2] First they are turned toward the entrance. They hear the music from the unseen musicians in the clouds above the alcoves but do not see how the food and drink are brought on and carried away.

First in the *Oriens*, the Air. During the princely banquet, suddenly and unexpectedly the curtain or *fuora* at Ӿ to V will fall to present at *Oriens* the *Prima Scena* lighted like day with the glow of lights or unseen oil lamps. For the delight of the guests, an *action* is presented in the *Parte Orientali*, a scene representing Air with charming red clouds and flying birds. In the

---

1. This use of several stages at an elaborate function continues a long tradition of princely entertainments. At the famous banquet of Philip the Bold at Lille in 1453, a large number of miniature scenes, some peopled with mechanical figures, were displayed on tables around the room (*Mémoires* of Olivier de la Marche, ii, 348 ff.). Sometimes there were two or more quite elaborate stages built in the same hall, as in the Palazzo Vecchio at Florence for the alternate presentation of the acts of *Mandragola* and *Assiuolo* with scenes on one stage by Francesco Salviati and on the other by Bronzino (J. A. Symonds, *Renaissance in Italy*. "Italian Literature," Chapter XI, "Drama"). The use of several stages may be looked on as a continuation in the Renaissance of the medieval practice of showing several scenes simultaneously.

2. At a banquet at Florence in 1608 the principal persons were seated at a table shaped like a new moon. Part of the entertainment was on a stage at the other end of the hall; part consisted of dancing and a foot-tourney on the floor of the hall. The knights were seated on wooden tiers at the sides. (Solerti, *Musica, Ballo, e Drammatica alla Corte Medicea dal 1600 al 1637*, pp. 54 f.)

*Prima Scena* appear the Oriental people with their characteristic costumes, houses, and plants. At the end of the *action* the scene is closed by the curtain pulled over it.

The Fire at *Meridies.* Then so quietly that it can hardly be noticed, the table is turned by the bars underneath to face the right side. The guests face the side marked *Meridies.* Suddenly the second curtain falls down and presents the *Secunda Scena* with a flaming *Ethna* or *Volcano* with extended beams. Here too an *action* is presented in the warm land of noon with Moors in costume, animals, buildings, and the fruit trees that belong to that land. In turn the second scene is closed by the curtain.

The *Occidens,* Water. The table is then turned to *Occidens;* the curtain falls suddenly and the *Tertia Scena* is shown. Here is the sea, first calm and quiet, then disturbed by enormous waves. In this raging sea the world-famous western mariners, the Netherlanders, Hollanders and Seelanders, pass in their ships. Between the ships are *balenen* or whales. The sea gets quieter. Finally two ships encounter, and amidst shots and explosions a naval battle is seen. With that the *Tertia Scena* is closed with its curtain.

At *Septentrione,* the Earth. Then the table turns again, to *Septentrione,* and the curtain falls to disclose the *Quarta Scena,* a fruitful land representing Earth with grain, trees, and woods. The farmer is plowing, the gardener is planting trees, the hunter is holding up his game. All is presented that can be done on a smooth ground. The people of the *Septentrione* likewise act a play for the guests in characteristic costume.

At the end the curtain here is closed and the hall brought back as it was at the beginning. After the meal is over, a foot-tourney, a bout, or a dance may be presented in the room according to the pleasure of the company. At 6 6 at the two sides of the front pit special little doors may be made, so that one may arrange the necessary convenience there.

*The Profile Or Cross Section Of The Schawspilsaal*

Here is the cross section of the building as if it were cut from *Oriens* to *Occidens.* At *Oriens* the front pit is marked *a* to *b.* On the *Prima Scena* the *periaktoi* are seen from the side. At *f* are the shutters in their grooves. Next is the rear pit, and at the back is the passageway for the actors. N is the rear window. Beneath is the side door through which the actors have access to the lower floor where they dress. They come up to the stage by the stairs at *h h* shown on the ground plan. At R and S is the Hell or space underneath the stage. T is the height of the rear pit laid with boards which can easily be taken up to permit the sea or other body of water to be shown.

From P to Q on the cross section is seen the capstan bar at which trained men stationed at the four handles can turn the platform with both the table and its guests. What is shown here of only one side is to be understood for the other. This ends the description of the Schawspilsaal.

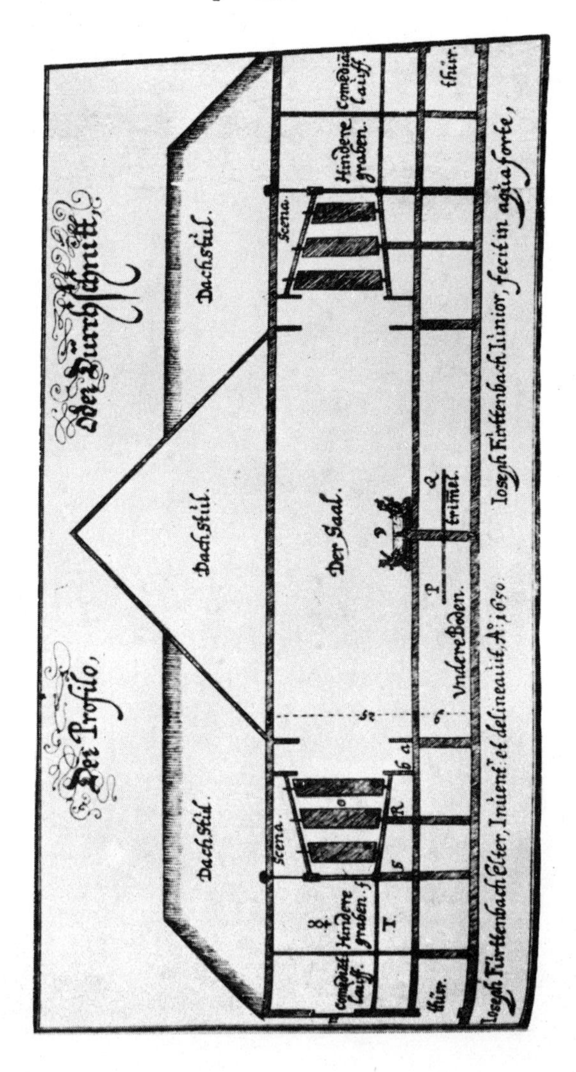

32. CROSS SECTION OF THE SCHAWSPILSAAL

# *Illustrations*

## SERLIO



## SABBATTINI

## FURTTENBACH